T0337450

A POLITICAL THEORY OF MONEY

Understanding money's nature as political, institutional and material answers today's big money questions. Money remains a foundational question of social theory. What is money? Why does something so insubstantial have value? How do money systems make promises function like valuable things? Why are money systems always hierarchical yet variable? The answer, *A Political Theory of Money* argues, is politics.

Money is institutionalised social power. Politics generates institutions that differentially lock into the future product of political and economic collectives. Money emerges from the institutionalisation of social antagonisms to encapsulate a collective's productive potential in a flexible, tradable instrument. This takes a system. Money is built in hierarchical layers out of the inherently variable material of politics and at various economic scales. This book outlines these variable processes theoretically and through case studies.

Anush Kapadia is Associate Professor in the Department of Humanities and Social Sciences, Indian Institute of Technology (IIT) Bombay.

A POLITICAL THEORY
OF MONEY

Anush Kapadia

CAMBRIDGE
UNIVERSITY PRESS

Shaftesbury Road, Cambridge CB2 8EA, United Kingdom

One Liberty Plaza, 20th Floor, New York, NY 10006, USA

477 Williamstown Road, Port Melbourne, VIC 3207, Australia

314–321, 3rd Floor, Plot 3, Splendor Forum, Jasola District Centre, New Delhi – 110025, India

103 Penang Road, #05–06/07, Visioncrest Commercial, Singapore 238467

Cambridge University Press is part of Cambridge University Press & Assessment, a department of the University of Cambridge.

We share the University's mission to contribute to society through the pursuit of education, learning and research at the highest international levels of excellence.

www.cambridge.org
Information on this title: www.cambridge.org/9781009331432

First published 2023

Printed in India by Nutech Print Services, New Delhi 110020

A catalogue record for this publication is available from the British Library

Library of Congress Cataloging-in-Publication Data

Names: Kapadia, Anush, author.
Title: A political theory of money / Anush Kapadia.
Description: Cambridge, United Kingdom; New York, NY, USA: Cambridge
  University Press, 2023. | Includes bibliographical references and index.
Identifiers: LCCN 2023023243 (print) | LCCN 2023023244 (ebook) | ISBN
  9781009331432 (hardback) | ISBN 9781009331463 (paperback) | ISBN
  9781009331449 (ebook)
Subjects: LCSH: Money. | Money–Political aspects.
Classification: LCC HG221 .K257 2023 (print) | LCC HG221 (ebook) | DDC
  332.4–dc23/eng/20230714
LC record available at https://lccn.loc.gov/2023023243
LC ebook record available at https://lccn.loc.gov/2023023244

ISBN 978-1-009-33143-2 Hardback
ISBN 978-1-009-33146-3 Paperback

Contents

FIGURES AND TABLES

Figures

Tables

PREFACE

This book is both a collection and a synthesis. While some of the case-study chapters started as responses to the global financial crisis of 2007–2008, the bulk of the theoretical section was written to synthesise the lessons learned from the cases and to connect them with all three major schools of monetary thought. The test of this synthesis, like all theories, is its generality: how many monetary contexts can it speak to?

The work synthesises elements from all three schools of monetary thought. Social theory is best seen as a resource from which we can select various elements from various theories to assemble our own social–theoretic machines fit to tackle our particular questions. Loyal adherence to a particular school therefore can end up damaging the work of social theory. As complex compounds assembled in particular contexts for particular questions, social theories are quite modular. Each element can in principle be recombined with elements from other theories. Theories are not infinitely recombinable, of course, and we will constantly argue over which elements are foundational, which are dispensable, which necessarily hang together and which are separable. But such arguments already concede the inherent modularity of theory.

The theoretical synthesis we attempt here combines elements from the Banking, State and Currency Schools with lessons from classical political economy and old institutional economics. The Banking School understands money as credit, as means of payment for settling debts public and private. It carries an implicit institutionalism because it recognises the futural orientation of all economic life: only institutions can help us collectively manage the uncertain future; institutionalism and futurity go hand in hand.

But the Banking School lacks an adequate account of hierarchy in money—why some monies are better than others—taking refuge in the nominal power of the law. This is the domain of the State School, which identifies the state as being central to money but does so by raising the state's nominal power to such a height that it ironically eclipses politics itself. This book seeks to improve upon the State School's understanding of money by placing it with a political understanding of the ontology of all social institutions including the state, an understanding inspired by Roberto Unger though it has many referents.

Finally, the book urgently insists on the materiality of money. This is a special kind of materiality to be sure—one that is futural, probabilistic, abstract, institutional and political all at once. As such, while this is not the materiality of money identified by the Currency School, it acknowledges the salience of the latter's materialist intuitions. In an age where 'printing money' has become a byword of government policy, social theory needs to rise to the occasion and account for why money, seemingly a confidence trick played on the populace by gnomic technocrats, is in fact anchored and rooted in material processes of production albeit at variable robustness and scale. Without the material dimension, there is no complete account of monetary variety and therefore no complete theory of money.

Those who work on money often recall the moment when they plunged down the money rabbit hole. I wrote this book to address the money gap I found in Karl Marx's theory of capitalism during my graduate work. While the reader will decide if the theory measures up, it is important to make the distinction between a theory of money and a theory of capitalism. Though naturally overlapping, a theory of money cannot substitute for a theory of capitalism in all its variegated, historically bound dynamics. That said, hopefully the reader will find herein some seeds of that broader theoretical formulation.

ACKNOWLEDGEMENTS

When you are down the money rabbit hole, you need a guide. I lucked out and found Perry Mehrling while browsing through the corners of the Columbia University course catalogue. Perry has that rare gift of being able to juggle the abstract and the concrete with consummate ease. This not only makes him a wonderful teacher but one of the most important social theorists we have. As I learned his institutionalist vision of money, I grafted it onto my own education in political economy to produce the work before you. It is no exaggeration therefore to say that without his teaching, scholarship and friendship, this book could not have been possible.

I have in fact been granted some outrageously good luck with fabulous mentors from all the way back to my undergraduate days when Amrita Basu, Pavel Machala and James Martel got me started on social theory. Partha Chatterjee, Sanjay Reddy, David Scott and Nick Dirks made up an eclectic and rigorous PhD dissertation committee. Each one will hopefully find some element of their thought represented in this work—perhaps, especially, Partha whose synoptic grip on theory and history continues to inspire and guide. As I moved on to postdoctoral work, I continued to luck out, finding Katharina Pistor, Akeel Bilgrami and Joe Stigtliz as mentors and interlocutors through the turbulent times of the financial crisis. Katharina in particular continues to be a model of scholarship and engagement.

My education continued while teaching social theory at the precious and unique programme of Social Studies at Harvard University. Social Studies under Richard Tuck created a special environment for lecturers and students alike, one that I was loath to leave. The anchoring it provided in classical social theory added a foundational layer to this theory of money. Around this time, I was blessed to encounter the scholarship of Chris Desan and through her the whole world of legal scholarship on money and political economy broadly, a vibrant and important scholarly community. Chris's seminal work on money deeply informed my own; she remains a wonderful mentor. I was also deeply fortunate to encounter the work of Roberto Unger at close quarters.

Several colleagues at Indian Institute of Technology (IIT), Bombay, especially the Sociology Group, have provided a warm and supportive environment. Others have once again provided important mentorship, particularly Rowena Robinson and Anurag Mehra.

One needs intellectual comrades of course, and there again I have had outsized luck. Siva Arumugam, Arjun Jayadev, Jason Jackson, Dan Nielson, Sanjay Pinto, Alex Gourevitch and Sandipto Dasgupta have all helped in the conceptualisation of this work in various ways.

Parts of this work were presented to audiences at Harvard University; King's College London; Centre for Policy Research, New Delhi; Azim Premji University, Bengaluru; Ashoka University, Sonipat; and Tel Aviv University. My since thanks to the organisers at these forums for their generous invitations and to the audiences whose questions sharpened the arguments.

The team at Cambridge University Press was extremely efficient in their handling of the entire process. My sincere thanks to Anwesha Rana for piloting the process as well as to Qudsiya Ahmed and Anandadeep Roy. My sincere thanks as well to the anonymous reviewers whose comments greatly improved the clarity of the work.

My family, who embrace my academic life despite it being so distant from theirs, have been steadfast in their support. The world knows no other more giving and loving person than Niloufer, my mother. My extended family in Palestine provided vital support at critical junctures of this project for which I am eternally grateful.

Finally, to Riham, who as a part of me carried the burdens and ups and downs of this project as her own—no acknowledgement could possibly suffice.

Abbreviations

AIG	American International Group
ASICs	application-specific integrated circuits
BoE	Bank of England
CD	certificate of deposit
CPU	central processing unit
DeFi	decentralised finance
ECB	European Central Bank
EFSF	European Financial Stability Facility
EMU	Economic and Monetary Union
ESM	European Stability Mechanism
EU	European Union
FX	foreign exchange
GDP	gross domestic product
ICU	International Clearing Union
IMF	International Monetary Fund
IPE	international political economy
LOLR	lender of last resort
MMT	modern monetary theory
NAV	net asset value
RBI	Reserve Bank of India
RMB	renminbi
SDRs	Special Drawing Rights
US	United States

PART I

1 | Money Anchored to the Future

Money is institutionalised social power, the power of people working together, implicitly or explicitly, in a division of labour to produce a collective output. Money is the result of an institutional process which encapsulates the power of productive collective action in a flexible, tradable instrument. Yet it takes an entire system of hierarchically concatenated institutions to transform a collective's powers of production into a highly liquid instrument. This book outlines the nature of that system. It discusses this process in theory (Part I) before moving on to a series of cases to illustrate how variations in the politics of collective action lead to variable monetary quality (Part II).

Why does something so seemingly insubstantial—a promise, a paper note, a digital ledger entry—have real value? This is perhaps the central mystery of money. Anecdotally, we know that many people still think money is backed by gold (or ought to be), something confirmed by emerging scholarship (for example, Kraemer et al., 2020). In order to fully account for money, we cannot dismiss such perceptions as mere error or false consciousness. Social theory has to explain how a credit instrument, a promise, can durably and systematically function like a real commodity. What is it about the money system that enables promises to function like valuable things? Why are some monies better than others? Why are money systems always hierarchical?

We propose a political theory of money as an answer. Social theorists have of course long argued that money is a social relation, but that still begs the question of why some social relations generate better, more widely acceptable money than others. To answer this question, we need a theory of types of social relations that map onto variable monetary robustness. We also need a theory of the social function of money because what counts as a 'better money' itself presupposes a particular historical social formation. The functional requirements of money change with the dominant social formation. As such, the prevailing form of money in any epoch tells us a great deal about how we have chosen to live and work together. The kind of money we have emerges from the kind of society we have.

As money has grown even more abstract, rich nations have become hyper-financialised, and inequality has grown to the point of breaking down the very legitimacy of states. The mystery of money and its value lies at the heart of these controversies, but at the end of the journey the citizen-worker will find that money reflects back her own future social product.

We argue that when promises—credit—are systematically institutionalised in a particular pattern, they can bear real value. As we outline in this chapter, this pattern of institutionalisation is *hierarchical and hybrid*, combining institutions formed of one type of social relation—political relations—at the system's apex with institutions formed of another kind of social relation—economic relations—at the system's capillaries.

Hierarchy emerges because political relations generate institutions of substantial scale and robustness. Politically institutionalised balance sheets generate highly creditworthy promises by being politically anchored across a national economy. Institutions formed through economic relations, by contrast, are easier to crack and moored to a much smaller part of the social product; they therefore produce promises that, while of substantial creditworthiness, are less creditworthy than those made up of political promises in the same jurisdiction. Different types and scales of social relations index differential creditworthiness. More creditworthy institutions set the terms for less creditworthy ones; the more creditworthy instrument is an 'outside' settlement instrument, 'money', for less creditworthy balance sheets—hence the hierarchy.

Yet these different types of credit are layered together in a single money system because only together can they combine the features of stability, flexibility and granularity, all of which are demanded by our dominant social formation of capitalism plus democracy. The dominant social formation therefore demands that money systems be *hybrids* of institutionalised political and economic relations. As we will see subsequently, this is not the same thing as a hybrid of public and private *ownership*.

Because institutionalisation and 'anchoring' vary with local political settlements and the size of economic catchment areas, creditary promises produced by various money systems vary in their money-ness. Some monies are so fragile that they barely function even on home turf, while others are so robust that they are used far beyond their home system as world money.

Politics operates at all levels of the system—both the micropolitics of market structures and regulations to the macropolitics of the society-wide political settlement. In all cases, money is designed and constructed in the teeth of a battle of ideas and interests. Money is Max Weber's 'weapon in the struggle for economic existence' (Ingham, 2004, p. 4), but because modern money is a promise—a credit note—and credit comes in systems, money is also the institutional milieu of such struggles. The contingent equilibria of such struggles instantiate themselves in a particular money's design, leading each money to have its own character and dynamic. A theory of money has to account for the huge variety of money we see in space and time.

Politics is foundational to money in two senses. At the level of the social contract, political contracts tie the future national product to state finances to 'back' national money. But more generally, all social institutions at all levels are collections of implicit political agreements—points at which we stop fighting to form what John Commons called 'working rules' (Commons, 1931). Political struggles instantiate themselves in the configuration of all institutions; ontologically, institutions *are* 'frozen politics' that can melt under enough political heat only to refreeze when the fighting inevitably stops (Unger, 1987). This politics-as-instantiation operates in all monies—public and private—because it operates in all social institutions.

Different types and scales of social relations lead to institutions of differing creditworthiness. Part of the complexity of modern money is that a well-institutionalised money system will not only combine institutions born of different types of social relations—political and economic—but each money system will do so in a different way depending on its own history and macro or micro politics. The range of combinatorial possibilities for possible money systems is therefore very large; we sample only a small subset of cases in Part II.

The relationship between the nature of a collective's social bonding, its internal political settlement and the dynamics of the resultant money is at the very heart of this theory of money. We establish this connection theoretically in Part I (Chapters 1–7). In Part II (Chapters 8–11), we explore the link empirically: the particular hybridity we see in developed economies (nationalised money plus privatised banking) is an instantiation of a local political settlement whose recent imbalance led to crisis (Chapter 8); a world unstably perched between national polities and global economies results in the absence of world money coupled with the urgent requirement for global governance of the hegemonic national money (Chapter 9); libertarianism and a hostility to credit animate the puritan cultures of cryptocurrencies, creating ingenious but malfunctional monies (Chapter 10); and, finally, the European Union's (EU) novel, non-national political contract results in a elaborately mutualised currency whose scale is global hegemonic even while suffering from fragility in a crisis (Chapter 11). Chapter 12 concludes by reflecting on the democratic possibilities for money.

In the remainder of this chapter, we sketch out the elements of a money or credit system in the abstract and then assemble them to illustrate why an ideal–typical system is both hierarchical and hybrid. In Chapter 2, we unpack some of the ontological properties of this system that enable promises to function as valuable things.

Money as Credit

We begin at the cellular level of a money system—credit. We know that modern money is a form of credit because it says so plainly. Many global monies such as the notes of the Reserve Bank of India (RBI) and the Bank of England (BoE) are literally signed by the central banker promising to pay the bearer the sum on the note. Later, we will return to the question of what the note actually promises to pay. To begin with, let us focus on its nature, or ontology, as a promise per se. Credit is a promise to pay something, a statement of debt to the creditor. Money is a form of credit to the holder and debt to the issuer.

Money promises come in two main forms of course: (*a*) cash, which is a bearer instrument, meaning the bearer is also the creditor of the issuing bank (the central bank), and (*b*) bank accounts, which state that the bank owes the deposit holder a specific sum of central-bank money, a portion of which can be repaid or 'withdrawn' on demand.

We are used to reading our bank statements as accounts of wealth (or, in the case of academics, poverty). They indicate wealth because they are statements of debt, of how much money the bank owes us; the money in question is central-bank money. For example, an account statement in India with, say, HDFC Bank Limited states that the bank owes account holder X a sum of RBI money. Another way of saying this is that HDFC's debt to the account holder is denominated in Indian rupees.

If central-bank money is itself a promise to pay (something), our deposit account is also a statement of promises to pay; only the 'something' is clearly defined: bank accounts are collections of promises to pay central-bank money. As promises that are tradable, bank accounts are themselves money in ledger form.

Thus, we have two forms of money right away: physical central-bank money, which is itself a promise to pay something, and 'bank money', a ledger or account form, which is a bank's promise to pay central-bank money. So bank money is already a derivative, a promise to pay a promise.

A theory of money is meant to denaturalise money systems to show how they work or break down. Seeing something as familiar as a bank statement as evidence of the existence of something called 'bank money' is the first step in this process of denaturalisation, enabling us to get out of our physicalist habits of mind.

Highlighting centrality of credit and promises is not meant to be an argument for the foundational role of trust in an economy, important as that may be. If credit appears too intangible to run an entire economy, it is so because we are used to thinking about the economy itself in physicalist terms; we have already seen that people assume that money is 'backed' by gold. If, on the other hand, we view the economy in relational and institutional terms, credit does not appear so insubstantial after all.

Credit as a Right to Future Control

The early-twentieth-century economist John Commons attempted to reorient economics by identifying an economy as transacting in commodities only *through rights*:

> [I]ndividual actions are really *trans*-actions instead of either individual behaviour or the 'exchange' of commodities. It is this shift from commodities and individuals to transactions and working rules of collective action that marks the transition from the classical and hedonic schools to the institutional schools of economic thinking ... the smallest unit of the institutional economists is a unit of activity—a transaction, with its participants. Transactions ... are, not the 'exchange of commodities', but the alienation and acquisition, between individuals, of the *rights* of property and liberty created by society. (Commons, 1931, pp. 651–652, emphasis original)

We do not actually encounter commodities initially. Between us and commodities there is always an irreducible layer of rights derived from society. We lay claim to each other's products by virtue of a system of rights and then swap them through our transactions. This system is not necessarily egalitarian: Commons identifies 'conflict' as well as 'dependence' and 'order' as attributes of all transactions (ibid., p. 656).

Working rules, formal and informal, are our collective hooks on the future-oriented world of the production and distribution of commodities. From the institutionalist point of view, 'legal control is future physical control' (ibid., p. 657). Rules and laws establish sanctions of various kinds (ethical, economic, jurisprudential) that *control* individual actions. This sociopolitical world of rules *is the very medium* of the world of commodities and their value, variably locking the commodity and its value to our transactional activity. Working rules are the connective tissue between production and circulation yesterday, today and tomorrow.

One of the most critical working rules or institutions of the economy is that which connects buyers and sellers. We naturally have to pay for our purchases, but, counterintuitively, most payments in an economy are *not* instantaneous. Most transactions occur in finite time; there is a definite period of time from purchase to final payment for the purchase. Until full payment is complete, *buyers are in debt to sellers.*

Any deferred payment immediately creates an implicit or explicit credit–debt relationship. This can take many forms—from a tab at the local shop to a credit-card bill or a mortgage. Until we pay our taxes, we are in debt to the state. Until we are paid our salary at the end of the month, we are creditors to our employers, advancing them our labour ahead of payment. Credit and debt are simply the obverse of most transactions.

If, following Commons, transactions deal in rights to commodities but also occur in finite time, then credit and debt are equally foundational to an economy. Transactions autochthonously generate credit–debt relations; this is equally true of 'transactions with nature'—that is, production processes given the finite time between input and output. Credit and debt are not epiphenomenal but definitional. 'Money' is the means of *settling* an economy's ongoing debts.

Credit, then, is a *right to future physical control of commodities or value*—a right which has all the force of formal or informal social sanction. Credit is a future-oriented right over valuable things and actions, a promissory relation created by our economic interactions and hardened into an institutional or legal form with the force of a right. This is an ideal type: actual creditary rights will of course vary empirically.

The value of this creditary right emerges from its two (inherently variable) elements: the strength of the claim to value and the value of the good or service claimed. We take up the first element in the next section, where we argue that creditary claims come in two broad types depending on the kind of social relation that institutionalised them.

Types of Mutualisation, Varieties of Money

We broadly classify credit claims into two kinds: (*a*) claims that economic units have against each other and (*b*) claims that the state has on citizens and taxation—namely political claims. Both these claims are of different social strengths in that one carries a lower penalty when violated than the other.

Our inspiration here is Emile Durkheim's distinction between organic and mechanical solidarity. Economic contracts are encoded in the civil law, whereas 'contracts' with the state are encoded in the criminal law. Civil remedies are less severe than criminal ones. For Durkheim, this indicated deeper social priorities that communities bonded around. We deploy the distinction between economic and political contracts as *an index of creditworthiness*, namely the likelihood that a credit claim will be paid.

Credit by definition is two-sided: one unit's credit is simultaneously another's debt; one's asset the other's liability. We use the term 'mutualisation' to describe this deep interlocking. Mutualisation occurs when one unit's cash commitment or liability is another's source of cash or asset. For example, if a company owes its supplier, this is an asset to the supplier and simultaneously a liability for the company. The balance sheets of the two units are interlocked, representing the two sides of a credit–debt relation. This kind of credit interlocking is both ubiquitous and asynchronous: debts come due at different times and do not always line up with cash inflows.

Mutualisation lies at the heart of the social ontology of any economy. If one unit's asset is literally another's liability, then these units are not merely interdependent but joined at the hip (along some margin). Individual economic units are radically incomplete without the broader division of labour. What appear as individual economic units are actually deeply social. Karl Marx and Durkheim both in their own way urged us to look beyond the fetish of isolated units, sanctified by liberalism and neoclassical economics, to the reality of the sociality of any economy. While this may be a hierarchical sociality, it is nevertheless a different paradigm from mainstream economics and much of economic sociology.

Yet classical social theory underplayed the dimension of time even though Marx's M–C–M' always occurs in finite time. Since all socio-economic relations are mediated by time, they are all inherently creditary: C–M' comes at some future date during which a creditary relation is in play. Credit, again, is not epiphenomenal to an economy but foundational, as irreducible as time itself. Following Hyman Minsky, we observe that this temporal dimension makes production like a bond instrument— money now for money later. This is not to flatten the distinction between real and financial operations but to illustrate their shared temporal properties. Mutualisation of balance sheets is one way to capture this level of abstraction, namely the ongoing, time-stamped interlocking of balance sheets in any economy.

Given the many-sided, uneven nature of economy-wide interlocking of balance sheets, coordinating agents are required to map asynchronous credit relations onto some means of paying off the debt—that is, 'money'. These agents are called banks. We will see here that banks always come in systems.

To understand mutualisation, we introduce the simple formalism of balance sheets represented as 'T accounts'. This abstraction is useful because it enables us to see how qualitatively distinct creditary promises can be commensurate by the logic of interlocking cash flows.

All economic and political units—households, firms, states—can be represented by (but not reduced to) two-sided balance sheets with assets and liabilities, sources of money and commitments to pay money. Whatever else these units do, they are imbricated in capitalism's cash nexus. Under capitalism, all units need cash, national money, to live and pay taxes; Minsky called this the 'survival constraint'. Cash connections are a critical layer of the map of the economy. Ordinary units secure cash by selling something or borrowing, with commerce and finance occupying the same ontological level.

Mutualisation is when one unit's cash commitment is another's source of cash. This interlocking of balance sheets is exemplified by institutions called 'banks', but *we are all banks* to the extent that we have cross-cutting, interlocking claims for cash with each other. A supplier that accepts delayed payment, like a salaried worker waiting for the end of the month, is implicitly a financier.

Banks borrow central-bank money and commit to repay their creditors, 'depositors', on demand. Their commitment is a source of cash for depositors: 'savings' is a physicalist expression making us think that we have placed some valuable *things* in safe keeping rather than engaged in a *promissory* relationship (see Chapter 2). By interlocking in this way, depositors and banks have mutualised their balance sheets to the extent of the deposit. This is economic mutualisation. We can think of the state's tax claims similarly—namely political mutualisation of the balance sheets of individual taxpayers (Figure 1.1).

While the balance sheet mechanics of mutualisation are the same in both cases, the relative strength of the credit claims is qualitatively distinct. An ideal-type state has better credit claims than an ideal-type bank because political claims are more robust than economic claims and operate over a much broader economic catchment area.

Mutualisation creates a 'collective' in the sense of a mutually dependent set of relations. Whereas private banks offer mutualisation on economic or commercial terms (that is, formally voluntaristic) to loan and deposit customers, states politically

Bank		Depositor	
Assets	Liabilities	Assets	Liabilities
Sources of money	*Commitments to pay*	*Sources of money*	*Commitments to pay*
	'Deposit'	'Deposit'	
	Loan from customer	Loan to bank	

Taxpayer		State	
Assets	Liabilities	Assets	Liabilities
Sources of money	*Commitments to pay*	*Sources of money*	*Commitments to pay*
	Tax	Tax	
	Future payment	Future income	

Figure 1.1   Economic versus political mutualisation

mutualise citizen wealth through taxation and social expenditure. Economic mutualisation is both of a different order and, although highly robust in itself, *less robust* than political mutualisation in that it can be violated at a lower cost.

By collectivising and institutionalising promises to pay, mutualisation allows us to understand why credit claims have real value and why different types of credit claims have different values. Balance sheets comprising economic mutualisation have a different tenor and scale than those made up of political mutualisation. Bank assets are a fraction of the economic projects of their loan customers. But the state represents the mutualisation of all citizens through the tax system: 'The state owns some part of each one of us, but we also own some part of it and, through its intermediation, some part of one another' (Mehrling, 2000a, p. 367).

Since robustness varies even within different types of mutualisation, it is certainly possible to have a particular bank money that is better than a particular national money; this has often occurred in the past or indeed in the present if we compare substantial multinational banks with certain developing states (see Figure 1A.1). But modern states in rich nations have enormously expanded capacities, with their tax revenues taking up over a third of gross domestic product (GDP) on average (Organisation for Economic Cooperation and Development [OECD], 2022). Of the top 100 units in the world by revenue generation, states occupy the top nine positions even in an age of world-spanning corporations which occupy seventy-one of the 100 places (Babic, Fichtner and Heemskerk, 2017). Democratic politics has made modern states economic leviathans; the well-ordered ones have liabilities that operate as money globally.

In the next section, we will combine the idea that credit is a right to future control with the idea that these creditary rights come in different types to answer how central-bank money and bank money are anchored in 'value'.

Banks Are Social Animals

The universe of transactions generates a complex, open-ended web of debtor–creditor relations; there is always someone who owes someone else money in an ongoing fashion. There is therefore a huge job to be done in coordinating and mapping these asynchronous credit relations onto one another and ultimately onto the means of final settlement—money. This mapping occurs from hyper-local to hyper-global levels of the division of labour.

Enter banks, specialist dealers in credits and debits that take on individual units' IOUs (I owe you) and replace their own credit claim for a fee. Our physicalist word for this is 'lending', but it is more accurately 'accepting', as banks accept or take on the liability of their loan customers and replace it with their own. Banks can do this because their balance sheets are composed of a large number of mutualised creditary rights, making their own credit superordinate.

Let us start with the liabilities side. Banks take loans from owners of central-bank money, 'depositors', that they promise to return on demand. The instantaneity of these loans makes it easy for banks to borrow money; depositor-lenders can recall the loan at any moment. As we have seen, we do not even take 'depositing' to be a borrowing or lending exercise.

By holding on to depositor's money, banks in effect are re-borrowing central-bank money (or national money) at every instant. The fact that bank liabilities can be exchanged for national money on demand makes bank money almost as good as central-bank money from the user's standpoint.

An institution whose liabilities are almost as good as central-bank money could up to a point create *more* near-money liabilities merely by writing up more ledger entries, generating more claims against itself offset by claims it has against others. Having durably mutualised large amounts of national money, banks are in a position to create fresh credit claims promising to pay national money, namely bank money. This is 'lending' (Figure 1.2), another physicalist term for a credit-relation operation.

Mutualisation of depositor liquidity makes bank money work almost like national money. This makes the bank a super debtor, owing money to its depositors. But this also enables a loan business whereby banks can create more money-like claims against themselves backed by future assets, namely loans which are promises to pay the bank national money in the future. This makes the bank a super creditor. In place of myriad individual credit–debt relations distributed across time and space, we have a super creditor or debtor that socialises these relations on its own balance sheet anchored by credit claims on future value. While this appears like the physical act of pass-the-parcel 'intermediation' or borrowing money to on-lend it, this appearance is itself an outcome of mutualisation or socialisation.

In a sense, a borrower has 'printed money' by issuing a credit instrument: an individual, non-monetary IOU. However, the bank accepts the borrower's credit note only after screening and the provision of collateral and legal protection. Yet the general public accepts the bank's liability furnished to the borrower because of its near-money qualities.

Bank		Borrower	
Assets	Liabilities	Assets	Liabilities
+Loan	+Checking account	+Checking account	+Loan

Figure 1.2 Expansion of balance sheets on both sides: a swap of IOUs

Thus, what has occurred in the process of 'lending' is in fact a swap of IOUs: the borrower has given the bank an individual IOU, and the bank has in return given the borrower a checking account—namely some bank money which can be used as means of payment. An *individual* IOU has been swapped for a *social* IOU, a claim on a socially mutualised balance sheet. The individual IOU is not socially acceptable as a means of payment: as an idiosyncratic instrument, it is entirely illegible to the public. But once it passes through a creditary process, it becomes part of a bank's larger set of borrowing or lending operations. The bank has assumed the risk of the borrower and replaced the individual borrower's IOU with its own socially legible IOU. Banks of course profit from this assumption of risk by charging interest, but we can read this as a kind of minting fee for turning individual IOUs into social metal.

This operation recalls John Searle's parable of the Chinese room. Locked in a room with a computer programme that can translate Chinese characters slipped under the door, a computer operator who knows no Chinese can appear to those outside as if he does. Similarly, by arranging a steady inflow of national money (from interest or repayments, fractional cash reserves and other borrowing), banks appear to those outside as cash warehouses sitting on a substantial physical pile of national money. Banks pass the monetary Turing Test by dealing so efficiently in interlocking *flows* of credit that flows appear to us as *stocks*. Yet bank liabilities are not money but near-money—just as the computer operator's knowledge of Chinese in Searle's parable is not the real thing but the functional equivalent.

There is clearly a constitutive precarity in balance sheets thus arranged, given the 'sight' nature of their liabilities. It is impossible to know exactly how much cash to keep in reserve for withdrawals, and a private bank's commercial interest is in issuing more of its own liabilities by way of loans. An individual bank can either be heavy or light on cash depending on the random flow of business. Loans can go bad. Banks need liquidity to survive, but they need loans to profit. Banks therefore arrange for backstop liquidity loans from each other, doing for each other what they do for their individual loan clients.

In this way, banks mutualise their own balance sheets in order to solve their own inherent liquidity issues, immediately creating hierarchy in a money system. This interbank mutualisation is constitutive of creditary operations, as Fernand Braudel's credit fairs of the thirteenth century, for example, make clear (Braudel, 1992, p. 112). In modern credit systems, interbank mutualisation takes the form of (global and national) clearing houses, interbank markets for central-bank money, central banks themselves and central-bank swap lines at the global level. Interbank mutualisation adds several layers to the hierarchy of money.

So critical is the refinance from other banks in compensating for the inherent fragility of banking that it is impossible to account for the money-like nature of bank liabilities without conceiving of a mutualised *system* of backstop liquidity. This includes a central bank whose liabilities can be created and destroyed (borrowed and repaid) as a last resort. Only the entire hierarchical system operating in sync can ensure the ever-ready transformability of any particular bank's money into central-bank money. The Chinese room misdirection works so well in normal times that we do not even perceive the difference between bank money and central-bank money. A stand-alone bank is therefore a category error. Banks are social animals.

This tendency to socialise liquidity is made all the more urgent by the nature of the banks' survival constraint: its liabilities are set at a fixed price of 1 to national bank money (see the following discussion). Without any flexibility on the price, banks have to secure adequate *quantities* of liquidity to meet this par constraint, a further element of thingification (Chapter 2). To meet this par constraint, banks keep reserves on hand and borrow as a first resort from each other and as a last resort from the central bank. It takes a system.

By acting as mutualised (twice over, at the level of both depositors and banks) pools of debts or credits, banks-in-systems are able to construct balance sheets that issue liabilities that are of superior creditworthiness than their loan customers. If the universe of transactions means that someone always owes someone else money, then insertion of a banking system into this universe means that someone always owes the bank money.

Banks are more creditworthy than their customers because they have mutualised individual depositors' balance sheets. This of course is the source of its profit: borrowing cheaply (and over the very short term) and lending dearer (over the longer term).

Still higher orders of credit are achievable at even wider scales but only by a different type of mutualisation. Banks can mutualise only so far and no further before they hit the limit of economic mutualisation; sometimes that limit is only discerned once the system is in freefall.

Banking with the State

If economic life has a temporality that autochthonously generates credit and lends itself to specialist dealers in liquidity or time, state–society interactions have a similar debt-generating temporality at a different scale and by means of a distinct type of mutualisation.

Taxes roll in over time (or not), but the war or development or any state function needs to happen today. Banking is the institutional art of turning future earning potential into cash today, not by lending an accumulated money hoard but by securing access to future cash to such a degree that the bank's own liabilities become near-money. Replace loan repayments and deposits with future taxes and bond issuance, and you scale up banking principles while turning economic bonds into political ones.

When merchant bankers found themselves in charge of city-states in fifteenth-century Europe, they figured out how to graft their banking technology onto future tax income. The result is what we call the *fiscal–monetary machine*, a concatenation of fiscal and banking power that was taken to world-conquering scale by 'fiscal-military states' (Brewer, 1989). When this machine was eventually democratised, its tax base became each and every domiciled resident, citizen and firm. A form of bank money was now backed by *political* mutualisation at a nation-state scale and set the task of providing for the republic.

Political bonding at national scale enables a combination of fiscal and banking technologies that generates a credit instrument, a promise, whose remarkable flexibility and stability win out in serving the often conflicting needs of expanding capital and a demanding *demos*. The fact that the state has a tax debt owed to it into the distant future makes the state both a political leviathan and an economic behemoth. Banking then turns this political asset into credit so good that it works as money.

We can see this combination of fiscal and banking technologies if we read back through the balance sheet of the central bank to a sequence of interlocking promises (Figure 1.3). Promises depend on what is in the vault, and central banks have government bonds as assets (gold is vestigial). Government bonds, in turn, are promises of the state through its treasury: the state effectively borrows from the bond purchaser and promises to pay them a fixed interest rate until the maturity of the bond, at which point it returns the face value. The treasury's promise is of course backed by the state's legitimate power to tax. Money is backed by bonds, which are backed by taxes, which in turn are backed by the production of citizens thrown into the indefinite future.

The national economy		The state		The central bank	
Assets	Liabilities	Assets	Liabilities	Assets	Liabilities
'Value'	Tax	Tax	Bonds	Bonds (Gold)	'Money'

Figure 1.3 The fiscal–monetary machine: interlocking of the state, the central bank and the national economy's balance sheets

We now have an answer to the question 'What is central-bank money a promise to pay?' From Figure 1.3, we can see that central-bank money is a promise to pay a share of GDP if we take that to represent 'value' created in an economy. This value is at once abstract (we cannot touch or smell GDP) and material (see Chapter 7). Central-bank money is not a promise to pay another instrument or commodity, but it is anchored by something broader and more flexible than any commodity—namely the productive power of people working together.

This institutional mediation between central-bank money and the economy, a mediation that runs through the fiscal system, is a necessary one. We have seen that money is a promise on a promise or, to use Chris Desan's phrase, debt on debt. Just as bank money is a promise to pay another promise (that is, central-bank money), so central-bank money is a promise based on another promise—that is, government bonds.

If central-bank money is a debt on debt, the asset-side debt is in the form of an interest-bearing asset and the liability-side debt in the form of money. The separation is vital and not accidental. The asset side fiscally anchors money to the future product of the nation; it therefore requires the form of an asset. Money itself cannot be interest-bearing since that would increase calculation and therefore transactions costs. Building a non-interest money-bearing instrument on top of a bond asset structure anchors this money in the material dimension. Central banking securitises government bonds, transforming them into a zero-interest, perpetual bearer bond that is money. The *indirectness* of the claim of money on the national economy is therefore functional, ensuring both robustness and scale, flexibility, usability, and so on.

Like layers of abstraction in computer architecture, money as a debt on debt enables simplicity and usability at the front end to be combined with complexity, robustness and scale at the back end. The institutional mediation of politically interlocking balance sheets is precisely what simultaneously socialises and materialises money.

Hierarchy and Hybridity

Still further layers of intermediation are required to deal with the complex division of labour of modern economies. A central bank standing alone could never offer banking services to an entire economy. Part of the reason for this, following F. A. Hayek, is because information is distributed in an economy in a granular, piecemeal fashion that is not necessarily discernible to a centralised credit operation. But this points to a deeper feature of an economy: the unevenness of any complex division of labour.

We have seen that credit is native to an economy. Credit is created and destroyed through transactions all the time as part of the natural metabolism of economic life. But because transactional space is uneven, credit is created or destroyed within and around particular zones of economic operation. Any economy has points of concentration and dispersion: spatially these are cities and their surrounding economies, functionally these are production and distribution supply chains, and so on. Catchment areas of credit that are smaller than 'the national economy' are therefore bound to emerge in healthy economic life.

Thus, if a central bank were to do justice to credit creation for an entire economy, it would have to construct its own vast branch network adequate to this unevenness. This would be the equivalent of having an entirely state-owned banking system as in China or India to a large extent.

But even where banking is formally nationalised, it would have to be cut according to the division of labour in an economy in order to work. Its form of mutualisation, in other words, would remain *economic*, bringing together smaller balance sheets in different areas of the uneven division of labour. The collective represented by the depositors and borrowers of a state-owned bank would be qualitatively and quantitatively different from that represented by the larger pool of the nation's taxpayers which ultimately backs central-bank money. There would be a substantial difference between the money liabilities of a state-owned bank and those of the central bank following their differences in type and scale of mutualisation. State-owned banks require surpluses for operational needs, and the orientation of discipline and elasticity of credit would not exclusively be profit for shareholders. But this is merely a different version of economic mutualisation.

If the central bank or the state-owned banking system declined to operate in such a disaggregated fashion, it would result in stagnation, the willy-nilly emergence of credit in various underground ways or (most likely) some combination of the two. There is no stopping credit creation, and, given the nature of the division of labour, there is no stopping economic mutualisation. The necessity of economic mutualisation is driven by the nativity of credit to an economy which always has an uneven division of labour. This is true whatever the formal ownership structure of the banking system—that is, whether it is owned publicly or privately.

We see evidence of the emergence of credit willy-nilly in all kinds of situations— from deferred payments during India's demonetisation to subprime lending in the United States (US), from the de facto emergence of the US dollar as a global currency to Bitcoin exchanges that are de facto Bitcoin banks. This is only to mention those instances covered in Part II. Credit cannot be eliminated, but because credit systems are inherently hierarchical, credit can be curated and controlled to serve a larger purpose. Given the centrality of credit to economic life, it would be folly to eliminate it—hence the irrationality of the cryptocurrency enterprise.

We should therefore not confuse the distinction between political and economic mutualisation with the distinction between public and private ownership (Table 1.1). For entirely contingent reasons, rich nations of the world have money systems wherein *money* has been nationalised, but *banking* has been privatised. Such systems have dynamics and contradictions all their own (Chapter 8). The hybridity of *ownership*, between public and private balance sheets, is contingent. After all, we have cases where the central bank itself is formally *privately* owned but over time operates with a public orientation. This of course is the story of the BoE founded in 1694, which politics made a public-oriented bank well before it was formally nationalised in 1946 (Chapter 4).

There is a deeper hybridity in all money hierarchies between political mutualisation at the system's apex and economic mutualisation at the system's capillaries. This hybridity is functional because it combines a highly secure 'outside money'—national money—with a highly flexible and granular 'inside money'—bank money. Outside money responds slowly and only in the last instance, thereby backstopping the entire system, whereas inside money responds with higher frequency and in a more localised fashion, mapping onto the uneven division of labour. Most money used in a mature economy (with some exceptions) is bank money rather than cash.

A healthy money system *has* to be a hierarchy, at once centralised and distributed, combining outside and inside money. This is most efficiently achieved by combining political mutualisation at the apex of the system with economic mutualisation at its capillaries.

Political mutualisation, with outsized scale and robustness, is best fit for the provision of outside money. If greater robustness leads to greater potential creditworthiness, it also leads to greater potential credit control. This is because in the competition for credit, the more creditworthy balance sheets set the terms for

Table 1.1 Hybrid money hierarchies

Credit system level	Type of money	Type of mutualisation	Formal ownership
Apex	National money	Political mutualisation	Public or private ownership
Capillaries	Bank money	Economic mutualisation	Public or private ownership

the less creditworthy. Political units at the largest scale will set the credit terms for smaller economic units. What we call 'monetary policy' is an asymmetric setting of creditary terms by the most creditworthy unit in a jurisdiction through its bank, the central bank. Globally, the most robust state covering the greatest politically institutionalised economic catchment area sets credit terms for the rest (Chapter 9). Robust mutualisation enables us to account for monetary power, a kind of market power in national and global credit markets rather than brute coercion (Chapter 3).

But while it is well suited for anchoring outside money and controlling it at a macro level, political mutualisation cannot replicate the smaller scale and granularity of economic mutualisation operating with the warp and weft of a complex division of labour. This is why all functional money systems are hybrids between political and economic mutualisation.

Capitalism, Democracy and the National Pillars of Globalisation

In conclusion, we say a few words about the broader social formation that imposes particular demands on modern money to give it its particular cast. This goes especially for the hybridity between political and economic mutualisation. Purely political or purely economic mutualisation would still lead to hierarchy in credit systems. But the hierarchical hybridisation of political and economic mutualisation in money systems occurs when flourishing capitalism must be combined with democracy.

The defining structure of our current epoch is the strained marriage between capitalism and democracy. This social formation, capitalism plus democracy, obviously varies widely over the surface of the globe. Yet however weakened democracy might be at present, no state is immune from having to legitimise its actions in the name of the people. This generates historically specific demands on money—that it be simultaneously flexible and stable at an economy-wide scale. Undemocratic but capitalist money need not be quite so flexible, especially at the apex of the system, since the state has fewer demands upon it for social expenditure.

This is why the archetype of 'sound money', the gold standard, was coterminous with both the absence of universal franchise and global empire. As Karl Polyani pointed out long ago, it was the undemocratic political settlement of the late nineteenth century that enabled the gold standard to operate, not its physicalist properties—hence the danger of fixed-by-design cryptocurrencies, whether their architects intend it or not.

We argue that only social relations—not gold, not cryptographic tokens—are capable of meeting the dual demand of capitalism plus democracy, but only social relations configured in a particular way—namely the hybridisation of political and economic mutualisation. Only social relations robustly institutionalised through fiscal, monetary and banking institutions are up to the task of producing money for democracy and capitalism together. Variations in political and economic mutualisation combine with scale to account for monetary variation and hierarchy.

Another money puzzle is how the currency of a particular nation state functions as world money. There are no gunboats directly enforcing the global writ of the US dollar even though many rich nations enjoy an American security envelope. Surely one of the major ironies of 'globalisation' is that it depends so much on the support of the balance sheets of hegemonic nation states. The explosion of globe-spanning capital flows and criss-crossing global supply chains means that the anchoring role of national monies is covered over. Yet this foundational role is revealed in times of crisis.

That financial globalisation is parasitic on certain national balance sheets gives us a sense of the power of robust mutualisation at scale. Some political communities have coupled high productivity with a particularly configured banking architecture to produce a money that combines security, flexibility and scale. Sometimes, a money instrument can have such robustness that it can be used extraterritorially— that is, by agents outside its home political contract. These external users free-ride on the robustness of the political community without diluting its fidelity up to a point. Issuers of world money are fiscal–monetary machines that have a surplus of robustness that allows their national monies to operate beyond their boundaries as world money.

This surplus compensates for the absence of a global fiscal constituency even while endowing such states with the exorbitant privilege of issuing world money. There is no world state, no global fiscal space that can politically mutualise balance sheets at a global level. But there are sub-global units with a surplus of robustness that allow their national monies to operate beyond their boundaries as world money.

Wretched inequality within the hegemonic nations of the Global North has meant that the monetary power of these states is truly flexed only when the entire system is in deep distress—for instance, during the financial crisis of 2008 and the Covid-19 crisis—rather than for the good of all its citizens, much less as a global public good. For all the world-spanning financial flows, when the crisis hits, the system collapses back onto the balance sheets of the central banks of hegemonic states. Swap lines between major central banks and the Federal Reserve, born in crisis, are now permanent backstops to the system, for instance. But politics means that only backstops to crises are conceived rather than ex-ante control mechanisms, even though the ability to backstop implies the ability to control.

Proliferating and criss-crossing global financial flows occlude the fact that the pillars of globalisation are firmly national, a fact only revealed when the cycle turns. Of course, not all national states form such pillars; this falls to a few large states configured in particular ways by their politics and economics. Globalisation of any kind is a political 'choice', the sum total of political forces within nations interlocking with those made in other constituencies; it is not an inevitable force of nature.

Another piece of evidence for the foundational role of certain national balance sheets for financial globalisation is the nature of the world's largest market—that for the exchange of foreign currency. The instruments traded in those markets are the monies of particular *states*. This centrality is mirrored in the size of the US treasury market, a foundational global market for the world's most risk-free asset which has an average daily trading volume of approximately USD 600 billion. If the centre of global money markets is the money and debt of a subset of states, this surely gives these states substantial degrees of potential leverage over markets.

Whether this potential is actually exercised comes down to the political equilibrium domestically within hegemonic nations as well as the equilibrium between nations. But the fact that some national monies anchor global capital ought to instruct us as to the nature of money itself.

Thus, even hegemonic states do not have untrammelled power over money. States face what Minsky called the survival constraint (Chapter 3). They need to have their liabilities, money and debt, accepted by both citizens and market operators. Legitimacy is the constraint on the first form of acceptance; value and security are the constraint on the second. The privilege of a sovereign is to bend the survival constraint further than others, not to break it. Those sovereigns who can bend it furthest are the furthest up the hierarchy of world money. Thus, while an appropriately configured state has the potential edge in money, we have to understand the nature and limits of monetary power if we are to democratically design money.

The contradiction of the global money system is of course that political mutualisation of any kind is almost absent at the global level. Global monetary power therefore defaults to the single largest politically mutualised economic block, which is the US (Chapter 9). The logic of political mutualisation shows us that we require some non-state form of political mutualisation at the global level to impel the national balance sheet providing world money to do so, at least partly, as a global public good.

Theories of Money

All theories build on others while marking themselves off from them. The space of money theories is marked by much contention between the three main schools of thought: commodity theories, state theories and banking or credit theories. We devote a chapter to each in Part I. Addressing state theories, Chapter 3 outlines the nature and limits of monetary sovereignty. Chapter 4 discusses how the Banking School does not apply its own creditary logic to the state resulting, ironically, in a residual Chartalism. Chapter 5 takes up the money view of a recent exponent of the Banking School, Perry Mehrling, to show how his vital account of hierarchy implies a political logic of mutualisation. Chapter 6 reads the work of Geoffrey Ingham to illustrate how the best version of Chartalism relegates politics to historical rather than logical status in money. Finally, Chapter 7 takes on the question of money's value—namely the material dimension that was critical to the Metallist School. This political theory of money shares much with all three schools while adding some new elements and reformatting others.

Commodity theories of money account for its value by pointing to a metallic monetary medium or a commodity referent. Such theories become normative in a world after gold, claiming that money *ought* to be backed by something of substantial value (or in the case of cryptocurrencies, contrived scarcity value). This impulse contains an important intuition central to classical economics: money cannot be the same thing as wealth. Yet our post-gold reality exposed what was always implicit in the system: the focus on the commodity referent is overly narrow, really just a means of *disciplining* a credit system rather than defining money's ontology. Discipline in credit is indeed required, but the elimination of something as foundational as credit is infeasible. On the other hand, a purely social or state theory of money lacks an account of variability in part because it forgoes the material dimension so critical to commodity theories. We argue that money does indeed have a material predication, but one that is anchored by a fiscal–monetary and civil–legal architecture to the *future* of a national economy for national money and sets of commercial 'economies' for bank money, rather than to a crude commodity referent.

State theories of money, Chartalism and its modern adherents, derive money's value entirely from its ability to pay off a state-imposed tax debt: 'taxes drive money'. But politics drives taxes, so politics must drive money. Chartalists are correct to focus on taxes as far as national money goes but take too nominalist a path. As such, they lack an account of economic mutualisation for bank money. But even on their home ground, they read taxes entirely as expressing an assumed constant called 'sovereignty' rather than the variable of state legitimacy. 'Sovereignty' becomes a black box containing the vast universe of state–society relations and all the variable institutional political economy of money. Finally, by focusing on the nominalist power of the state, they miss the material dimension of money in accounting for its value. The politics of acceptability can vary independently of the materialist dimension. The theoretical status of taxation is completely different in the theory outlined here, a creature of dynamic fiscal sociology rather than brutally coercive 'sovereignty'. As such, Chartalists miss the entire space of variation of robustness and scale that allows us to account for monetary diversity. Chartalists have no theory of monetary hierarchy. Theirs is an account of the special case.

Credit theories of money locate its value in what, as an IOU, it promises to pay. In a post-gold world, such theories hew dangerously close to state theories by failing to identify what money now promises to pay. Credit theories necessarily focus on futurity, and their acknowledgement of differences in creditworthiness goes a long way in accounting for monetary variation. Yet being more concerned with system dynamics, they bracket the ontology of central-bank money. Unlike bank money, central-bank money does not fulfil its promise in *instrument* form. Central-bank money is a promise to pay 'value' anchored by fiscal and banking institutions in the national economy in more or less durable ways. While the best credit theories acknowledge that all credit money is intrinsically hierarchical, they do not account for the source of hierarchy because they skip over the differential ontology of the underlying balance sheets. We argue that these differences emerge from different types of mutualisation, types of social relations, economic or political.

Our political theory of money, then, takes on board the *materialism* of commodity theories but not their reductionism, the implicit *political focus* of Chartalism but not its state fetish, and the *institutionalism and futurity* of credit theories while adding a sociopolitical account of hierarchy in credit systems. By pointing to the future value of a social economy anchored politically and institutionally, the theory's materialism is not reductive. By rendering the state as the institutionalised expression of a legitimate political settlement, its statism is both grounded and capable of accounting for monetary difference. And by seeing IOU-issuing balance sheets as differentially socialised at different scales, its creditary imaginary is hierarchical because it is anchored in the material productivity and robustness of mutualisation of particular political or economic communities.

Conclusion

Combining the scale and certainty of future taxes with the institutional magic of credit, the modern fiscal–monetary machine turns the national economy itself into the reserve asset of a special kind of bank. Molten, future-oriented, politically intermediated economic activity outstrips both congealed metal and cold cryptography as the dynamic anchor of a credit system subject to the demands of capital and democracy. While the system's core is made up of political mutualisation, its outworks comprise economic mutualisation (whatever the formal ownership pattern) and banks which are more granular in their operation and require constant propping up from the core. Different types of social relations lead to mutualisations of variable robustness and scale, giving us monetary variation and hierarchy.

The core–outworks or apex–capillary distinction is functional; it does not follow that retail banks will be privately owned. Yet because money has everywhere been nationalised while banks in rich nations are privatised (the hegemonic model), the entire credit system is wrapped in a fetish of 'fiat money' (Chapter 2). Mutualisation works like Marx's commodity fetish, making the social–abstract relation of credit appear as a money-thing. In normal times, we cannot even tell the difference between the core and outworks, between promises and things.

The promise-on-promise nature of modern monetary systems makes it appear as if the currency pyramid is floating in air, inherently self-referential; one reason for this could be that we still do not have a good way of thinking about economic value, itself abstract yet social and material. But money-as-credit is struck by a set of balance sheets locked together and built on real economic productivity. The more there is of this activity, and the stronger knitted together the balance sheets are, the better the credit note struck against them. Robust mutualisation at scale drives hierarchy in money, but both political and economic mutualisation vary greatly, leading to monetary variation.

Appendix 1A

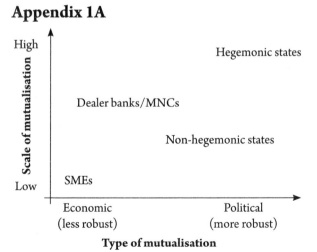

Figure 1A.1   Robust mutualisation at scale

2 | THE MONEY FETISH
Making Promises into Things

In the last chapter, we saw that credit is not epiphenomenal but constitutive of political and economic life. The economist's fiction of a barter economy 'veiled' by money leads to a thing-based monetary science of quantities, velocities and value from scarcity. But a *monetary* economy is ontologically distinct, a social entity that requires a social science.

Yet the economist's intuition is not entirely misguided: money does in fact behave like a thing with value, a commodity. The question is *how* it does that, and why different money-things have different values.

Money is the outcome of an institutional process by which creditary *promises* acquire the attributes of *things*, commodities with value. This of course recalls Marx's idea of the commodity fetish whereby social relations between people take the necessary form of appearance of relations between things because the social element, 'value', being abstract cannot be perceived as such. With money, this process occurs through a particular kind of institutionalisation, 'mutualisation', a ubiquitous socio-economic relation which is at the core of the social technology of banking—namely the business of dealing in credit. The relation with bank money especially is obscured; given its form of mutualisation, we never encounter it as such.

The magic of credit, and the outcome of mutualisation, is the *functional thingification of promises*: promises remain promises, but they can move about the world like value-bearing things. So successful is this process that common sense takes money to be a fiat-thing, a token rather than a credit-promise. Mutualisation is the variable process of making promises operate as things. Erroneous as an account of money's essence, 'fiat' nevertheless refracts the institutionalised source of money's power.

One of the main ways in which a money fetish is created in the credit system comes from hierarchy itself. One level's credit (inside money) is simultaneously another's money (outside money), and outside-ness confers thing-ness. We consider this first

An earlier version of this chapter was published as the article 'Money and "Demonetisation": The Fetish of Fiat' in the *Economic and Political Weekly* 51, no. 51: 36–42 © Sameeksha Trust 2016. All rights reserved.

before outlining four further elements of fetishism: 'lending to the bank' appearing as 'depositing', system-wide flows of liquidity appearing as localised stocks of cash, and credit creation appearing as dishoarding cash. Finally, we consider how the 'exchange rate' of 1 between bank money and central-bank money, the par constraint, amplifies the money fetish. We conclude by discussing the irony of the cryptocurrency enterprise attempting to copy the fetishised *projection* of the credit system by trying and failing to make bare tokens work as money.

The Fetishism of Outside Money

Mutualisation is an inherently hierarchical operation: a *promise* of one level of the hierarchy of money simultaneously functions like a *thing* at another level. To the issuer, credit is its own 'inside' promise or IOU. To those who use *another* unit's credit instrument as money, it is something *outside* them which they can only acquire by earning or borrowing. In short, it functions like a commodity. A third party's IOU that operates as money takes the same ontological form as a commodity to users of that money. It may be an IOU in essence, but because it is issued by a third party, to everyone else it may as well be a commodity for all intents and purposes.

Hierarchical chains of inside–outside relations develop: bank money is inside credit to banks but outside money to borrowers; central-bank money is inside credit to central banks but outside money to banks and everyone else; US dollars are inside credit to the Federal Reserve but outside money to everyone else. Credit money is endogenous to the issuer and exogenous to everyone else. Units at the top of the hierarchy could paraphrase that infamous monetary one-liner: 'It's our IOU, but it's your money.' *Outside-ness confers thingness.*

My IOU is my inside money: I merely have to expand my personal balance sheet to issue more (whether this is prudent or not, or accepted or not, is a separate matter). But bank money is an outside asset to me: only the bank can create it; I cannot. Bank money is simultaneously an inside liability for the bank and an outside asset for me: this simultaneity is the method by which our balance sheets interlock. The same distinction occurs all the way up the chain. Bank money is a promise to pay central-bank money, which is an outside asset to the bank but an inside liability to the central bank; one nation's central-bank money is an outside asset to another central bank. The outside asset has to be borrowed or earned just like a commodity.

Gold is no one's liability, an outside asset without simultaneously being an inside liability at any level. Promises to pay gold can be as good as gold: the gold standard was always a *credit* system, just one configured for discipline rather than elasticity, thanks to its arbitrary commodity referent.

From the point of view of the lower rungs, the outside asset one level up might as well be gold or indeed any commodity because it is a hard constraint to units at the lower level, something that it has to earn or borrow. This is why Minsky called it the 'survival constraint': most units need a form of outside money to live. The outside asset cannot be produced by a mere expansion of a unit's balance sheet unless that unit is a bank or a sovereign, and even then there are limits to monetary power (Chapter 3). Outside-ness therefore reads as 'commodity-ness' to units at lower levels; a creditary outside asset is the functional equivalent of a commodity.

The hierarchical logic of the credit system fitted out certain commodities as appropriate outside money, not some intrinsic property of commodities themselves. Following Ralph Hawtrey (Chapter 4), gold was demanded *because* it formed part of the credit system; not the other way around. The function of the commodity anchor is the function assigned to it by outside-ness—namely to modulate the discipline of the survival constraint.

The *commodity* anchor merely represents draconian discipline of credit because it tethers the human economy to an arbitrary quantity of an arbitrary physical commodity. Marx's commodity–money fetish then kicks in to make users and analysts like Marx read money as a commodity and the economy as barter. Denying the monetary nature of the economy has been highly detrimental to classical and neoclassical economics.

Promises Are Good for Capitalism Plus Democracy

But why go through the entire rigmarole of turning promises into money-things? Why not have precious things with actual (or cryptographically rendered) scarcity value do the job? The fact is that mere things are just not up to the job of being money under conditions of capitalism and democracy, *both* of which demand a money that is *simultaneously* elastic and stable. Elasticity is essential for the basic function of payments: economic units do not always have ready money on hand to pay their bills as they come due; they can borrow of course, but that just shifts the burden elsewhere in the system.

The deep fact is that economic activities of production and distribution are conducted in asynchronous time and therefore require payment coordination. Ultimately, we need a system that can *create and destroy* acceptable means of payment to bridge the inevitable temporal gaps that emerge in the division of labour; this is the hierarchical and hybrid credit system. The alternative is to simply conduct fewer or, what amounts to the same thing, slower payments—that is, have less capitalism. That also means less for democratic states to tax. This in turn would mean redistribution, rather than growth, would have to ensure legitimacy under current conditions, something unattainable in capitalist political settlements by definition.

Credit is certainly elastic, and stability is attainable in principle because credit systems are inherently hierarchical, thereby enabling technocratic management. But hierarchies are also subject to political capture. The politics of money is all about balance between elasticity and discipline, for whom and on what terms. Often that politics produces booms, busts and even stagnation, whose benefits and costs are unequally distributed. This only politics can change. We can escape this perpetual cat and mouse, eliminate credit and permanently petrify money only by brutally suppressing capitalism or democracy or both. Again, the kind of money we have emerges from the kind of society we have.

Very few entities are configured so that their mere promises can operate as money; to be so configured is of course to enjoy enormous social power, an exorbitant privilege, and therefore to incur the requirement of public accountability, if not outright public ownership. Banks are such entities, and central-bank-centred credit systems enhance the mutualised logic of banking by politically anchoring its collective balance sheet at the nation-state scale.

If the system's mutualisation is poorly done or the mutualisation process is damaged or overextended, the promissory element will bleed through the money fetish; the magic wears off and promises are mere promises again. How well mutualisation is done, and at what scale, tells us how well a particular credit instrument can operate like a money-thing. This is a dynamic fact that changes over the course of a business cycle: a boom can be defined as an expansion of the set of IOUs that are accepted as money; a bust sees a 'flight to quality'—namely a contraction of that set. A dynamic spectrum of more or less money-like credit is then conceivable—some credits so money-like that they operate well beyond their home base.

Monetary power results from a sociopolitical process rather than brute coercion. Bank money as a creditary right emerges from commerce as private entities constructed their own credit hierarchies; even if bank money now comes to be *measured* in the state's unit of account, its *value* derives from a (more or less contingent) commercial claim. With national money, coercion has to operate within the bounds of state legitimacy. 'Fiat' is more apt as a description of the thingification process in mutualisation than an account of the use of coercion in money. While it is true that central-bank money is no longer a promise to pay another instrument and is therefore 'irredeemable', it still derives its value from a creditary arrangement locking into a real economy; money is not a 'fiat' instrument.

Fetishism in the Credit System

Fetishism in the credit system occurs whereby individual creditary relations between the state and citizens and between customers and banks are necessarily concealed through a process of aggregation or socialisation. Just as Marx's commodities appear to have a life of their own but are in fact the products of collective labour, so does modern money appear to have a 'fiat' character, thanks to the nature of its production process through a combination of state and private credit.

One of the main ways in which a money fetish is created in the credit system, we noted earlier, comes from hierarchy itself. One level's inside money is another's outside money, and outside-ness confers thing-ness.

This section outlines three further elements of fetishism: 'lending to the bank' appearing as 'depositing', system-wide flows of liquidity appearing as localised stocks of cash, and credit creation appearing as dishoarding cash. The next section considers how the braiding of bank money and central-bank money through the par constraint amplifies the money fetish.

Our bank deposits are loans from the point of view of the bank. They are special types of loans that can be called back on demand by the lender, the depositors, at any moment. The any-time callability of our bank deposit gives us the impression that we have merely stored a thing called money in the building marked 'bank'. In fact, when we 'make a deposit' we are engaging in a creditary relationship, lending the bank money, and the bank stands ready to return our loan at any moment. This is why they are called 'demand' deposits.

Here is the most primary level of the money fetish. A bank is not a cash warehouse or a communal mattress under which we store our cash. It is a dealer in liquidity, borrowing in short-term, liquid form and lending out over longer periods in illiquid forms. In exchange for assuming this liquidity and maturity risk, the bank earns a profit called interest. By mutualising individual liquidity and generating a socially legible and acceptable IOU that functions as money, the bank is *transforming* individual liquidity into social liquidity.

Yet we do not observe this operation on the surface, in the sphere of credit circulation. We systematically mistake a social relationship—lending money to the bank—for a physical action: depositing a thing in a particular building. Social relations have taken the form of things and physical actions.

By themselves, banks are quite fragile creatures, given the nature of their promise to depositors. They have committed to stand ready to return their deposit-loan at any time, night or day, on demand. One way to make good on this promise is to simply have large stocks of cash on hand at all times. But that would be cash warehousing, not banking. It would also be a huge waste of society's resources.

Again, we do not appreciate this fragility from the communal-mattress point of view because of the fetishised credit relationship. This is further camouflaged by banks that go out of their way to cover over their fragility with the rhetoric of safety and stability. Banks keep only a small fraction of liquidity on hand at any time ('fractional reserve banking'). The entire hierarchical credit system matches liquidity so effectively that only a fraction of total outstanding liabilities is required at the user-facing front end to generate the outward appearance of a cash warehouse.

This is a second element of the money fetish, whereby *flows* through the system—fractional reserves plus interbank lending plus central-bank backstops—take on the appearance of *stocks* in a lone cash warehouse.

A third element occurs in the process of making loans. When a bank makes a loan to a borrower, it accepts the borrower's private IOU based on the borrower's creditworthiness and creates a checking account—that is, higher-quality claims that, unlike the borrower's personal IOU, can be used as a general means of payment. As we saw earlier, the bank's IOU is of higher quality or creditworthiness because it has so arranged or mutualised its balance sheet as to attract a substantial flow of liquidity towards it, be it in the form of deposits or interest on payments of other loans. In the act of the loan, banks create more socially legible liabilities against themselves in exchange for individual illegible IOUs that traditionally sit on their balance sheet until maturity.

Lending involves the creation of the bank's own IOUs for its loan customers by way of a brand-new checking account, *not* the physicalist idea of recycling cash items. Yet because its two liabilities—existing deposits and new loan-created checking accounts—are indistinguishable as balance-sheet entries, the processes of borrowing from depositors and lending to loan clients are subtly equivocated. Borrowing from depositors entails writing up the liabilities side of the bank's balance sheet, whereas lending entails writing up both sides simultaneously. But in both instances, more liabilities are created albeit by two distinct processes.

Unable to view this distinction, users and analysts alike build on the first element of the fetish—that we have deposited a thing in a building—to draw the conclusion that lending must operate the same way—that is, by banks borrowing physical money and on-lending it. Again, we have a physicalist misreading of the bank's loan operations as recycling some value substance rather than appreciating the social power of liquidity mutualisation and maturity transformation that the bank's balance sheet expresses. Banking is not money lending; banks are dealers in central-bank liquidity, creating and destroying their own near-money IOUs in the process.

Having engaged in the business of banking rather than cash warehousing, the bank can only make good on its promise to depositors in one way—ensure not just a sufficient stock of cash on hand but a potential inflow of cash should the need arise. That is, banks have borrowing and lending relationships with other banks and ultimately the central bank in order to manage temporary deficits or surpluses of cash-liquidity.

These refinancing arrangements are another layer of social relationships that banks themselves construct in order to produce a promise that is at once solid and liquid—solid in the sense of reliable and liquid in the sense of instantly available. The collection of promises that comprise our checking account with a bank is not the same thing as cash: they are merely balance-sheet entries in a ledger that promise to pay central-bank money, national money, on demand. That we equate these balance-sheet entries with actual cash in hand is a testament to a particular kind of collective achievement: the transformation of a social relationship into the universal equivalent.

Nationalised Money Plus Privatised Banking

Part of the misdirection in modern money is that an implicit fixed-price system between our two kinds of money, central-bank money and bank money, is read as a physical relationship between things. 'Depositing money in a bank' is a physical act. 'Lending central bank money to a money dealer in exchange for bank-money IOUs struck at a fixed price of 1 recallable on demand' is engaging in a creditary relationship. We think we are doing the first when we are actually doing the second. Working backwards from the familiar to denaturalise money helps us understand how two types of money emerging from distinct types of bonding or mutualisation are made to function as one most of the time. The process of making bank money and central-bank money function as the same 'thing' has another feature—that of giving promises the appearance of things.

These two types of credit—national money and bank money, outside money and inside money, respectively—are both highly robust, but one more than the other. Both are forms of *credit*, promises that function as money—that is, a means of payment, exchange and a store of value. But, as we have seen, they emerge from distinct forms of contracting.

Observe that in all modern banking systems, whether in rich economies or poor ones dominated by private or publicly owned banks, *money has been nationalised*. What we call money is the liability of a public bank: the RBI, the Federal Reserve, the European Central Bank (ECB), the BoE, and so on. Yet in most rich nations and many poor ones, *banking* remains in private hands. This division between money and banking is itself contingent: it instantiates collective action configured under the twin pressures of capitalism and democracy in those locales. This arrangement has not been fantastic for democracy of late even though, ironically, democracy's political legitimacy provides a much broader economic anchor to capitalist money than it has ever enjoyed.

Under modern arrangements, bank money is obscured by the legal fixing of its price in terms of national money at par: the 'exchange rate' between bank money and national money is a fixed price of 1 set by the law. This is also called the 'par constraint' since banks are constrained to market their own liabilities at par (one-to-one) with those of the central bank.

As we noted earlier, our bank statement is actually a statement of the bank's debt to us. It says that we have X units of bank money payable to us in central-bank money on a one-to-one basis. It is as if the price of one unit of bank money is set to one unit of central-bank money.

We know this is an implicit fixed-price regime because of the practice of fractional reserve banking. Our money is not waiting for us in storage at the bank. On the contrary, the bank is a dealer with whom we have contracted to lend our central-bank money. This dealer promises to return our central-bank money on demand. This promise is so tenuous that it takes an entire complex system to fulfil; it is fulfilled so effectively that we do not even realise that it is a promise to begin with.

But a promise it is—one to set bank-money liabilities at a fixed price of 1 to central-bank-money liabilities. (If this sounds like a money market mutual fund setting its net asset value (NAV) equal to USD 1 and promising not to 'break the buck', it is; see Chapter 8.) This equivocation makes users think bank money and national money are the same thing—that the bank and we are engaging in the physical depositing, borrowing and lending of money rather than creditary operations. The fixed-price system between central-bank money and bank money functions so smoothly that it reifies social relations.

Bank money is locked behind national money because it is a debt denominated in national money. The only form bank money takes is a ledger entry of a promise to pay a matching sum of national money. We never encounter bank money directly; it is a promise so credible and so neatly fitted to national money that it is erased, recoverable only by analysis or in a crisis when the promise breaks down. What we deal with normally is a thing-like projection of bank money—'deposits'.

While national money and bank money are *substantively unequal* in creditworthiness, they have been *formally equalised* by the law. This does not eliminate their difference of course. It merely leaves the differences to be worked out behind the scenes on the system's concatenated balance sheets rather than through visible price fluctuations. These differences become visible again at the water's edge—that is, with foreign currency or in a financial crisis when bank money does not pay out one-to-one with central-bank money.

Why do we observe systems wherein money has been nationalised with banking remaining private? While no capitalist democracy has managed to survive without the nationalisation of *money*, whether banking itself is nationalised is down to the local political settlement. While the separation of nationalised money and privatised banking is entirely contingent, the hybridisation of political and economic mutualisation is not. The public–private distinction does not map onto the political–economic mutualisation distinction.

Socialisation and Matching Liquidity

We have outlined four elements of fetishism in credit money: first, a relationship appearing as a thing when depositing; second, flows of liquidity appearing as stocks when making payments; third, credit creation appearing as physical recycling when lending; and fourth, the equating of bank money and central-bank money to occlude creditary operations. All four have a critical common feature: they all enable the socialisation or aggregation of liquidity, which, as we have seen, is an index of time.

Deposit-loans are the most basic way in which liquidity qua time is shared. From the individual unit's point of view, cash balances can be in either surplus or deficit at any given time. Deposits of course represent a collection of surplus agents who have mutualised their balance sheets to some extent by lending their surpluses to a social institution: my deposit-asset is simultaneously the bank's deposit-liability, with our balance sheets interlocked at that margin. Smaller and weaker than state-wide political mutualisation, bank mutualisation of customer deposits creates an entity that is substantially more robust at scale than individual surplus agents—hence the hierarchy from individuals to banks to state banks.

'Flows of liquidity' are actually a poor, physicalist shorthand to describe what is in effect a matching of payments and complementary liquidity demands across the economy. The payment system is more than a just-in-time inventory management system for physical cash, although it has elements of it. Because the 'inventory' in question is the liability of a bank, the (central) bank can magic up some more inventory to meet a payment demand if and when, at the end of the payment period, the banking system still has a mismatch between inflows and outflows. This extra inventory will be destroyed the following day and created afresh the next day, and so on, as the daily matching metabolism of the payment system creates and destroys credits to keep the interlocking network of balance sheets—that is, an economy—coherent.

Mutualisation of liquidity enables the creation and destruction of high-quality IOUs. It is what differentiates a credit system from a physicalist, just-in-time inventory system. Note parenthetically that cryptocurrencies are an ingenious invention to manage what is actually the physicalist projection of the credit system whereby finite tokens are tracked and transferred. In other words, they are based on an entirely false premise of how a money system works.

Lending is the process by which banks and loan customers swap IOUs, personal for social. As we have seen, the bank's IOU is more socially acceptable because it is a super-surplus agent, with its (in)flows substantial and robust enough to be mistaken for stocks. Individual banks cannot achieve this by themselves: they form relationships with other super-surplus-agent banks. Collectively, banks mutualise into clearing houses backed by the agent with the widest and strongest claims—the state. The seemingly alchemical ability for banks to produce money when lending comes from this systemic aggregation of liquidity.

Without a reliable source of refinance from other banks in the system, a lone bank would have to keep a much higher proportion of liquid cash stocks on hand in case depositors come calling. All its liquidity management would occur in the arrangement of the tenure of its loan book and the spatial or temporal spread of its depositors. But given various contingencies from the repayment of loans to the pattern of depositor behaviour, at any given time banks might have either more or less liquidity than is required, let alone optimal.

A lone bank would therefore have to approximate a cash warehouse; a lone bank is a category error. Banks come in systems. Hierarchy in these systems is driven by the scale and nature of the socialisation or mutualisation of the constituent balance sheets. At the bottom we have individual banks, then the pool of the interbank market, then the private clearing bank and finally the state's bank representing the largest and most robustly mutualised pool.

Fetishism Is Functional for Discipline but Not Democracy

Through several rounds of profit-driven expansion and contraction, banks grew into social systems evolving hierarchical credit arrangements that pooled liquidity at ever-greater scales. The inherent fragility of banking, borrowing short and lending long in an uncertain world combined with the crisis-prone nature of capitalism to create a credit system that posed a systemic risk to any nation that was not able to manage it.

One mode of management was to tie credit to some hard asset that lay *outside* the system of interlocking balance sheets—an asset that was not at the same time some other balance sheet's liability. This of course was monetary gold.

A metallic monetary base does not mean that the ontology of money was a metallic commodity. Commodity money was simply the anchor on the asset side of interlocking and hierarchical balance sheets. These balance sheets issued IOUs that promised to pay gold, but it was these IOUs in the main that functioned as the money supply rather than gold. This was true from early modern capitalism all the way to the Bretton Woods system (Eichengreen, 2011).

The credit system's functioning, and its politics, is all about the balance between elasticity and discipline: who gets which at what price. Credit is such a powerful institution that it can be hard to discipline regardless of who wields it—states, banks or individuals. Some situations require credit discipline, but not all: that was the folly of the gold standard.

The fetish of fiat money makes it appear as if the only entity requiring discipline is the state and, by implication, democracy. If we see the fetish as a by-product of the credit system's intrinsic operations, then the anti-democratic bias inherent to the fetish of fiat might dissipate.

Once the 'barbarous relic' of gold was supplanted at the apex of the credit system by government debt, the final nail ought to have been driven through the money fetish as a commodity fetish. No longer could the vestigial presence of gold offer its false reassurance that our money was worth something after all. Yet without gold we assumed we lived in a world where pure state fiat drove money. The fetish of fiat replaced that of the commodity.

What actually happened was more radical: the democratic state interpolated the logic of banking to make a living, human economy—the national economy—the reserve asset of the banking system. As the outermost inside money, the central bank's IOU has the most 'outside-ness'. But because it is anchored by fiscal power, this outside-ness is read as 'fiat'. Government debt held by central banks is a promise to pay future tax receipts. It represents the commodification of a sociopolitical relation, pure and simple.

This is a fairly thin method of commodification missing as it does the predication of a complex social division of labour. The longer the supply chain of a particular commodity, the easier it is to fetishise the composite social relations. Yet with government debt it is one step, which is why government bond traders are keen political observers. It also means that disciplining money can take the form of disciplining democracy itself under current conditions—that is, limiting government bond issuance. Yet there is such a thing as democratic credit discipline on banking principles (Chapter 12).

Fetishism for Marx is not some conspiratorial veiling of the operations of capital. It is a necessary attribute of a system defined by a complex division of labour where concrete labours relate to each other not directly but abstractly as different components of a widely distributed but mutually concealed supply chain. Concrete labours relate to each other abstractly through the commodity and its value, but we read the commodity merely as a concrete thing rather than a 'social hieroglyph' as well.

Just so, monetary fetishism is as necessary an attribute of a modern money system, turning individual IOUs into socially accepted IOUs at three levels of socialisation or aggregation. It turns individual IOUs into social money through the bank's loan operations; it turns bank liquidity into higher-powered IOUs through interbank lending; and it concentrates all this socialisation of liquidity at the apex of the national credit system in the central bank. Central-bank swap lines go a step further by making central banks themselves part of a larger mutualised block along some margin.

Again, these levels of socialisation are necessary mediations to achieve scale, security, flexibility, usability and granularity. This is not at all to say that banking and finance cannot develop baroque, unstable structures. It is merely to note that some level of hierarchical mediation is axiomatic. Here again cryptocurrencies fail.

Once the logic of banking is fused with that of government debt; 'money' is given a social predication that is the entire economy itself via the intermediating balance sheets of the central bank and the state. The state is a leviathan, itself a synthetic fusing of individual wills into a social will. The monetary expression of this sociopolitical mutualisation is the flow of taxes to the state. Chartalists make a basic error: ironically, they fail to see the political in the state (Chapter 6). They therefore fail to see how democracy is critical to the legitimacy of the state and therefore the acceptability of its money (Chapter 12).

Why Tokens Are Bad Money

Two sets of thinkers on money have recently gained notoriety: Chartalists, or the state money school, who also go by the name of modern monetary theorists, and cryptocurrency enthusiasts. While we engage both in the chapters that follow, we conclude this chapter by foregrounding how they trip up on the money fetish.

'Money' is that instrument which terminates credit–debt relationships. 'Money' is the means of payment or settlement of ubiquitous debts, economic and political. But who decides which instrument will terminate debts? Debtors cannot simply settle affairs by offering their IOU since that would count as rolling over the debt, not settling it. Settlement therefore requires some 'outside money', an instrument exogenous to the debtor. Instruments that are themselves IOUs of some third-party issuer can perform a settlement role, but which issuer can transactors agree on? The creditor can of course accept their own IOU acquired somehow by the debtor, but few creditors other than the state have IOUs that circulate this way. The need for multilateral agreement naturally points to some coordinating authority.

As for the state, it can of course nominate the instrument that will settle tax debts; this is the Chartalist axiom. But it by no means follows that this particular instrument will become the means of settlement even domestically. That would be a significant and often fragile political achievement—namely the political consolidation of national economic space. However, several putatively 'sovereign' nations in the developing world experience extensive 'dollarisation', the de facto or de jure substitution of the domestic currency by a foreign currency (Corrales et al., 2016). Pace the Chartalists, formal or nominal sovereignty is far from sufficient for substantial monetary sovereignty.

An intrinsically worthless *item* could in principle be endowed with some debt-settlement value if the law nominates it as legally valid for terminating debts, especially tax debts. Yet this legal, 'nominalist' power of the state, irreducible as it is, is often misunderstood and insufficient by itself for a complete account of money (see Chapters 6 and 7).

For cryptocurrency believers, the ontological difference between a token (a physical or digital *item*) and a promise (a social *relation* set down in ink or computer code) is especially noteworthy. An intrinsically worthless token could in principle acquire stable value, but *only* if it is placed *within* a stable credit–debt relationship. This much Chartalists agree with. A political theory of money goes further, however, to show that even if that relationship were with the state, we ought not believe that mere state declaration ('fiat') can create value. Put differently, sovereignty is nothing but a political settlement which has its own inherent limits.

Thus, only state actions within a *creditary* register are capable of creating some degree of value unlike, say, when a state creates a standard of monetary *measurement* or a unit of account (Chapter 6). Like all creditary actions, the tax relationship is two-sided, not necessarily one of equals but certainly one of countervailing forces. Constituent units only accept a 'tax' imposition from a legitimate entity, with legitimacy thereby forming the limit of acceptance.

Any creditary relation's value has two elements: the strength or nature of the claim and that which is being claimed. The nominalist power of the state can endow value only to the first element, and there too it faces the limits of its own legitimacy and the balance of political power. But the second element—that which the credit relationship actually claims—is the subject of material production and distribution. The state can of course substantially influence this material element through industrial policy. But by its nature, that which is claimed points to a domain outside the creditary relationship itself. Material productivity forms another limit of the nominalist power of the state.

Worthless tokens placed into a creditary force field acquire the latter's attributes including value, but it is the creditary relationship that bears the value rather than the token. Bare tokens *outside* such a creditary relationship might have cryptographically contrived scarcity value, beauty-contest exchange value, and so on, but will not make for good money under current conditions (Chapter 10). The recent drift in cryptocurrencies from *money* pretenders to decentralised *finance* (DeFi) attests to this fact.

Bare tokens, outside creditary relationships, would be pure creatures of code, be it legal code, computer code or the code of the fairground. Their value stands as it were on one leg—hence their volatility. Creditary promises, on the other hand, are backed by both the fidelity of the promise and the nature of the assets of the institution making the promise. National money is not an intrinsically worthless *thing* but a *credit* of such superior quality that it behaves like a valuable *item* because of the (variable) quality of both creditary elements, the fidelity of the promise and the asset or value promised.

Like all credit instruments, the value of both national money and bank money stands on two legs—the nature of the claim and that which is being claimed, the contractual *and* the materialist, namely the future product of the borrower or the taxpayer. The first leg points to the 'robustness' of mutualisation and the second to the 'scale' of economic activity.

Bank money is a promise to pay an instrument, national money, but its value is also backed by commercially mutualised assets. National money is a promise to pay something more abstract, 'value' from the national economy, backed by politically mutualised taxation assets. Outside of a credit relationship, tokens or items are not promises and do not pay anything.

The superiority of national money over bank money is the function not of the nominalist power of the law but of robust mutualisation at scale. Indeed, the nominalist 'fiat' power of the state is better understood as the expression of the (better or worse) institutionalisation of a particular form of collective action. In the case of contemporary monetary arrangements, the law actually puts individual banks in a tough spot through the par constraint—that is, by mandating quantitative equality between qualitatively unequal promises. Banks are also incentivised to take on this par constraint to make their own promises credible. This creates contradictions that can be either managed or politically weaponised (Chapter 8).

The legal mandate for banks to *fix the price* of their liabilities with those of the state's bank at 1 is the point at which our two forms of money, national money and bank money, appear to merge. It is also the point at which the tokenised fetish of 'fiat' obscures the most. It might appear as if individual banks have been given a *licence* to print money, but they are in fact being mandated to do something impossible— namely to equivocate their relatively inferior liabilities with those of the state's bank.

They naturally fail to do so on their own and therefore have to be integrated into a system that ensures that national money is used only in the last instance: most of the means of payment we use is bank money, 'deposits'—namely promises to pay national money. The rigorous demands of the par constraint mean that this system must be tightly regulated and backstopped by the state and the central bank such that de facto, banks become public undertakings, whatever their formal ownership may be. In a system when money is nationalised but banking remains private, the discipline of the par constraint can only be met by a deep mutualisation of public and private balance sheets, albeit on unequal terms.

The common sense reads 'fiat' as a sovereign will imbuing worthless tokens with value. The reality is somewhat more complex. Yet this has not stopped many cryptographic initiatives from working off this common sense to create fiat digital tokens based on distributed ledger technology (Chapter 10). These designs encode a hostility to credit—that is, the ability to create and destroy tokens—lest it be abused.

Public credit has indeed been abused. Yet if the creation and destruction of credit is native to economic life, the righteous anger of cypherpunks perhaps ought to be directed to the abuse of credit rather than its very existence. Designing better token-based systems will not help if money needs to be something else.

The bare token view of money sees the monetary system as a simple intermediating mechanism, a logistical layer moving money-things around, floating above 'the real economy'. But when the state engages in a creditary relationship with we, the people, we are implicitly engaging with each other through the intermediation of the state. Analogously, depositors and lenders implicitly relate to each other through the intermediation of a bank.

But this 'intermediation' is not, pace the token view, of the pass-the-parcel kind. Even the most sophisticated 'real-time' gross settlement systems between mainline banks require huge amounts of intraday *credit* from the central bank (Borio and Van den Bergh, 1993; Bech, Martin and McAndrews, 2012). Economic life at every level requires more than moving money around: it requires credit creation and destruction in real time. This is doubly so under conditions of democracy where the pastoral care-giving state has to flexibly respond to crises. The trick is to design this hierarchical, hybrid money system for democracy.

The interlocking mutualisation of balance sheets is the very ontology of the economy and society, including, in a fortified and scaled-up mode, the state. The balance-sheet logic of credit, banking and the state run together, rendering bare tokens a monetary category error. In a sense, cryptocurrency enthusiasts want money without community, without mutualisation of any kind. This is because they have misrecognised the thingified appearance of money for its social essence.

3 | BENDING, NOT BREAKING

Monetary Sovereignty and the Survival Constraint

This chapter explains the nature and limits of monetary power using Minsky's idea of the survival constraint. This is the idea that all agents, including the state, need 'cash' to survive. The constraint binds more or less depending on the acceptability of a unit's liabilities. Banks accept borrower liabilities if they deem them solvent; citizens accept a state's liabilities, bonds and money, if they deem it legitimate. Political mutualisation drives super-acceptability, giving the state's bank disproportionate market power rather than untrammelled coercive power ('fiat'). This enables the state's bank to bend the survival constraint much further than other domestic private entities.

(Neo-)Chartalism misreads this as pure coercive power. Since illegitimate coercion ceases to be state action and becomes a 'crime', state coercion is limited by legitimacy in principle. Put differently, brute coercion is less effective than legitimate violence, so a 'state' engaged mainly in brute coercion will be less effectively mutualised and therefore issue a poorer form of money.

Monetary power is the ability to modulate the survival constraint of other units, imparting elasticity or exerting discipline on a credit system. For the state and its bank, acceptability qua legitimacy forms one of its outer limits.

Capitalism is a cash nexus: we all need whatever is conjuncturally defined as 'cash' to fulfil our basic material needs. Minsky's 'survival constraint' is a Banking School rendition of this axiom. Most of us sell our labour power in order to avail ourselves of cash, which represents an 'outside asset' to us. By whatever method—earning, selling, borrowing—we must arrange our personal balance sheets to ensure that cash-in is greater than cash-out. This is what Minsky called the 'survival constraint': an economic unit cannot survive without positive cash flow; often it has to incur debts to get it.

Given that the state is itself embedded in capitalist relations of production, we will demonstrate how the survival constraint applies to the state itself albeit within much wider bounds. Political mutualisation at scale enables the state to bend the survival constraint further than any other domestic entity. The robustness and scale of a particular political mutualisation effort determine where the state sits in the international hierarchy of money.

The very logic of credit requires *acceptance*; this is another expression of the survival constraint. Chartalists assume away the problem of acceptance applied to the state because they have an inadequate conception of sovereignty. The privilege of any sovereign is to *bend* the survival constraint rather than to break it. Sovereignty is an inherently variable phenomenon. The further a given sovereign can bend the survival constraint, the higher up the hierarchy of money it will be.

Depending on the configuration of the apex of the credit system, the survival constraint for down-hierarchy units can be either elastic (loose) or disciplined (tight). In the lead-up to the Credit Crisis of 2007–2009, monetary abuse manifested itself as excessive elasticity for all on the way up, but elasticity for the bankers and discipline for the rest on the way down. Justified anger in the wake of the financial crisis led to a period rich with monetary experiments. Cryptocurrencies are the obvious one, but talk about ending the Fed, 100 per cent reserve banking, sovereign money, Chartalists who now go by the sobriquet of modern monetary theory (MMT), and so on indicate that money's legitimacy has been badly damaged (Weber, 2018).

These experiments point to our main message: money is rooted in a political settlement which comes to be expressed in the design and configuration of the credit system. This includes both macro- and micro-social politics. The disruption of this settlement will reverberate across the institutional landscape and can often come to a head in monetary debates. There is no one-to-one link between the political settlement and the configuration of money, but the former will leave its imprint on the latter. Politics in particular contexts—the Eurozone, the US, the international political economy (IPE)—led to particular configurations of the relevant credit system, which often amplified the inherently unstable nature of future-oriented credit and/or ignored the political moorings of money to their peril.

Political Mutualisation Bends the Survival Constraint

The state deploys political mutualisation to overcome the survival constraint, but only in a manner dictated by the self-same constraint. The state is both a critical site on which the political settlement is played out and an institutionalised expression of that same settlement. The social technology the state uses to access value is state banking and state finance—balance sheets which represent the socialisation of claims on future labour power. Socialisation makes these claims both stable and liquid. But the balance sheet has two sides; the state is both enabled and hemmed in by the logic of credit. We will first explore the general attributes of the state versus the survival constraint before outlining some of the historical–institutional ways in which the constraint can be relaxed or tightened.

Having politically constructed an economic leviathan that gives it disproportionate degrees of freedom from the survival constraint, the state is in a position to modulate the same constraint for the rest of the domestic economy. Just as banks' economic mutualisation allows them to attenuate individual liquidity needs even while being subject to bank runs, so too states' political mutualisation enables them to alleviate banks' liquidity needs while leveraging the national economy itself (subject to the size and international location of that economy). A 'run on the state' (which could proceed at various speeds) is a systemic political crisis.

This political access to value can of course be configured in myriad ways. The state could, for instance, access value production directly by owning some part of the economy, 'the commanding heights' or a few public sector undertakings. Alternatively, it could monopolise banking or take a lead role in development banking and thereby financially control private industry. Or it might preside over a largely private economy and harvest passive ownership rights on a portion of value produced through the tax system. The varieties are endless, limited only by our imaginations interacting with local political realities. But they would all be versions of the same move—namely the state using its political settlement to durably access value and thereby relax the survival constraint's hold on its operations.

Political mutualisation at scale enables wide bounds for the state or central-bank provision of money, but its degrees of freedom are not infinite.

In the political dimension, the degree to which states can issue more IOUs ('print money') or borrow domestically is limited, in the final instance, by the carrying capacity of the political settlement. How much will citizens and residents support the state's money? If citizens are barred by administrative controls from using foreign money or buying foreign assets, this too will have to be borne by the settlement.

The material outer limit to the state's ability to commandeer national resources, whether through purchases or confiscation, is having the entire economy on its balance sheet. Politics will kick in well before that.

Internationally, where the nation sits in the global division of labour and consequently in the global hierarchy of money will determine how acceptable its money is. A fetter can be created by capital controls, but ultimately the qualitative difference between national money and world money will compel sub-hegemon sovereigns transacting internationally to arrange their balance sheets so as to acquire some amount of world money if only defensively. This fact marks a qualitative difference between the international sphere, where no sovereign writ runs, and the domestic sphere, where money can (falsely) appear as an attribute of state fiat. Political mutualisation stops at the water's edge; lower-order political contracts like treaties can of course be obtained internationally with the EU being an intermediate case. But what is at play between national boundaries is simply another variety of the inside–outside money distinction projected onto national economies themselves.

The constraint felt by sub-hegemon nations, namely world money, is therefore not dissimilar from that felt by an individual citizen towards national money or bank money. Citizens at home and nations abroad both face the constraint of having to acquire what counts as 'money' at their respective levels of monetary hierarchy. 'Money' is an outside asset needed to transact in the world. Just as my personal IOUs are not money domestically, most nations cannot use their own money (their central bank's IOUs) in international commerce. Again, Chartalists seem to miss the global cash nexus as a limit to monetary sovereignty applying to all but the global hegemon.

Capitalism produces value through a complex division of labour. These two elements—value and the division of labour—stand in the way of the state, completely brushing aside the survival constraint. Because capitalism is a cash nexus, the price of admission into material life is money itself. To overcome this entirely, the state would have to subsume the entire economy onto its own balance sheet, something that is both technically and politically impossible, not to mention dystopian. What it does instead is to deploy political mutualisation to durably access valuable goods and services, taking its place in the division of labour albeit as a superordinate part.

Both states and banks are leveraged operations. Where we marked the distinction between economic and political mutualisation in the first chapter, we now point to their similarities as operations of mutualisation at scale. The political conglomerate may be more robust than its economic counterpart, but they are both 'banks' in their creditary logic. The state's banking logic is given explicit institutional form in the central bank, which wields a particular kind of power: monetary sovereignty. This is the power to *modulate the survival constraint* as it operates on both the state itself and balance sheets lower down the hierarchy. This is not purely coercive power in either its operation or foundation. It is infrastructural power or non-sovereign power (Mann, 1984; Foucault, 2003). Legitimate coercion might be used to sure up the boundaries, but by definition such coercion occurs within the envelope of a given political settlement.

Operating the credit machine from the inside while moving in a fog of war, mistakes will be made by monetary technocrats and political leaders. The point at which credit modulation tips a complex system into incoherence is inherently unknowable—hence the need for a substantial margin of safety. But politics can either eat away at that margin or replenish it. The space for the operation of monetary sovereignty is wide, finite and blurred at the edges.

Taxation Takes Time, Credit Buys Time

To understand the creditary logic of the state, we need to examine how the process of state formation in early modern Europe generated existential demands for liquidity. These demands were met by constructing a state bank backed by taxation powers turned into financial assets on one side with bank-liability money on the other. Like all banks, the state's bank operated to span timescales: money today for money tomorrow for a price. But politics in these locales took the banking game to a whole new level (Ingham, 2004; Chapters 6 and 7). Thanks to the scale and robustness of political mutualisation, these timescales could be intergenerational.

It is important to mark the uniqueness of the early modern European experience of state formation. Focusing on the particularity of early modern Europe, namely its credit system, is not to say that Europe has some intrinsic, essential properties that fated it to be the home of such developments. Conjuncture piled upon conjuncture to produce a pathway of development that led to world empire. Thus, when we refer to the fiscal–military state below, we do not mean the mere existence of a military–taxation nexus; this is indeed ancient and universal. What was revolutionary about early modern Europe is that public debt was invented so that sovereigns could borrow from the collective *future*.

Fiscality was thereby linked to the future through a national debt. To our knowledge, admittedly that of a non-historian, no ancient state, eastern or western, managed this task. David Graeber's opus on debt makes no mention of any public debt in the 'Axial Age', while Earl J. Hamilton noted, 'A national debt is one of the few important economic phenomena without roots in the Ancient World' (Hamilton, 1947). Speaking of the British financial revolution of the seventeenth century, John Munro cites Forest Capie claiming that 'the word revolution has perhaps been overused in economic historical studies, but perhaps this is an occasion when it is appropriate' (Munro, 2003).

For states to be able to spend *in advance* of accumulation, a particular political revolution had to be institutionalised, deeply locking the state into the economy. Brute commodity accumulation substituted for this institutional articulation prior to the financial revolutions of the early modern period in Europe. War and empire then spread the fiscal–monetary machine across the world through conquest and imitation.

State-making historically meant war-making, and war obviously costs money. Taxation and borrowing are operations in finite time. Taxation is of course slower than borrowing—hence the need for borrowing in the first place: to tide over periods between the influx of liquidity from tax receipts. While taxation arrives in a discontinuous, lumpy flow and takes its time, the needs of the state are continuous and arrive at unexpected moments, paradigmatically in the time of maximum uncertainty, namely war. People and material require liquid cash.

The survival constraint will bind differently depending on whether the prevailing money at that historical conjuncture is metallic or some credible promise to pay. Metallic money as an outside asset to the state needed to be earned or borrowed. Issuing the state's own credit as money entails acceptance that can be driven by the politics of taxation, but such acceptance already implies a financial or political revolution.

In either case, the sovereign power to tax, exercised over the medium-to-long term, is severely qualified by the ever-present and uncertain need for liquid cash. Put differently, *taxation power, sovereign power, is merely a potentiality, an illiquid potentiality at that*. For that power to literally flow, it must be turned into cash.

There are only two ways for a state to hedge itself against this risk of being caught short of liquid cash, but what operates as outside money is critical. If cash is defined as metal, then the state has to generate the mother of all metallic hoards so that it has cash on hand to meet any contingency. This itself places a material constraint on coercive power: there is only so much taxing, looting and pillaging a prince can do. If we are in a historical epoch where cash is state credit, then the state has to have the ability to write huge amounts of IOUs instantly without the state's credibility being called into question if it is to overcome the liquidity constraint. But this already assumes that a politically and economically relevant set of citizens and bondholders are willing to accept the state's IOUs. Accepting the sovereign's money is an outcome of political mutualisation.

There is a system, evolved over the centuries, that specialises in turning potential future solvency into liquid credit on demand. This is the banking system. The state that effectively internalised the logic of banking would therefore have drastically eased its problem of liquidity, giving it differential power on the battlefield and elsewhere.

This is the significance of Britain's Glorious Revolution of 1688, pace the new institutionalists: a political revolution led to a world-historical relaxing of the survival constraint (North and Weingast, 1989; Hodgson, 2017). This revolution is a necessary but far from sufficient condition for successful state-making.

The state can issue IOUs in diverse forms and seek to have them accepted either through a central-banking operation or by issuing interest-bearing debt (bonds).

There will always be some baseline demand for the state's IOUs since citizens and residents need to accumulate them for paying taxes, but it is entirely unclear that this demand itself can drive demand for money adequate to the state's needs. Increasing taxes can simply stifle an economy, to say nothing of igniting political outrage. The MMT motto might be 'taxes drive money'—the idea that money demand can be finely calibrated by moving around tax rates to manage liquidity—but to hold such a position is to have a political tin ear.

As we will examine in detail in Chapter 6, for Chartalists, the state has the power to nominate the asset that will satisfy the debt to the state itself. The state can always drum up demand for its own IOUs since this is what the state will accept as settling the tax liability it imposes on society. By increasing the tax burden on society in the wake of a flourish of expenditure, taxes drive (demand for) money. The state can never have a borrowing problem because the state is always already owed, can always be owed more and can simply create more IOUs-as-money that cancel out this debt.

Yet Chartalists seem to have confused solvency with liquidity. They have also ignored the temporal dimension of economic life. The state never has a solvency problem: it will always have (taxation) assets that outstrip its (IOU's) liabilities in some final accounting. But taxing takes time. Just because the state can issue IOUs today and tax them away tomorrow, it does not escape the survival constraint which binds *now*. Taxation takes time, but the state needs to fight a war today.

The time-bound nature of economic activity, indeed of life itself, asserts itself once again; in a sense, liquidity is just stored-up time, a collection of claims on future value. State-making, and especially war-making, drives the demand for liquidity, which in turn drives political bargains with those who have access to stored-up time by means of controlling a real production process (including trade which 'produces' a material change in location). Modern state formation is unthinkable without a politically fortified banking function becoming part of the very logic of the state, with its futural fiscality turned into money today. Taxing takes time, credit buys time, taxation power gives you excellent credit—until it does not.

Accepting the Sovereign: Credit and State Formation

Money as credit is, like all credit, a form of leverage: the issuance of more state credit money is a form of leveraging the economic heft of the (future) national economy by issuing IOUs against it. So long as creditors, both internal and external, accept the sovereign's IOU, leveraging can continue in a growing economy subject to their relative rates of growth. Acceptance is naturally predicated on a degree of stability, and issuance or elasticity beyond an inherently unknowable-because-indeterminant point will lead to incoherence: inflation, financial distress, capital flight. This is true even if citizens, as daily users of the sovereign's money, are its main creditors; beyond a point, abuse of monetary sovereignty constitutes a violation of the legitimate political settlement, not to mention the arithmetic of debt. Citizens react by withdrawing acceptance (tax strikes and even tax havens implicitly).

'Acceptance' therefore takes on a dual meaning in our context. In the vernacular of credit systems, banks 'accept' the creditworthiness of their loan customers and substitute their own IOUs in their place. The political usage is analogous: accepting the money or debt of the sovereign also means acknowledging its creditworthiness. But for citizens, 'accepting the sovereign' simultaneously entails a swap of political IOUs: taxation for representation, a swap that renders the sovereign creditworthy in the first place through a collective pledge of future value to the state. In a Rousseauvian vein, we accept the sovereign's IOUs because it is us: the state is merely the institutionalised expression of this fact.

Accepting the sovereign means enabling the state to make payments with its own (central bank) IOUs. Here the commercial logic of banking is turned political. Banking is the socio-economic process of mutualisation at scale. Commercial acceptance turns private IOUs into publicly acceptable IOUs. The totality of the state's borrowing and money issuance is a similar process by which citizens accept their own collective solvency, but only through the agency of their state and their bank. The social process of acceptance makes the state's IOUs 'money'. Accepting the sovereign arms it with leviathan-class borrowing power, enabling it to stretch liquidity further than any private agent—further, but not infinitely. Politics at the national scale inhabits the logic of credit to stretch it further than economic mutualisation. This is different from the coercion-centred approach of Chartalism.

This state is also subject to the survival constraint. This is not notional but tangible; the more so, the further down the hierarchy of global money a nation finds itself. This is often overlooked because we live behind the fetish of fiat money, assuming that the state's writ can create money (Chapter 3).

Indeed from the user's point of view, the nature of monetary power does not matter in the least: all we know is that we need liquid cash to survive. That too is a bit of fetishism: from the outside or at the individual level, the 'credit' of the central bank performs like an asset; at one level up in the system, we can see that the central bank's IOU is in fact backed by our collective assets.

Thus, 'outsideness' or 'assetness' depends on which perspective one adopts in the hierarchy of money. From the domestic apex, money represents national equity, a 'real bill' backed by national wealth. The elasticity of money is limited by the extent of the national economy. How far are money and debt holders, both domestic and international but especially the former, willing to leverage this economy?

Taxes rest on a political settlement; moving them around can shatter the social peace and choke off the flow of funds to the state. A casual reading of world news illustrates this truism: massive street protests have recently erupted in reaction to changes to taxes in no less than three separate countries (Chile, Ecuador and Lebanon). Taxes are a critical component of a political settlement which forms the limit of sovereign power itself and by extension monetary sovereignty.

The privilege of the monetary sovereign is to bend the survival constraint; it breaks it at the risk of unstitching the very mutualisation that brought it into being and gave it its super-solvency. Sovereigns with well-integrated fiscal and credit systems presiding over large economic catchment areas can bend it further than those with less articulated systems atop smaller ones. Relative power is what matters in a crisis. Credit just buys you time, but that can be enough to win the war if you can out-mobilise your enemies; the last bit of British war debt from the eighteenth century was still being paid off in the twentieth.

From the crucible of centuries-long fighting in Europe emerged a ruthless, world-conquering war machine that was the 'fiscal-military state', its operations pioneered by Britain's 'financial revolution' that was simultaneously a political revolution, bringing Dutch finance to Britain along with a Dutch sovereign (Brewer, 1989; Dickson, 1967). Walter Bagehot (1920 [1873], p. 90; Chapter 4) understood both sides of this particular coin, finance and politics: the BoE was for him 'not only a finance company, but a Whig finance company'. The terrifying success of this state formation stimulated global mimicry that continues to this day. How successful a human community is in equipping itself with such a state determines its location in a global division of labour and thence the global hierarchy of money. That location, in turn, defines the state's external liquidity constraint.

'Banking', says Minsky, 'is not money lending; to lend, a moneylender must have money. The fundamental banking activity is *accepting*, that is, guaranteeing that some party is creditworthy' (Minsky, 1986, p. 256, emphasis added). As Minsky wryly observed, anyone can issue a credit note; the problem is to get it accepted.

But with state credit, 'accepting' is at once an economic and irreducibly political relationship. If accepting defines the business of issuing credit money ('banking') and accepting is fundamentally political, then credit money is itself a political thing, not merely something with political attributes. Acceptance can thereby be read as the financial expression of legitimacy, a canonical attribute of the state. The central bank is merely the institutional expression of the creditary logic of state power.

Unlike the Chartalists, we do not assume that sovereignty by itself confers acceptance of the state's IOUs. Rather, solvency reflects a particular pairing that has to be assiduously built and maintained: a stable political settlement anchored in a productive economy. This pairing is brought together in taxation: it forms the basic ingredient of sovereignty and the core of what might be called a financial theory of state. Whence Burke's aphorism: 'Revenue is the chief preoccupation of the State. Nay more, it is the State.'

As we noted earlier, Chartalists argue that the very existence of tax obligations to a sovereign state implies that states do not face a hard budget constraint. The state merely has to nominate the instrument that will adequate the tax liability to it, and that very act turns the nominated instrument into money. This is, as it were, *credit by fiat* rather than through the socio-material process of mutualisation.

Acceptance is never an issue for the Chartalist state: 'A sovereign government, according to MMT, occupies the top tier of the money pyramid. It is easy for it to find acceptors, because many of us owe payments to it' (Nersisyan and Wray, 2016, p. 1303; see also Bell, 2001). For these thinkers, 'affordability is not the issue for governments operating with their own sovereign currencies' (ibid., p. 1313). The state 'writes the dictionary', so the existential struggle that is acceptance simply evaporates.

This is a thin reading of what a state is, often held up by little more than pieties such as 'the only thing certain in life is "death and taxes"' (ibid., p. 1310). By skipping over the politics inherent in the logic of credit, the politics of acceptance, and how it is expressed in the institutions of the state, Chartalist economists simply miss the political ontology of money itself. Geoffrey Ingham, a social theorist among the Chartalists, takes up a somewhat different position regarding the role of politics and coercion in money and sovereignty; we take up his view in Chapter 6.

With the evolution of Dutch finance, states took the 'social technology' (Ingham, 2004) of banking to even greater heights, having an 'asset base' that is the nation itself via a tax deal with capital. As Ingham notes, private credit monies circulating in closed networks could never have achieved this scale unless they were wedded to a state (Ingham, 2004, p. 122).

Hegemonic national states hit upon the ability to retrofit their ancient, pre-capitalist powers of taxation to the infinite horizon of capitalist futurity. The secure tethering of tax and capital, of state and economy, is achieved by the incorporation of the technology of banking into the very logic of state formation. But this remains a *creditary* logic fortified and scaled up by politics.

Through several centuries of competitive state formation, the nation state emerged as the winning state formation, beating out city states and multinational empires as the most robust formation economically and militarily (Tilly, 1990). Notwithstanding globalisation, we live in a world of nation states arranged hierarchically, and this is why we live in a world of national monies arranged hierarchically. New state forms can always emerge—the EU, for example—but they remain species of political mutualisation.

Staying Alive: The International Survival Constraint

The limit of monetary sovereignty is the point up to which people are willing to hold sovereign IOUs, whether in money or debt form. As we have seen, taxes account for some portion of this willingness but not all of it. Taxes-as-political-contract is critical when we aim to define the political ontology of national money and try to uncover the core of its *value*. But taxes only tell part of the story of the nature of monetary *power*, which is the story of the nation's balance sheet versus the survival constraint. *National* balance sheets have sources of cash flow much broader than taxation flows even though the latter form their politically mutualised core. In terms of the state's degrees of monetary freedom, *all* flows accruing to the nation, both internal–political and external–commercial or geopolitical, are to be taken into account since its monetary power leverages the national economy.

To understand the external survival constraint, we should ask the question: what is national credit money a promise to pay? We have seen that in an economic sense or in terms of its internal sociopolitical relations, the answer is value itself fiscally anchored. But in terms of its external and largely economic relations, national money is a promise to pay not value but another instrument, namely other national monies through the international money market (Mehrling, 2013). As a medium of *international* exchange, money does in fact promise to pay other monetary instruments. Given that there is an international hierarchy of money topped by a hegemonic currency or 'world money', we can think of a national money as a promise to pay world money for all sub-hegemon nations.

The issuer of world money is something of a global sovereign because its IOU functions as a means of global payment, giving it a truly global 'exorbitant privilege' (Charles de Gaulle's famous jibe at the dollar). As with all hierarchies of money, this privilege rests in the final instance on political mutualisation at scale. Mutualisation over a substantial share of the world's economic catchment area (both domestically and internationally) creates an asset available for leverage. That is a necessary but not sufficient condition for the provision of world money.

In addition, the aspiring hegemon's credit system will have to be so configured to allow it to function as a liquidity provider to the world. This requires a political settlement that will tolerate the dominance of the class in control of banking, be they technocrats or financiers. We explore the dynamics of world money and the dollar in Chapter 9.

The hegemon is clearly the exception rather than the rule. Further down the hierarchy, in most of the world, national monies will be subject to the market discipline of the constant threat of flight to the better currency. As with all balance sheets, national balance sheets have cash inflow and cash outflow, thanks to their balance of payments—that is, receivables from international trade and borrowing. If their trade earnings exceed expenditure, they might accumulate reserves of world money and use them to buffer potential bad weather. Sustained accumulation might see their economies grow.

But if a nation earns less on its trade account than it spends, it has to borrow like any down-hierarchy balance sheet, but now from non-domestic sources. This puts it at the mercy of nations or indeed other private balance sheets with better access to world money. As the source of (cheaper access to) world money, creditors will determine how tightly the survival constraint binds for the debtor nation. At this level, the lack of *monetary* sovereignty shades into sovereignty itself.

Being qualitatively superior to most national monies, world money sets up a currency–credit or outside–inside dynamic with national monies, subjecting national balance sheets to the survival constraint just as individuals are subject to it under the auspices of, from their point of view, outside national money or bank money. For all countries save the hegemon, world money is outside money.

For once-colonised nations, desire for the substance of real, economic independence is what drove freedom movements. On gaining independence from immiserating imperialism, post-colonial nations resolved to overturn their wretched dependence situation. One method—universally accepted at the time, thanks to the havoc caused by 'hot money' during the Great Depression—was capital controls. International markets can only speculate in a currency for which there is an open market. But capital controls administratively limit the play of market opinion; when well enforced, they strictly determine how much trading activity can occur in the home currency. As a fetter on 'free markets', capital controls form an essential predicate of sovereignty, especially for debtor economies rather than merely Polanyian 'protection'.

Capital controls cannot by themselves alter hierarchy of course. But they can serve as limits to the operation of the international survival constraint and thereby earn nations critical degrees of freedom. That space, in turn, could potentially be used to build a growing economy and initiate a move up the hierarchy. The local political settlement determines whether this space is used for 'development' or not.

The epoch in which capital controls were seen as legitimate has now passed (though this is shifting marginally). Some nations took advantage of the conjuncture to build industrial machines and achieve real, economic independence. East Asian nations now use their hard-earned export surpluses as the functional equivalent of their now-absent capital controls—namely to relax the international survival constraint (China of course has both surpluses and controls and therefore even more room for domestic manoeuvre). Yet most nations cannot achieve export surpluses by construction (trade balances net to zero at the global level). With their capital accounts now forced open and unable to create massive reserve firewalls, most developing nations are now condemned to suffer the whims of global finance capital. The result has been a diminishment of both their money and their democracies.

The degree of acceptance, in both senses of the word, determines the degree to which the survival constraint binds the nation state domestically and internationally. There is obviously a minimum threshold of acceptance given the denomination of taxes in the sovereign's money of account, and to that extent the state's survival constraint is relaxed. Yet tax-based hoarding will only get you so far in terms of bending the survival constraint. Over and above any cash kept aside for settling a periodic tax liability, citizens' holdings of its sovereign's money will be determined by the degree of administrative closure (capital controls) of the sovereign's economic catchment area combined with its general management of the currency.

Gold as Imperial Discipline

The grip that the survival constraint has on the sovereign varies with the nature of outside money in both the domestic and international spheres. The nature of outside money—commodity or credit—is a key element in determining the survival constraint's balance between discipline and elasticity.

A commodity regime is one in which national money is a promise to pay some amount of a physical commodity rather than a share of GDP. Both are credit systems but with very different elasticity or discipline settings. Commodities have to be produced, earned or borrowed, whereas credit notes require long-term coherence with 'value'. As such, a commodity outside money is much less forgiving, more disciplining of the credit system than the credit-note outside money of our present systems.

Indeed, commodity discipline was too rigid for a post-war capitalism that needed to incorporate both a scaled-up democracy at home and a more clientelistic empire abroad. It was belatedly eliminated with the formal end of the Bretton Woods system in 1971, only to be replaced with a more technocratic method of discipline fortified by neoliberal nostrums ('inflation targeting', open capital accounts). As per imperial ethics, this combination turned out to be not so disciplining for the hegemon but harshly disciplining for the rest.

The logic of the survival constraint operates when there is a better-quality outside asset that 'money' is a promise to pay, an asset (world money) that nations need to operate in the global markets since that is globally acceptable. In our contemporary arrangement, that outside asset is another sovereign's inside credit, namely the US dollar. But at several historical conjunctures, this outside money was either gold or silver or both. Domestic gold coins might have had distinct denominations and gold content as compared with internationally accepted bullion, but the market price of the metal would link the two through an open capital account.

A commodity outside money differs from a credit outside money in how tightly the survival constraint binds on the state. Before the rise of democracy in the early twentieth century, commodity outside money constrained even the issuer of world money, the United Kingdom. But democracy demanded elasticity for fiscal freedom, so the Victorian discipline of gold was sacrificed under the Bretton Woods system (Polanyi, 2001 [1944]). Democracy-consistent discipline was then achieved by non-market, administrative controls both at the borders and within them: capital controls and financial regulation.

This 'financial repression' only lasted as long as the post-war political settlement itself, notably in Anglo-American constituencies. Financial control was the obverse side of post-war democracy. Once democracy in advanced capitalist countries added its demands to those of capital itself, credit had to be freed from the imperial discipline of gold as nations were required to silence global capital through capital controls. Developing nations, those further down the hierarchy of money, continued to face imperial discipline now shorn of its golden fetters, but they were also sheltered in part by capital controls until the neoliberal era.

An arbitrary stock of some commodity is a sterner disciplinarian of a credit system than a flexible-credit outside money because it is not possible to conjure it up by a simple balance-sheet operation. Put another way, any such balance-sheet operation would not be credible before certain political and institutional conditions were met. Credit structures hitherto built on top of commodities could only free themselves from their rigid discipline once the state was stably fiscally articulated with a healthy national economy. Tax-backed credit structures could then make the economy itself the 'reserve asset', a more flexible and scalable anchor for money. The national economy would replace gold as the reserve asset of the central bank. Techniques of control also improved as crisis by crisis central bankers learned their imperfect art.

Democracy stretched the state's survival constraint domestically and potentially internationally; it also helped format the domestic monetary space for capital by offering a more secure and scaled-up monetary asset (Ingham, 2004). In the post-war period, capitalism and democracy achieved a brief modus vivendi that saw advanced capitalist states use their monetary sovereignty, fortified by capital controls and regulated finance, to serve the people in substantial measure.

This interregnum collapsed as a new global division of labour destroyed the bargaining power of labour (Streeck, 2014). Credit discipline was now meant to be ensured by gold-like means. But now, in the presence of democracy, discipline had to be less harsh than gold. The need for discipline in credit is obvious, but under the auspices of neoliberalism, discipline was formatted in the undemocratic, technocratic garb of constructing monetary policy as 'independent'. And, of course, discipline was not felt equally by the citizenry.

Thus, national economies could in practice have abandoned the 'barbarous relic' of gold long before they formally did in 1971. Indeed, they had functionally dropped it under the Bretton Woods system, which operated as a dollar standard with the discipline of gold almost entirely vestigial, save when the dollar itself became highly undisciplined, and even then it signalled systemic collapse. The role of gold or any commodity outside money is always to provide discipline to the global credit system, the threat of conversion to an inflexible outside money containing the elasticity of world money by acting as the sword of Damocles over the issuer. *A commodity outside money serves to tighten the survival constraint in a credit system rather than determine the ontology of money.* It is the outsideness or superior creditworthiness or acceptability that matters in a creditary relation; a commodity anchor merely represents a particularly brutal institutionalisation of credit discipline.

The commodity anchor thus takes its place *within* the logic of credit (the logic of the survival constraint) of discipline and elasticity. The Bretton Woods as a system collapsed in 1971, but the world economy did not because it had by then long been anchored to the reserve asset of the American economy itself rather than an arbitrary precious metal. In 1960, the US economy was 40 per cent of the global GDP; it was 35 per cent in 1971, and today it is still a substantial 25 per cent. This national economy rather than gold was the new anchor of the world economy.

As with previous empires, this scale both enabled and was enabled by a particular global political project. While it may be true that the absence of the discipline of gold has enabled this project, what we ought to focus on is the absence of commodity-based discipline. For the US at least, both democracy at home and empire abroad were facilitated by this absence.

Our current conjuncture is unique because we lack both competing outside credit monies that could provide hegemon-disciplining exits from the dollar and a commodity outside money whose Victorian discipline would in any case be too much for populist democracies to bear. This means that the present global hegemon has enjoyed an epically relaxed survival constraint and has behaved accordingly. In this unique scenario, global acceptance of an over-expanded dollar might ultimately come down to the lack of competitors that could correct the global balance of power, at least at the distended margin.

Solvency Is in the Eye of the Counterparty

Also critical to the operation of the survival constraint is the identity of the class of people that holds the nation's debt (or, equivalently, in which currency the nation's debt is denominated). If citizens and residents are the major holders of government debt, either directly or through their pension funds, postal savings banks, and so on, they have thereby agreed to pledge their liquidity to their government *over and above* the amount they require to settle their tax liabilities. These holdings further slacken the state's survival constraint and represent a deeper political contract often fortified by a broader sense of patriotic duty (exemplified by war bonds, for example) as opposed to the everyday duty of paying ones' taxes.

Citizens are seeking riskless assets for their savings but are still being patriotic to the extent they have options to place savings abroad or with the private sector. If they lack such options thanks to capital controls, such bond holdings represent coercively corralled liquidity. If these bond holdings are in a relatively institutionalised form as opposed to a marketised form (say, deducted from payrolls and lent to a state-owned development bank as in Brazil), they are even more illiquid for the holder and therefore relax the state's survival constraint commensurately.

However, if non-resident parties hold the majority of the nation's debt, this already represents a substantial breach of the financial border, given that foreign holders would not invest in domestic debt unless they could rely on a swift exit. Formal empire precluded the need for such an exit by eliminating local sovereignty itself. The rupee was anchored to silver at a rate that suited British investor interests, while the absence of an Indian sovereign meant that there was no institution to impose capital controls.

The ever-present threat of capital flight out of national debt and domestic currency and back to the 'safe haven' of world money itself represents a substantial tightening of a state's survival constraint—if not immediately, then when the credit cycle invariably turns. This gives foreign bondholders a seat at the *fiscal* table. Sovereignty is diminished commensurately.

Where the state sits in the global division of labour and consequently the global hierarchy of money is therefore critical in determining how tightly the survival constraint binds on a given sovereign. The nature of outside money—IOU or commodity—the degree of capital controls and the pattern of currency and debt holding can all partially mitigate a subordinate position in the system if they are set to survival-constraint-relaxing positions, but they cannot by themselves change it.

A nation's relative position in the hierarchy can only be altered by real economic growth, sufficient earnings on external account combined with institutional density in the fiscal superstructure. Such a national balance sheet would be 'hedged' in Minsky's terms and have substantial rather than merely formal sovereignty. Whether or not its IOU could be used as a competing world money further depends on scale and the configuration of its credit system in terms of its accessibility to foreign punters; this in turn depends on the relative power of the 'money interest' (which could be a subset of technocrats in a state-dominated structure) within the local political settlement.

Bending to Breaking Point

Pace Chartalism, a bending of the survival constraint is emphatically not a result of the monopoly of coercive power as if that fully accounted for 'sovereignty'. Monetary sovereignty reflects the power of conglomeration rather than the power of coercion. Enabled by the logic of political mutualisation, monetary sovereignty operates through the logic of credit: the state is an economic leviathan because it is a political leviathan. Operating through that logic means being limited by it.

As two-sided balance-sheet operations, individuals are commensurate with firms and governments that also have balance sheets with sources and commitments of cash. Distinct from the economist's 'intertemporal budget constraint', the survival constraint shows us a *social* world tied together by complex, interlocking cash commitments (Mehrling, 2017). The gearing of our collective balance sheet is provided by the survival constraint: how tightly does it bind the constituent balance sheets?

This is the definition of monetary power: the ability to calibrate the survival constraint to impart elasticity or exert discipline on a credit system. Because the credit system is hierarchical, the decision on the elasticity or discipline of credit is determined at one level higher than the concerned unit, ultimately resting at the system's apex. In the language of social theory, this is not coercive power but 'infrastructural power' or 'non-sovereign' power—namely power that operates through a particular arrangement of things into systematic relations (Mann, 1984; Foucault, 2003).

Following Charles Kindleberger, we might say that it is the kind of power that operates by the force of circumstance rather than the force of arms, although we would add that the circumstances are themselves highly contrived rather than simply emergent (Kindleberger, 1967). But this power is hemmed in both domestically or politically and internationally or economically.

'Coercion', like the 'commodity', becomes subject to the internal logic of such systems rather than some exogenous force determining their operations. We are indeed compelled to pay our taxes, but this coercion only works because society has conferred legitimacy on the state; it is simply a truism in our turbulent times that such legitimacy can be withdrawn quite quickly: outrage against new taxes is a frequent phenomenon globally. Domestic political settlements, whether legitimate or not, set the limit of coercion.

Political mutualisation can potentially create a balance sheet that can operate within the rules of the credit game to winning effect because it enables legitimate coercion and thus highly secure future cash flow at scale. Just as we fetishise commodities by forgetting that their value comes from our collective labour, we fetishise the power of the state because we forget its ultimate source is our grant of legitimacy. Within that legitimate political envelope, a state can run a credit system that issues an IOU securely locked to the future labour of its citizens. Some communities might be productive enough to attract foreign buyers of their social product.

Weber's definitional claim was that 'a state is a human community that (successfully) claims the monopoly of the legitimate use of physical force within a given territory' (Weber, 1991 [1919]). Rearranging, we might say that *a state is a human community that successfully claims the apex of a hierarchical credit system because it is legitimate within a given territory.*

The state is subject to the survival constraint; it bends it through political mutualisation. But it cannot break it any more than it can break the legitimate political settlement of which it is a creature. Breaking the survival constraint would mean tearing up its legitimacy, turning the state into a criminal gang. This does occur of course, but for that reason such states issue bad money.

Taxation is wedded to capital through state banking. The irony of contemporary advanced capitalism is that the most secure, large-scale anchoring for capital is achieved by a *democratic* sovereign embedded in capitalist relations of production. The entire national economy is made the reserve asset of the central bank which issues national credit money. The scale and robustness of this operation is only conceivable if citizens across generations pledge a portion of their future surplus to their state.

Democracy, popular sovereignty variously configured, is at the heart of modern capitalism and its money. But capitalism, especially in its neoliberal avatar, requires a continual limit placed on democratic ownership of the economy and polity. This unsteady peace is coming apart as we speak, a theme we explore in our concluding chapter.

Of course, money itself is often seen as inherently undemocratic because credit systems are inherently hierarchical. As such, well-intentioned and completely justified attempts to make money more democratic end up taking aim at hierarchy itself. This is wrong-headed because hierarchy is a *technical* attribute of money, not a moral attribute. While this technical fact makes it harder to engineer monetary systems for democracy and makes the monetary system more susceptible to capture, the fact that democracy is at the heart of modern money can balance the scales.

Credit systems are inherently hierarchical because credit is a relation of variable quality, not unlike sovereignty itself. In the previous chapter, we traced hierarchy in credit to two dimensions: the nature of balance sheet mutualisation and the scale of such mutualisation. In the next two chapters, we will theoretically test the robustness of this claim by comparing it to other answers to the question 'Why are credit systems hierarchical?' We start with an overview of a subset of the Banking School tradition before examining the work of someone who has developed the idea of hierarchy, Perry Mehrling.

4 | Mystical Kernel within the Rational Shell

The Banking School's Residual Chartalism

... practically, and for the purposes of their daily life, [bankers] have no need to think, and never do think, on theories of currency.

—Bagehot (1920 [1873])

Why, according to the Banking School, is central-bank money better than bank money? What is its account of the hierarchy of money? This chapter will illustrate that the answer is paradoxically Chartalist, albeit in a residual manner. 'Outside money' is rendered by several stalwarts of the Banking School as 'fiat', defined by legal tender laws and/or monopoly grants to an issuing bank. A political theory of money, by contrast, bases the superior quality of central-bank money in its robust (political) mutualisation at scale.

The Banking School oddly agrees with Chartalism that legal tender laws drive hierarchy in money. We interpret this as being anchored in the former's argument that a qualitatively superior, 'outside' instrument is required to settle debts. For the Banking School, the law is not the ultimate source of the distinction between money and credit because the logic of debt settlement itself implies such a distinction. 'Promises precede deliveries' (Hicks, 1989), so transactions inherently proliferate chains of credit that only a qualitatively better 'money' can stop. The logic of hierarchy is inherent in debt which, in turn, is inherent in the economy itself.

This generates unstable dynamics that again requires hierarchy to manage. Ralph Hawtrey identified a constitutive tension between value and liquidity. Transactions proliferate credit, but the 'inherent instability of credit' pulls against a stable value of money. This incoherence can be managed 'on banking principles' – that is, through the hierarchy, by modulating banks' survival constraint.

Reading the Banking School somewhat against its own grain, we can also see the more political elements of money—namely how political settlements are expressed in the configuration of the credit system (Bagehot, 1920 [1873]) and how money is linked to value (Hawtrey, 1919).

For a tradition of thought that emerged in eighteenth-century Britain out of real banking practice, this school of thought naturally considers the fact of outside or Chartal money as only the very beginning of the story (Arnon, 2011). For the Banking School, the credit system has its own sui generis dynamics built out of interlocking claims on outside money—dynamics that must be understood in all their interactive complexity if the system is to be managed. The technocratic means of management themselves emerge from banking itself—namely hierarchy, elasticity versus discipline, and so on. Notwithstanding its residual Chartalism in its understanding of outside money, all the action for the Banking School happens in the credit system capped by the central bank.

In a sense, it is precisely because much of the action happens endogenously for the Banking School that they can perhaps neglect a deeper look at the ontology of outside money. This neglect runs with the hierarchical nature of the credit system itself: the outside instrument always shows up as an exogenous constraint whether it is a commodity or the liability of another, 'high-powered' issuer. The Banking School can bracket the nature of outside money because its thought emerges from within a system where such bracketing is part of daily operations.

We have been theorising outside money or national money as a claim on real wealth written into (central) banking institutions by a political contract. By foregrounding the political essence of taxation, we embed the traditional Chartalist argument from sovereignty within a political horizon defined by state legitimacy even while recognising that divergent types of mutualisation generate monies of differing qualities.

Here, we will outline in detail how two key figures of the Banking School end up taking another tack, defining outside money as having superior quality to bank money, thanks to the law, a recognisably Chartalist position.

For a political theory of money, the central bank's power is derived from a politico-legal locking of state or central-bank liabilities to the national economy rather than the debt-imposing law itself constituting and generating value. For the Banking School, the credit system is an engine for generating near-money claims that cyclically approximate the real thing, namely 'money' or 'currency' as defined by legal tender laws. In other words, the Banking School is focused on the dynamics of economic mutualisation, *given* some definition of outside money.

The tendency to handwave in a Chartalist direction is quite widespread in the Banking School. Thus, even John Hicks, an illustrious member of the Banking

School and someone more on the free-market end of its spectrum, concedes that coinage, a critical step in the development of money, could not have occurred without the state 'since the circle of people who might be expected to have faith in the [state's] guarantee would be wider [than the private sector guarantees]' (Hicks, 1989, p. 45).

Having outlined our reservations with Chartalism here, we must therefore extend these to this aspect of the Banking School even while taking on board its lessons regarding economic mutualisation. We will take Walter Bagehot (1826–1877) and Ralph Hawtrey (1879–1975) as our star witnesses.

The Banking School tradition of monetary thinking is often associated with a more laissez-faire, pro-market ideological mode of thinking. There is some justification for this. The so-called real bills doctrine came freighted with a 'law of reflux' that suggested that left to itself, credit could not be over-issued: the market would simply 'reflux' bills surplus to requirements back to issuers either as loan repayments or purchases of securities (Sproul, 2018). The view that the credit system is dynamic in this way might be read as equivalent to saying that regulations are bound to fail as banks will simply innovate around them (Goodhart and Jensen, 2015, p. 22). Charles Goodhart, another Banking School stalwart, did after all coin Goodhart's law with all its similarities to rational expectations (Goodhart, 1983).

Yet from Bagehot to Hawtrey and from Keynes to Minsky and Goodhart, there are many acclaimed adherents of the Banking School who are of the opinion that money has to be actively managed by a central bank which is either owned by or operates in close coordination with the government. There is no perfect overlap between the School and laissez-faire—far from it. As Goodhart observes, '[T]hose supporting the Banking School argued in favour of a central authority, a central-banking institution with the capacity and power to influence both the quality and volume of bank expansion' (Goodhart, 1995, p. 208).

The real thrust of this School is to make the *distinction* between money and credit and focus on the sui generis dynamics of a system built to connect the two rather than to dwell on the nature of money. As Hawtrey observed in his textbook *Currency and Credit*, 'We have treated money as subsidiary to credit. In a highly developed system of deposit banking, such as that of England or the United States, the justification for this is obvious' (Hawtrey, 1919, p. 380). Credit, 'inside money', comes first as a promise to pay 'outside money'. To use Hicks' language of 'circles', outside money is a claim on some entity outside an established circle of creditors or debtors (Hicks, 1989).

The Banking School is born out of pragmatism and lessons hard won from 'concrete realities' (Bagehot, 1920 [1873]) through an almost ethnographic immersion in real banks. Yet for all its emphasis on credit and inside money, its conception of outside money betrays a Chartalist predilection. As a consequence, the Banking School somewhat overlooks the critical fiscal compact that underlies both the value of money and the hierarchy of the system itself, thereby limiting the institutional imagination required for system management, leave alone social transformation. This ends up creating the impression of a managerial conservatism.

Bagehot's Bank

Walter Bagehot is of course famous for outlining the role of the central bank in the management of a liquidity crisis. Even though he was the editor of *The Economist*, son of a bank manager and a member of a bank's board of governors, he was far from an untrammelled free marketeer. His manifesto, *Lombard Street: A Description of the Money Market* (Bagehot, 1920 [1873]), was meant to outline the principles that ought to guide the operation of the central bank, most particularly as the lender of last resort (LOLR). Such a bank, as we now know, ought to lend freely in a liquidity crisis, but, in order to stave off moral hazard, it should do so only against the best collateral and at a high rate of interest (Mehrling, 2011).

At its core, *Lombard Street* is an argument about how the central bank is a very special kind of bank and ought to behave as such. Britain's peculiar constitution had chalked out a very particular role for the BoE which was at the time still a private, profit-driven bank owned by its shareholders and run by a private board. Bagehot was writing in the wake of Peel's Act of 1844, which had bowed to Metallist dogma in splitting the BoE into the Issue Department (which emitted notes strictly backed by gold) and the Banking Department, which was meant to compete, like any other private London bank, by taking in 'self-liquidating' bills, issuing notes (subject to a legislated limit) and creating deposit accounts.

Bagehot's entire argument is that contrary to this ideological legislation, the BoE is emphatically not just any old private bank. To think of it as such would be pure folly and might result in the bank's failure to play its crucial role in managing the money markets and averting financial crises. The BoE is special and ought not behave like any other private, profit-driven bank.

But what exactly made the central bank special in Bagehot's eyes? We will argue that there are strains of both Chartalism and a political theory of money in Bagehot's understanding of the BoE. His emphasis on the 'legal tender' nature of money is very much of a Chartalist bent, while his account of how the bank got its massive scale and subsequently sat at the top of the hierarchy of money foreshadows a political theory of money in that it foregrounds the bank's DNA as emerging from a political settlement.

London's Lombard Street—that is, the money market—was in Bagehot's time where the world came to bank: businesses and foreign governments alike came to this financial emporium to raise money. And it is finance for Bagehot that had driven the English industry forward. 'Democratic' access to credit had allowed eager newcomers from all social backgrounds to compete with comfortable 'merchant princes' and thereby create an economy alive to new and varied opportunities for profit: 'The rough and vulgar structure of English commerce is the secret of its life; for it contains "the propensity to variation", which, in the social as in the animal kingdom, is the principle of progress. In this constant and chronic borrowing, Lombard Street is the great go-between' (ibid., pp. 10–11).

London had grown by orders of magnitude to become the clearing house to the world. Why did the world have confidence in London? A necessary part of the story is of course sheer confidence: in the face of a deeply uncertain future, this is a key element:

> Somehow everybody feels the Bank is sure to come right…. Neither the Bank nor the Banking Department have ever had an idea of being put 'into liquidation'; most men would think as soon of 'winding up' the English nation. (Ibid., pp. 40–42)

But more than the 'confidence fairy' holds up the credit of the BoE. Part of Bagehot's narrative is that the BoE practice has long since departed from the letter of the law as outlined in Peel's Act. In particular, when panic strikes and market liquidity dries up, the special nature of the BoE reveals itself. A sovereign exception is declared, and 'letters of licence' are issued by the government that in effect suspend the law in an emergency. The letters allow the Banking Department to expand its note issuance over the legislated limit. The effect, Bagehot makes clear, was to signal that the entire faith and credit of the British government was behind the putatively private bank:

> The 'effect of letters of licence' to break Peel's Act has confirmed the popular conviction that the Government is close behind the Bank, and will help it when wanted. (Ibid., p. 41)

So here is the first sense in which the BoE is special. The second comes from its liabilities being made legal tender. Bagehot first outlines the central role of 'legal tender' as outside money to the banking system:

To put it more simply—credit is a set of promises to pay; will those promises be kept?... All that a banker wants to pay his creditors is a sufficient supply of the legal tender of the country, *no matter what that legal tender may be*. (Ibid., p. 22, emphasis added)

In practice therefore bankers are content to black-box or bracket the nature of outside money. All they know is that they have to deliver 'money' when a demand is made of them:

> [P]ractically, and for the purposes of their daily life, [bankers] have no need to think, and never do think, on theories of currency. They look at the matter simply. They say—'I am under an obligation to pay such and such sums of legal currency; how much have I in my till, or have I at once under my command, of that currency?' (Ibid.)

Bagehot even cites the most Chartalist of examples, the greenback:

> In America, for example, it is quite enough for a banker to hold 'greenbacks', though the value of these changes as the Government chooses to enlarge or contract the issue. But a practical New York banker *has no need to think* of the goodness or badness of this system at all; he need only keep enough 'greenbacks' to pay all probable demands, and then he is fairly safe from the risk of failure. (Ibid., p. 23, emphasis added)

And it is the law that has made the BoE special: 'By the law of England the legal tenders are gold and silver coin (the last for small amounts only), and Bank of England notes' (ibid.).

Another Chartalist principle operates in Bagehot, namely the limits of Chartal reach. State power is operative within the realm, but foreigners require an internationally accepted money—gold:

> But then what is 'cash?' Within a country the action of a Government can settle the quantity, and therefore the value, of its currency; but outside its own country, no Government can do so. Bullion is the 'cash' of international trade. (Ibid., p. 45)

Foreigners are subject not to the law but to confidence: 'this foreign deposit is evidently of a delicate and peculiar nature. It depends on the good opinion of foreigners, and that opinion may diminish or may change into a bad opinion' (ibid., p. 35).

And where do foreigners acquire their bullion when they want to exit a nation? 'Now, the only source from which large sums of cash can be withdrawn in countries where banking is at all developed, is a "bank reserve"' (ibid., p. 45).

This 'bank reserve' is outside money as defined by the law: at the time, it was composed of both gold and BoE notes (which, if we recall, were supposedly limited in number by the frequently suspended law: NB crypto enthusiasts). Since foreigners want gold rather than legal tender notes, the holder of the bullion part of the reserve has special responsibilities when faced with a foreign drain of gold:

> Whatever persons—one bank or many banks—in any country hold the banking reserve of that country, ought at the very beginning of an unfavourable foreign exchange at once to raise the rate of interest, so as to prevent their reserve from being diminished farther, and so as to replenish it by imports of bullion. (Ibid., p. 47)

Raising rates to coax gold back in and prevent capital flight preserves the crucial bank reserve.

Law might confer reserve status on BoE notes, but how is it that the bank has come to acquire much of the nation's gold? What accounts for the particularly concentrated nature of banking in England, for Bagehot?

Real versus Conjectural History

Notwithstanding notions of natural hierarchies, Bagehot takes England's 'one-reserve' system to be highly 'artificial' and indeed quite dangerous. Contrary to 'conjectural history' or just so stories that Bagehot lampoons, he outlines a 'real history' of banking. In Bagehot's own story, politics looms large:

> The first banks were not founded for our system of deposit banking, or for anything like it. They were founded for much more pressing reasons, and having been founded, they, or copies from them, were applied to our modern uses. The earliest banks of Italy ... were at first only companies to make loans to, and float loans for, the Governments of the cities in which they were formed. (Ibid., p. 77)

Note well that for Bagehot, the doyen of the Banking School, banking was *invented* for government finance. If the political origins of banking per se were clear to Bagehot, this went double for the BoE, which in its origin it was not only a finance company, but a Whig finance company. It was founded by a Whig Government because it was in desperate want of money, and supported by the 'City' because the 'City' was Whig. (Ibid., p. 90)

As Bagehot tells it, the 'monstrous robbery' of Charles II's Stop of the Exchequer in 1672 ruined the otherwise good credit of English kings. Indeed, the credit of most sovereigns was superior to that of the private sector and enabled banking to get a leg up:

> In many European countries the credit of the State had been so much better than any other credit, that it had been used to strengthen the beginnings of banking. The credit of the State had been so used in England: though there had lately been a civil war and several revolutions, the honesty of the English Government was trusted implicitly. (Ibid., p. 91)

This sentiment is itself quite contrary to other adherents of the Banking School. Take Hicks, who notes that 'one does not get the impression that the kings of olden times were a reliable lot' (Hicks, 1989, p. 45), or Perry Mehrling, who observes, 'Pace the strong [C]hartalist position, my reading of history is that the king's money was typically not very good money, and tended to depreciate against the private money, sometimes dramatically so and sometimes intentionally so as a mechanism of state finance' (Mehrling, 2012b, p. 10). Bagehot demurs, 'The post-Glorious Revolution (1688) regime however was not trusted by the markets, "Government created by a revolution hardly ever is"'. With ruined credit and dire need from continental wars, the revolutionary state had come up against the survival constraint. A huge debt needed to be raised from the Whig City. Bagehot cites three weighty privileges that were extracted from the new sovereign in exchange for the incorporation of the BoE and the national debt (Bagehot, 1920 [1873], pp. 93–95).

First, the government would bank exclusively with the bank so that it would become the government's creditor over time. For Bagehot, this created a huge demonstration effect: the common man would naturally bestow disproportionate trust on a bank that housed the government's own account. Second, the bank alone had the privilege of being a limited liability company, a principle Bagehot claims was unheard of in English common law. This induced several prudent merchants to join its board who might have otherwise stayed away, burnishing its prestige and creditworthiness. The third privilege was the most potent: the bank was the only joint stock company allowed to be a bank of issue in England. This gave the bank a virtual monopoly on note issue in the monied metropolis of London; private banks (unlimited liability partnerships) might issue notes, but they would be at too small a scale to compete, thanks to the joint action of limited liability and the ability to issue common stock. This was robust economic mutualisation at scale in action but facilitated by law and politics.

The fount and origin of these privileges, says Bagehot, was the political contract of the revolutionary settlement. The 'fundholder' or buyer of the National Debt was considered a cornerstone of the revolution, completely opposed to the Pretender whom it was assumed would return only to repudiate the debt: 'For a long time the Bank of England was the focus of London Liberalism, and in that capacity rendered to the State inestimable services' (ibid., p. 93).

It is this concatenation of politics and banking that gave rise to what was for Bagehot a peculiarly English system:

> With so many advantages over all competitors, it is quite natural that the Bank of England should have far outstripped them all. Inevitably it became *the* bank in London; all the other bankers grouped themselves round it, and lodged their reserve with it. (Ibid., p. 97)

Bagehot is at pains to stress that this was *not* a 'natural' monopoly or hierarchy: 'I have tediously insisted that the natural system of banking is that of many banks keeping their own cash reserve' (ibid., p. 309). Left to itself, the banking system would distribute the nation's bank reserve to a number of equally sized banks: 'In all other trades competition brings the traders to a rough approximate equality' (ibid., p. 66). He is not suggesting another revolution to change things of course; this is the system as it is; people are used to it, and it has to be managed as such. But the political logic of the BoE's unique scale and position in the hierarchy of money is clear in his history.

Such is Bagehot's story about how the BoE became special, how it came to be in charge of both legal tender note issue and the empire's gold reserves. It is from here that Bagehot derives his famous formula on how to stem a panic.

'An alarm,' notes Bagehot, 'is an opinion that the money of certain persons will not pay their creditors when those creditors want to be paid' (ibid., p. 53). Some entity therefore has to be ready to lend during a storm if it is to be quelled. But lending too freely might result in a drain of bullion, 'cash' to foreigners, especially in panic. An 'internal drain' for domestic cash is frequently accompanied by an external drain for gold, creating a 'compound disease'. The remedy for the external drain is to raise interest rates high enough to attract gold back to the reserve. Whence the formula to lend freely but at a high rate: this attacks both internal and external drains simultaneously.

It is the duty of the keeper of the nation's banking reserve to be a LOLR. Bagehot dismisses other arguments for the BoE acting in a publicly minded manner: neither having its notes being legal tender nor being the keeper of the government's money is a sufficient reason. No, the possessor of the reserve is impelled by that very fact to lend it in a panic; this is what a bank reserve is for:

> The real reason has not been distinctly seen. As has been already said—but on account of its importance and perhaps its novelty it is worth saying again—whatever bank or banks keep the ultimate banking reserve of the country must lend that reserve most freely in time of apprehension, for that is one of the characteristic uses of the bank reserve, and the mode in which it attains one of the main ends for which it is kept. Whether rightly or wrongly, at present and in fact the Bank of England keeps our ultimate bank reserve, and therefore they must use it in this manner. (Ibid., p. 63)

Since the duty stems from the possession of the reserve, the conditions that led to the BoE possessing the banking reserve in the first place are of prime importance for a theory of money and its hierarchy. As Bagehot traces it, a political contract led to the creation of a bank of such scale that other domestic banks lodged their reserves with this bank. This unnatural monopoly, flowing from the nature of the revolutionary settlement in English politics, makes this entity far from your garden-variety private London bank. While '[w]e are ... solemnly told that the Banking Department of the Bank of England is only a bank like other banks' (ibid.), this flies in the face of real history. We might not like it, but the BoE is special; politics made it so.

Bagehot goes out of his way to tell us that he does not like this arrangement:

> I shall have failed in my purpose if I have not proved that the system of entrusting all our reserve to a single board, like that of the Bank directors, is very anomalous; that it is very dangerous; that its bad consequences, though much felt, have not been fully seen; that they have been obscured by traditional arguments and hidden in the dust of ancient controversies. (Ibid., pp. 65–66)

It is 'dangerous' but manageable if we understand the system's dynamics. Critical to this is understanding that the BoE, the repository of banking reserve of the nation and empire, is a special bank. It is special because it expresses a society-wide contract— that transforming political settlement into economic fact both enables it to operate at superordinate scale and as such requires it to act as an LOLR.

Hawtrey's Institutionalism

Being born out of practical experience with real institutions, there can be little surprise that the Banking School makes several moves that would find favour with the 'old' institutionalist school of economics. While Mehrling (1998) focuses on the American tradition in this respect, it might be argued that the focus of the British Banking School on legal tender laws, debt as a form of contract, and so on, also chimes with American institutionalism as we saw with John Commons.

The institutionalist focus on the transaction as the cellular unit of economic life is exactly where Hicks begins his own theorisation of money. He begins by observing that most transactions in real economic life are not in fact spot transactions but transactions across time. While the importance of the temporal dimension derives from the Austrian School, the way in which it is made operational in Hicks is quite institutionalist.

For Hicks, a transaction is divided into three moments: first, a contractual promise to deliver is swapped with a promise to pay; the second and third see actual delivery or execution of the promise to pay. In spot transactions, exceptionally, these moments are compressed into a single instant. But the vast majority of the time, these moments are not simultaneous: 'promises precede deliveries' (Hicks, 1989, p. 42).

We are here in the space of transactions in rights, of working rules of collection action, the space of institutional economics. If transactions are constituted by debt, then money is the instrument that legally extinguishes that debt and completes the transaction. Preceding Hicks in this institutionalist approach was the English economist and treasury official Ralph Hawtrey.

Hawtrey's opening move is to illustrate the centrality of debt–credit relations at the very cellular level of the transaction: 'If a man sells a ton of coals to another, this will create a *debt* from the buyer to the seller' (Hawtrey, 1919, p. 2, emphasis original). By illuminating the creditary architecture of the most basic element of economic life, the transaction, Hawtrey illustrates the absolutely foundational nature of debt to economic life. The classical conceit of money as a neutral veil stands defeated.

What is true of exchange is also true of production: 'In the processes of production *a service rendered creates a debt* from the person to whom the product belongs to the person who renders the service' (ibid., p. 3, emphasis added). Debt and credit are part of the deep structure of the economy precisely because of the temporal nature of economic action.

As with Bagehot, Hawtrey too wants to emphasise the distinction between money and credit. The economic requirement is not for credit to be anchored to some 'real' commodity; that is a Currency School conception. The economic requirement is for *closure*: how does a chain of transactions end?

> [I]n the absence of money there is a certain difficulty in closing transactions.... The need for a medium of payment which cannot legally be disputed is obvious. (Ibid., p. 15)

Since transactions are open-ended and futural, how do we get closure? Some exogenous element is needed to close the chain, so the law defines legal tender. Hawtrey's emphasis on the debt-generating transactional chain leads him to a more general definition of money whose creditary logic necessitates legal closure:

> We started by saying that money is a medium of exchange. This is true enough.... But legally money is the means of discharging a debt, and this is really the more general conception. It is used as a medium of exchange because a purchase creates a debt, and money provides the means of paying the debt. (Ibid.)

The requirement for legal tender emerges from the creditary logic of transactions that require closure. Legal tender is a codification of 'customary tender' and thereby fixes what is already in circulation. Institutional fixing is distinct from 'fiat' as value generating since valuable debts emerge from economic life; Hawtrey passes over the debts that emerge from political life.

Now, a particular *credit instrument* could in principle be designated as 'legal tender' and thereby perform the functions of money; this was the case with BoE notes after 1833. But it would be the law doing the designating, in Hawtrey's argument. By his logic, nothing in the qualitative nature of the particular credit instrument marks it out as being capable of bearing the functions of money because in the most general conception, the economic function of closing a transaction can only be performed by an act of law.

From the point of view of a political theory of money, however, the law is constrained in its choice of instruments to serve as legal tender. Any old credit note or commodity will not do. The law puts the seal on the logic of robustness and scale; it does not act independently of it if it wants to produce good money.

There is, for Hawtrey, another economic function of money that cannot be performed by the law itself. This is the requirement for a stable standard of value against which all other goods and services can be measured. Prefiguring Minsky and coterminous with Keynes, Hawtrey pioneered the idea that the credit system is characterised by 'inherent instability'; it tends not to equilibrium but to cyclical swings as profit-seeking banks expand and contract their balance sheets in response to merchants' and producers' demands:

> In the practical business of credit regulation it is vital to take due account of the inherent instability of credit. When credit is normal, and the resistance of the banking system to the pressure of borrowers is just sufficient, the banking system is in reality balancing upon a razor's edge. (Hawtrey, 1933, p. 168)

This definitional instability creates a problem for money qua a measure of value. Debts after all are denominated in units of money; the credit embedded in the transaction is merely a promise to pay money. Transactions occurring across time require a stable unit of value. Transactions are nothing but concatenations of credit–debt relations; the more complex the pattern of exchange in an economy, the less likely it is that debits and credits will perfectly cancel each other out at the end of the trading day. Debts are carried forward in time, and therefore the unit of their measure must have some stability if today's debts are to be legible tomorrow. Dealers in debts, banks, emerge to interface between debits and credits, interposing their own balance-sheet liabilities, which can be used as a means of payment and as a bridge to carry over perpetually outstanding debits or credits. Debt is always already outstanding because it is always already created by ongoing transactions.

Therefore, money for Hawtrey has two functions: first, to legally discharge debts in order to close transactions and, therefore second, to anchor the intertemporal legibility of the interlocking web of transactions by providing a stable standard of measure. But the creditary–temporal nature of transactions *constantly militates against stability* in the provision of the standard of value:

> We now see the part that money has to play. First of all, it has to provide the means for the legal discharge of a debt; secondly, by supplying a standard of value, it has to correct the instability of credit.... The second function of money, that of providing a standard of value, arises naturally out of the first. The value of a debt immediately due is necessarily equal to the value of the means by which it can be legally paid. Thus the problem of stabilising credit is transformed into the problem of stabilising the value of money. *We shall find that the expansive tendencies of credit are in perpetual conflict with the maintenance of a fixed standard of value*, and a great part of our subject is taken up with the problem of how best to reconcile this conflict. (Hawtrey, 1919, pp. 15–16, emphasis added)

The credit system comprises layers of profit-seeking actors coordinated only by the profit motive. This generates a system of credit that is perpetually tottering on a 'razor's edge', constantly prone to bouts of instability as the various parts of the system attempt to coordinate with each other in the face of an abyss of uncertainty. The 'art of central banking' inheres in managing this 'perpetual conflict' by keeping money in some stable relation to 'value'. In the language of the previous chapters, transactional ease or liquidity requires elasticity, while stabilising value across time requires discipline. The system is shot through with contradictions which have to be actively managed.

Note parenthetically that cryptocurrencies aim to manage the trade-off between the expansion of credit and the stability of value *by eliminating credit itself*. But this has not yielded stability in value because the universe of transactions constantly peppers money with its asynchronous demands; if money cannot expand and contract in response, all such demands will be reflected in the price in real time—hence the inherent volatility in cryptocurrencies rendering them unsuitable as stable standards of value (Borio, 2019).

Bank credit is a promise to pay 'money', and money is defined legally. In a fractional reserve system therefore, even in the absence of any concrete regulations, banks will keep stocks of that which is legally defined as money on hand to meet randomly arising demands to convert banknotes or deposits into legal tender money. The level of bank reserves is to the individual banker a barometer of how risky their operations are: the lower the level, the less likely they would be able to fulfil random demands for 'money'. Thus, for Hawtrey, control over the expansion and contraction of the banking system can be achieved by a central authority targeting the level of legal tender money in the system through its price, namely the interest rate. This is because interest rates drive the creation of credit, and credit in turn drives demand for legal tender money.

This is a delicate dance between private and public balance sheets, far from lockstep control. Contractions and expansions of credit feed through balance sheets of merchants, manufacturers and consumers, but the dynamic state of those balance sheets will determine the degree of traction of control over credit by a central bank. But a legally defined monopoly on money 'note issue' does enable centralised control nevertheless:

> The best organ of Government for [the control of a paper currency] is a State Bank, or else a central bank which, while not itself a part of the Executive Government, is willing regularly to co-operate with it. Such a bank can regulate the paper currency *on banking principles.* (Ibid., p. 50, emphasis added)

The fact that banks must maintain adequate reserves of legal tender money to ensure that they can meet their demand liabilities, *while legal tender money can in the last resort be obtained only by borrowing from the central bank,* gives the central bank great power of control over credit. The market rate of interest will always tend to approximate to the rate charged by the central bank, the 'bank rate' as it is called. (Ibid., pp. 50–51, emphasis added)

It is obvious that a central bank, which advances to the other banks, at what rate of interest it pleases, the cash [legal tender money] necessary to provide their reserves, *holds a very commanding position.* (Ibid., emphasis added)

By rigorously maintaining that the distinction between money and credit is a legal one, and by subordinating the functioning of money or currency to credit, Hawtrey is trying to instruct us in how a modern economy works. While money might indeed be defined by the law, it absolutely does not follow that the monetary economy behaves in the 'classical' fashion—that is, by treating money as a neutral veil or just another commodity that conventionally represents value.

The aforementioned might sound like the Chartalist notion that legal definition allows untrammelled monetary control. Yet this is not the case, not least of all because the rest of the world cares not for legal tender of a particular sovereign. In a modern economy, *credit drives money,* not the other way around. Whatever the state defines as 'money', the banking system can in principle create credit on top of it thereby driving demand for 'money'. This is not a free-market platitude but a recognition of the role of credit in economic life, a role that is eminently subject to management 'on banking principles' (Hawtrey, 1919, p. 50).

This after all is what banks are doing—namely socialising the credit inherent in the economy. As we know, profit-seeking banks will tend to overshoot, which creates the need for a central bank:

The only effective method of controlling the issues of paper money is to control the creation of credit, for *the demand for legal tender money for circulation is consequential upon the supply of credit.* Hence the need for a central bank of issue. (Ibid., p. 52, emphasis added)

The residual Chartalism of defining outside money as 'legal tender' is not the Chartalism of sovereign control. But nor is it, according to Bagehot and Hawtrey, an account of an 'inherent hierarchy of money' that ends with the state. In contrast to Hicks' view, there is nothing from Bagehot and Hawtrey which suggests that they identify a natural monopoly of scale operating in the credit system. What monopoly exists is on account of the law:

> Till Bank of England notes were made legal tender in 1833, the only exclusive privilege of the Bank in regard to note issue was that, among the note-issuing banks, it had a monopoly of the constitution of a joint-stock company. It was this privilege which gave it its pre-eminence. (Hawtrey, 1933, pp. 131–132)

Given some instrument defined by custom or law as 'money'—that is, that which indisputably and legally settles transactions—certain dynamics of a money-credit system apply. Control is possible (indeed, given inherent instability, *required*), but only by understanding and applying the internal, sui generis logic of the system—namely inherent instability. Control is possible but only by operating with the grain of the system, *'on banking principles'* (ibid., p. 50, emphasis added). This is the principle of credit being a promise to pay some outside instrument called 'money'.

The residual Chartalism of Bagehot and Hawtrey is in terms of how they identify outside money and *not* the operation of the credit system: this is what is meant by subordinating currency to credit. Demand for credit drives demand for currency: this is an endogenous dynamic that subordinates currency to credit. Monopoly of legal tender enables the central bank to control this endogenous activity through modulation of the price of money. This is the residual Chartalism.

But the mode of operation of this control is through the credit system itself by modulating the survival constraint ('on banking principles'): this is non-sovereign, market or institutional power rather than coercive control.

If Bagehot points the way to a political theory of money by recounting how political contracts turn to nation-scale creditary operations, we must now examine how Hawtrey helps us understand another element of the political theory of money—namely how currency and credit come to acquire value in terms of their ability to command real wealth. Unlike with Bagehot, the explicitly political element is missing for Hawtrey.

The Command of Wealth

What we are somewhat apologetically calling the residual Chartalism of the Banking School ought not lead to the confusion that Bagehot and Hawtrey view the *value* of money as deriving entirely from an act of legal fiat. The legal element in their argument has one main economic function: it serves to demarcate the end point in an otherwise infinite chain of transactions of debt and credit. It also enables control of an endogenously dynamic credit system, given that money is a means of final settlement. It also provides the unit of measure for the ramifying credit–debit relations inherent in all trans-actions.

In operating as such, the interval between 'temporary' and final settlement allows for specialists in debt and credit to emerge in the temporal gap before final settlement; transactors might tarry at an intermediate stage for some time and indeed use temporary or customary means to settle other debts without engaging outside money at all.

Hawtrey spins out the creditary logic of the transaction in order to open up the banking dimension: '[I]t is necessary to understand that an undischarged debt due from a solvent debtor is, from the standpoint of the creditor, purchasing power' (Hawtrey, 1919, p. 367). An incomplete transaction leaves an outstanding debt unpaid that can be turned into a monetary instrument by the operation of some entity intervening to assume that outstanding debt in a particular manner (repayable on demand). This method of accepting a third party's solvency generates near-money means of payment. But it takes an entire system of refinance to achieve this nearness.

Hawtrey renders production itself in terms of debt: 'Production may be regarded as making society the debtor of the producer' (ibid., p. 186). Yet society will only pay off its debt to production to a certain extent, depending on the market for the product. And society will only pay its debt at the end of the production process: in the meantime, the producer has overhead costs, a wage bill, and so on. 'In the interval the banker undertakes society's debt (subject, of course, to discount)' (ibid.). This social debt is transformed through banking into purchasing power *today* for the producer to get busy with the production process.

Thus, the law does not endow the monetary unit with real economic value. Transactional time is native to all economic processes from trade to production, so the means of payment are required to span these timescales. Demand for means of payment comes from the temporal nature of economic life. For Hawtrey, such demand supports the value of the means of payment. This is true even in a gold-standard system where bank notes are promises to pay gold:

> In fact there is a demand for the means of payment *as such*, and this demand gives a value to whatever is established by law or custom as the means of payment, quite apart from any value it may possess for any other purpose. Gold itself derives part of its value from the demand for it as a means of payment. (Ibid., p. 33)

What Hawtrey is implicitly nodding to here, by way of contrast with strong Chartalism, is the fact that whatever law or custom defines as money, people will demand it not to pay their taxes, at least not in the first instance, but because capitalism is a time-bound cash nexus. Now, the state can indeed drive such a process of marketisation, but to hold that taxes are the main driver of money to the exclusion of the monetisation of material relationships is to hold a very narrow view of the relations between state and society.

Hawtrey shows that the distinction between money as a medium of exchange and a means of payment (of debts) is somewhat flawed if all transactions entail time-debt to begin with. The distinction is only meaningful in a world dominated by spot transactions, but that is not our world.

Transactors demand means of payment, banks supply credit money, and governments, through their banks, supply legal tender credit money. The link to production will enable us to see how the value of money is determined and exactly what role the commodity anchor plays.

The value of money, for Hawtrey, comes from what you can buy with it. More precisely, the entire stock of money derives value from the entire stock of wealth to which it refers. As we are familiar with today, Hawtrey defines the stock of purchasing power as outside (legal tender) money in circulation *plus* all the liabilities of banks (that is, deposits) (ibid., p. 34). This universe of money instruments derives its value from the universe of commodities in a quantitative ratio. This is Hawtrey's version of the quantity theory of money; he calls the entire stock of money 'the unspent margin':

> The quantity theory, in the form in which we have enunciated it, merely equates the unspent margin of purchasing power, which is a total of monetary units, to the *command over wealth* which the people hold in reserve. It equates, in fact, a total of monetary units to a total of wealth [fn.: a *potential*, not an actual, total of wealth], and so *determines the value of the monetary unit in terms of wealth.* (Ibid., p. 39, emphasis added)

Money has value because it has 'command over wealth' where wealth is set in *futural* terms. Yet by rendering outside money as legal tender, Hawtrey misses an opportunity to embed money's ability to command wealth in the fiscal relations of society which are also creditary in nature. From his perch, he focuses on the economically mutualised element of the credit system. For Hawtrey, money commands *wealth* because it can settle debts through *market* transactions, while debts are legal obligations to deliver *money*:

A debt is fundamentally an obligation to give not money but wealth. Legally the use of money enables the debtor to close the transaction. From the economic standpoint, however, the creditor's claims are not fully satisfied till he has spent the money. *He must go into the market* and draw from it so much wealth as is represented by the purchasing power he has received. (Ibid., p. 14, emphasis added)

Thus, for Hawtrey, wealth is linked to money through (the potential for) *market* transactions that transform money into wealth. Legally, the debt is paid on the delivery of money, but economically for wealth to change hands, M must be converted back to C, to use Marx's terminology. The market, a set of *economic* relations, lies between money and wealth and links money to wealth, whereas for a political theory of money *fiscal relations*, a political contract forms a channel sui generis that legally locks national money (the central bank's liability) to national wealth over and above a market-based command of wealth.

Hawtrey outlines a definite link from money to wealth and 'value' in a classical sense, but like the classics, he misses the fiscal–political institutions that (more firmly) bind money to value. This, ultimately, is the price of residual Chartalism. While a political theory of money does not ignore the economic dimension of market-based purchasing power as regards the value of money, it relates it to fiscal relations as the latter form a qualitatively more robust bond to value (see Chapter 7). Fiscal relations are the creditary core that enables the economic relations to operate as more or less stable outworks. Fiscal relations enable a political command over wealth. But both are species of mutualisation of creditary relations.

Yet by configuring money as 'command over wealth' per se, Hawtrey enables us to avoid the fetishisation of the monetary commodity gold as that which delivers value to the credit instrument under commodity-based systems. He lampoons classical theory which decries that '[p]aper money which is not convertible into coin is a sham, a fraud (ibid., p. 364). Indeed, for Hawtrey, the whole function of commodity gold is seen in terms of its ability to ensure the stability of the standard of value given the unremitting fact of the instability of credit. Gold is merely a means of discipline in the face of the elasticity credit. Commodity 'backing' does not render money valuable; command over wealth does:

A credit in Capetown is the means of making payments in South Africa; a credit in London is the means of making payments in England. Each credit therefore gives a command over wealth in the region where it is due. This is the real basis of its value; convertibility into gold is merely a device adopted to steady the purchasing power of the monetary unit. (Ibid., p. 57)

If a gold-based system worked, it did so because it helped stem the inherent instability of credit, and emphatically *not* because it contained any deep truths about the nature of money. 'To recommend a dogma on account not of its inherent validity but of its good practical consequences is a dangerous method' (ibid., p. 367).

Of course, this begs the question: worked for whom? The assumption by both Hawtrey and Bagehot is that the ability to preserve the value of the currency, namely gold, is predicated on the issuing bank's action to raise interest rates. The contractionary toll this method of discipline takes on the poorest in an economy and most of those in poorer, imperially held economies would be too severe for democracies to endure. Imperialism and the absence of democracy are clearly part of the deep, shared assumptions of both Bagehot and Hawtrey. As we will see in Chapter 8, it was a particular combination of democracy at home and empire-without-empire abroad that enabled Pax Americana to eliminate gold and achieve both stability and democracy for some, and only for some time. Bringing politics in means appreciating the political preconditions of a stable anchor.

Hawtrey's version of the quantity theory tied inflation to the dynamics of credit: inflation simply means the unchecked and ill-disciplined expansion of credit. There is, he freely concedes, a danger in credit, namely its inherent instability, but the temporal nature of economic life means that the overly disciplined dogma of metallism does not provide a way out of this danger. Only artful management of credit can achieve this.

Since the value of gold, so to speak, is to regulate the stability of the credit by means of discipline, there can be more rational and equitable modes of discipline than anchoring money to an arbitrary precious metal. Following Irving Fisher, Hawtrey points to index numbers as potentially forming these disciplining anchors:

> Credit possesses value, and it is more correct to say that the value of gold is due to its convertibility into credit than that the value of credit is due to its convertibility into gold. Convertibility into gold certainly sustains the value of credit, because it facilitates the regulation of credit. *But were the union between the two dissolved, credit might still be judiciously regulated, in relation for example to silver or to an index number,* or as under the Bank Restriction, to nothing in particular. (Ibid., p. 371, emphasis added)

'But were the union between the two dissolved' shows how a post-gold world was imminent in the credit system because gold was itself internal to the latter's logic. The advantage of index numbers as anchors is that they can be transposed to the world of commodities, to wealth as such. 'Value,' Hawtrey reminds us, 'is not a quality, but a relation, and fixity of value must be fixity of value in terms of some other thing or things' (ibid., p. 374).

In the end, Hawtrey does make a brief nod to politics and justice, albeit a somewhat conservative conception of justice as the continuation of the status quo:

> The monetary unit is employed for the measurement of debts. The purpose of fixing its value is to preserve justice as between debtor and creditor. We are not here concerned with the fundamental economic conception of justice, justice in the distribution of wealth, but with the strictly limited conception of securing the fulfilment of legitimate expectations. So long as we base the economic management of society on bargains which relate to the future, the stability of the unit in which those bargains are calculated must be of paramount importance. (Ibid., pp. 374–375)

The black-boxing of politics means that Hawtrey cannot relate stability in money to a broader notion of democratic justice qua the distribution of wealth. To that extent, he was of course a creature of his imperial time. But in pointing to time, wealth, and the inherent tension between discipline and chaos in 'bargains which relate to the future', Hawtrey was already well ahead of his time.

Goodhart's Control

Our burden in this chapter has been to show that there is a residual Chartalism lurking within the creditary logic of the Banking School. While this illustrates a theoretical inadequacy of the School's account of hierarchy in money, it is more like the School does not really care about the ontology of outside money so as long as it is clear that there is some hierarchical distinction between money and credit. It is the *distinction* that matters—the fact that money ends chains of debt, that credit is a promise to pay money and that money is subordinated in value and dynamics to credit. Everything follows from there.

But settling on legal tender laws as the source of outsideness or higher quality in central-bank money has theoretical costs. While Hawtrey is at pains to note that legal tender laws do not imbue money with value, the foregrounding of the law as the source of the central bank's monopoly power might lead one to that conclusion. On the other hand, by making the distinction between money's purchasing power in the market and legal tender laws, Hawtrey misses out the political–fiscal predication of national money's value.

However, through a close reading of Bagehot and Hawtrey, we can glean several elements of a political theory of money. In reading Bagehot, we see the notion that the central bank attains scale, thanks to it being the institutional expression of a society-wide political contract. Yet for Bagehot, this contract takes the legal form of monopoly privileges rather than the politico-economic form of an asset base that is the economy itself. Hawtrey also relies on a Chartalist definition of outside money but does not make the argument for Chartal-type control: this does not follow given the inherent instability of credit. Control is available if the central banker maintains a link between money and value qua wealth by modulating the survival constraint—namely the availability of outside money.

What of contemporary Banking School adherents? What is their view of modern money? Goodhart, an economist and historian of central banking, illustrates the point of this chapter by being both a Chartalist as well as a member of the Banking School. Wearing the latter hat, for instance, Goodhart recognises that the 'money supply' is endogenous to bankers' decisions to lend or not; what the central bank controls is the price of bank refinance through the functional equivalent of the bank rate, not the quantity of money (Goodhart, 2002).

Over the years, Goodhart's view on how the central bank operationalises its control over the system has evolved. He is, like Bagehot, clear that historically it started as the government's bank. Initially, again like Bagehot and Hawtrey, he appears to have thought that the legal mandate that bank credit ought to be a promise to pay 'fiat money' at par is key:

> The ability of a Central Bank to maintain its influence over interest rates, and a generalised pressure on the rate of monetary expansion, depends ultimately on commercial banks needing to retain balances with itself. That need would appear likely to continue so long as the banks themselves need to maintain the convertibility of their own liabilities, whether deposits or notes, into a more 'fundamental' store of value, whether that be (a basket of) commodities, or into fiat money. (Goodhart, 1995, p. 58)

However, more recently, Goodhart stresses that the legal constraint can in fact be done away with since ultimately the central bank can operate in the (domestic) market free of the constraints of profitability precisely because it is the government's bank. Unmatched balance-sheet depth becomes a source of its power:

> Indeed, while it is true that such control appears to rest on the central bank's ability to vary its monopsonistically supplied monetary base by

open-market operations, I shall argue that this is, in fact, a superficial epi-phenomenon. What the ability of the central bank ultimately depends on is the fact that it is the government's bank, and thus has the power to intervene in (financial) markets without concern for profitability (let alone profit maximisation). It can, consequently, force its profit-seeking commercial confreres, in the last resort, always to dance to its tune. (Goodhart, 2000, p. 190)

This of course leads us right back to debates over Peel's Act of 1844. The central bank is special for some quasi-Chartalist reason that exculpates it from run-of-the-mill profit-making: this reason is either because it holds the bank reserve of the country (Bagehot, 1920 [1873]), its notes are legal tender (Hawtrey, 1919) or the government's bank can afford to operate in the money markets guided by policy rather than profit (Goodhart, and indeed Mehrling, as we explore in the next chapter). Either way, control is effected *on banking principles*. This means using price-based controls over outside money to modulate the elasticity or discipline of the credit system to control its inherent instability.

For economist and historian of thought Perry Mehrling, Goodhart's Chartalism is meant to provide a theory of outside money in a post-war world without gold. As we have seen earlier, convertibility to some higher unit is the key to central-bank control for the Banking School. For Mehrling, it is in order to make sense of the post-war hierarchy of money that ends with fiat money (which is not a promise to pay anything) that Goodhart increasingly embraces Chartalism: 'Goodhart's Cartalism [*sic*] served as a bridging device that allowed him to step between the vanished pre-WWI world and the lived experience of his own time' (Mehrling, 2003, p. 33).

However, as this chapter has shown, a residual Chartalism of the kind Mehrling ascribes to Goodhart is in fact a constitutive part of the Banking School going back to Bagehot. 'Gold' was always read as coterminous with legal tender as outside money; fiat money was simply paper gold. The abandonment of the commodity anchor after the war merely served to bring to the fore the Chartalism that was always present in the Banking School—the residual Chartalism of having the chain of payments stop with legal tender money domestically and gold internationally.

As such, Goodhart is perhaps less of a bridge than a throwback, insisting as he does on the well-worn Banking School distinction between currency and credit now shorn of the gold fetish. Goodhart sees himself as providing a salutary reminder that a world without gold is by no means a world without the possibility of central-bank control on banking principles, the very core of the Banking School message.

The presence of gold internationally in a certain period might seem to bolster the Metallist case until we remember that a particular global political settlement was operative in the period of its ascendance. Taking our cue from Hawtrey that credit drove demand for gold, we might say that the international acceptance of gold was driven by the acceptance of sterling in the empire and beyond (see Chapter 5).

The post-war scenario sloughed off its golden skein and thereby eliminated a commodity as the ultimate means of payment; national 'fiat' monies seem to end the chain of payments. As Mehrling read it at the time, this served to blur the distinction between money as a means of payment or means of final settlement (currency) and money as a promise to pay or medium of exchange (credit) (Mehrling, 2003). The line between credit and currency having been blurred, mainstream monetary theory went astray by forgetting about money as a means of payment or settlement and focused solely on money as a medium of exchange.

With the elimination of gold, the political foundations of national money stood exposed. We (mis)read these political foundations as 'fiat' because of the fetishisation or objectification of money through the mediation of state-based institutions (Chapter 2). We ought to read 'fiat', we argue, as an index of the congealed political relations that are represented by the political settlement and expressed in the configuration of the state and the credit system. Bagehot and Hawtrey give us suggestions on how to do that in passing, but their real concern is credit-system operation and not the ontology of money. Unlike the Banking School, we argue that hierarchy in credit comes from mutualisation at scale which is then codified in law. This matters for credit-system operation because it tells us how far we can bend things before they break.

The modular nature of the hierarchy of money itself allows the Banking School to bracket the question of the ontology of national money. Hawtrey lays bare the tension between value and credit by foregrounding time, uncertainty and instability. He shows that one can be both a constructionist in value—positing a socially synthetic value invariant like index numbers—even while remaining a materialist by anchoring money's economic value to command over real wealth. He runs the link through the market rather than fiscality, but markets also encode a political logic of acceptance, the inverse of coercion (see Chapter 6). Both the market logic qua purchasing power and the fiscal logic of taxation link money to material wealth, but the latter now anchors for the former, given the more robust nature of the social bonding that undergirds it. There is today no money as such, only national monies—that is, politico-legal claims on the wealth—present and future—of national economies.

5 | BETWEEN CURRENCY AND CREDIT
Mehrling's Money View

> The state owns some part of each one of us, but we also own some part of it and, through its intermediation, some part of one another.

> —Mehrling (2000a)

Monetary systems are clearly hierarchical, but why? One answer comes from Chartalism: the state has sovereignty and can therefore impose itself on the monetary system. We have already seen why this is a very limited answer based on a too-thin reading of the politics of accepting credit. We will explore these limitations further through a close reading of Ingham's work in the next chapter. We have also seen earlier that a residual Chartalism can be paired quite consistently with the Banking School in terms of a 'fiat' or legal-tender understanding of outside money, 'currency' that then comes to be deployed within a system of inside money complete with its own creditary dynamics, namely 'inherent instability'.

Mehrling gestures towards a non-Chartalist account of hierarchy. He seems uncomfortable with the Banking School's residual Chartalism without fully abandoning it. In line with Banking School practice, Mehrling brackets the ontology of outside money to focus on the economists' level of abstraction, the evolution and control of credit system dynamics, rather than the ontology of money. He develops the difference between money and credit into a unique vision of hierarchy stitched together by market-making, but he does not say why money is better than credit. 'Credit' points to the system's unstable but endogenous elasticity while 'money' refers to the discipline of the survival constraint.

Yet Mehrling makes an initial step towards a political theory of money by rendering politics and the state *within* the logic of balance sheets to defeat the argument from fiat and coercion. This enables us to see different types of social bonding, economic versus political, leading to more or less money-like liabilities. This then opens up a pathway to a non-Chartalist account of hierarchy and heterogeneity in money.

As we saw in Chapter 4, the Banking School does not really need to have a complete theory of the ontology of money: all it has to assert is that there is some qualitatively distinct 'currency' which originates *outside* the credit circle (that is, not the liability of an 'internal' operator) which 'credit' is a promise to pay. All the Banking School needs to assert is a *qualitative distinction* between currency and credit rather than a fully articulated theory of the source of that distinction. Once we have the distinction between currency and credit, we are off to the races in terms of a Banking School analysis of *credit*.

Such an analysis, in other words, can bracket theories of money as the latter operate on a distinct, albeit connected, level of abstraction. As we saw Bagehot saying of bankers, 'practically, and for the purposes of their daily life, they have no need to think, and never do think, on theories of currency' (Bagehot, 1920 [1873], p. 22).

Since currency is subordinate to credit in this view, all the emphasis is on the latter. Yet as we have seen, the nature of outside money—commodity or credit—is a critical feature in determining the elasticity or discipline within a credit system. The more credit-like the outside money, the more explicitly *institutional* the form of discipline has to be, making monetary management all the more susceptible to outright politics in a way that the naturalising commodity fetish of gold foreclosed.

The problem for the Banking School in a world without a *commodity* outside money is of course that it begs the question: if 'money' is a credit note, a promise to pay, then under modern conditions, what is it promising to pay? The chain of payments seems to stop abruptly at national monies. Gold at least partook of a commodity fetish in terms of its ability to deliver 'value' embedded in a commodity.

In the last chapter we saw that it was this order of question that led Banking School advocates like Goodhart to embrace Chartalism as an account of where the buck stops—that is, as an account of outside money. Where Bagehot and Hawtrey defined outside money 'legal tender' as both minted gold and central-bank notes, having the commodity and high-powered liabilities sit side by side, the post-gold world saw the latter-day Banking School simply drop the commodity and focus instead on fiat qua the sheer force of the state.

Given the focus on the ability of the economy to generate its own means of payment, this residual Chartalism was always going to sit uneasily within a Banking School frame. The burden then is on the Banking School to come up with a non-Chartalist account of the hierarchy of credit systems and the nature of outside money.

This chapter will argue that Mehrling started this ball rolling towards what we are now calling a political theory of money. However, being more focused on traditional Banking School concern with credit-system dynamics, Mehrling brackets this theory-of-money concern and does not develop further what might be called a financial theory of the state (he has, however, invoked a 'financial theory of society' [Mehrling, 2017]). This bracketing can downplay the state and political economy in his analysis. Though he sees credit systems as 'essentially hybrid' (Mehrling, 2013), Mehrling means hybrids between states and markets, the money interest and the public interest rather than political and economic mutualisation.

Yet as we shall see, hybridity, as with hierarchy, is not fully theoretically accounted for. The missing dimension, as we saw in Chapter 1, is an account of institutions as frozen politics and credit systems as differentially mutualised balance sheets. This allows us to see the state itself as expressing a political settlement that binds central-bank money to value with a robustness and scale disproportionate to private bank money. Such a view, we argue, provides a route to a non-Chartalist account of the hierarchy of money. If Mehrling asserts a qualitative difference between layers of the hierarchy of money, a political theory of money provides a theoretical accounting of that qualitative distinction. By operating at the level of credit dynamics, Mehrling operationally partakes in the residual Chartalism of the Banking School. Yet his own discomfort with this position leads him to offer us a way out by pointing to a political theory of money.

What Is Inherent about Hierarchy?

Mehrling positions himself carefully in relation to the Banking School. He achieves a balance between the warring factions of currency and credit by means of his most central move, namely seeing the credit system as 'inherently hierarchical'. Part of the source of 'hierarchy' is the usual Banking School induction. 'Monetary thought arises from monetary experience, but with a long and variable lag' (Mehrling, 2011, p. 30). Or as Goodhart and Meinhard Jensen observe, 'Banking School adherents have been more inclined to work backwards from practical empirical observation towards general principles, whereas Currency School have tended to work forwards from certain theoretical axioms to more general conclusions (Goodhart and Jensen, 2015, p. 25). Just so, for Mehrling, it is simply a fact that '[a]lways and everywhere, monetary systems are hierarchical' (Mehrling, 2012a, p. 394).

But how do we account for hierarchy? Unlike much of the Banking School, Mehrling has always been dissatisfied with the Chartalist answer even in residual form.

The deep source of this dissatisfaction is again empirical and historical observation: private actors generate their own means of payment; some of these instruments have historically been more robust than those of several states.

Yet it is also equally true empirically that modern states have the best credit domestically. And their banks, central banks, do seem to be able to modulate the inherent instability of credit if they are minded to do so. Putting together the endogeneity of money on the one hand and the fact of the state's superior creditworthiness and ability to control credit on the other, you get the idea of an inherent or endogenous hierarchy of money, a system whose very logic is hierarchical. This is Mehrling's position:

> I have used the word 'inherent' in my title, and now I want to explain why. I use it to emphasise that the hierarchical character of the system, and its dynamic character over time, are both deep features of the system that emerge *organically* from the logic of its normal functioning. That is to say, the hierarchy is *not* something simply imposed from the outside, e.g. by the power of government, or the force of law. Rather, monetary systems are inevitably hierarchical, from the inside, by the logic of their internal operations. (Mehrling 2012a, p. 399–400, emphasis added)

Note Mehrling's dissatisfaction with the residual Chartalism of the Banking School: not by 'the force of law'. Notwithstanding this, he does not do more than point to hierarchy as 'logic' while outlining its dynamic expression in contemporary institutions of, for example, the American money market or the forex market.

For Mehrling, the credit system is hierarchical with profit-driven market makers knitting together layers that are qualitatively distinct. Given the inherent instability of credit, this hierarchy is cyclically dynamic; the balance of the political economy can amplify or dampen this instability, but this is in any event exogenous to its functioning. But identifying hierarchy and its layers is not the same thing as theoretically accounting for the source of their qualitative differences. What accounts for the qualitative differences between money and near money? For this we need a theory of money rather than a theory of credit dynamics.

Mehrling and the Banking School are after the sui generis dynamics of the credit system, exactly how its inherently instability manifests under contemporary institutional settings. This analysis can in principle be unbundled from a theory of money. Thus, we saw that for Hawtrey, the demand for credit drives the demand for gold: inside money is where all the action is. Or again, for Goodhart and many others, the central bank sets the *price* of outside money while the banks then decide how much credit they will create given that constraint: the *quantity* of credit money in the system is not a variable the central-bank controls (Goodhart, 2013).

Whatever the set of answers provided, the Banking School question is: given a certain definition of outside money ('currency'), how does the credit system behave? This is what makes it a kind of economics rather than social theory. The Banking School's bracketing of the ontology of national or outside money does have some explanatory costs, however, since plain 'economics' explains less than political economy. Since the ontology of national money is in large part political, bracketing this fact leaves politics out of the analysis of money. This makes it hard to identify the deeper roots of elasticity and discipline in a particular credit system.

Imperial Money

One of the ways in which this bracketing of the political nature of money operates in Mehrling is his reading of the gold standard. Gold was imperial money: the frequent forgetting of this fact is a clear demonstration of the cost of bracketing the political ontology of money.

One of the things that distinguishes imperial states from regular states is the balance between legitimacy and coercion. Imperial states are by definition born of conquest. The prominence of the coercive element sets the limit of their legitimacy especially once legitimacy came to be defined in democratic terms. Interstate relations in general are the space of war rather than the space of political contract, and this makes it much harder to bracket off the political dimension of money when discussing the global monetary system. Robustness at scale still operates at the international level but with this political element more visible (Chapter 9).

Mehrling renders the fact that the chain of monies now ends with national monies as a *negation* of hierarchy: 'recognizing the pervasive role of the state throughout the system has the effect of flattening the hierarchy' (Mehrling, 2003, p. 33). This view stems from an overemphasis on gold as international money and a downplaying of the imperial or coercive element of world money even under the gold standard.

While gold was the means of *final* settlement internationally even during the heyday of the gold standard, many users were happy to keep balances in sterling; the city as a global bank would be inconceivable were this not the case. Yet it is also a fact that many colonies had no choice but to accept sterling balances on their earned export surpluses: they could not convert these into gold. The fact of a national money acting as international money encodes an imperial fact of global life then and now.

As we saw with Bagehot and Hawtrey earlier, it is the credit system that drives demand for currency, not vice versa. The gold standard was in effect a sterling standard, trusted by foreigners because the city could be trusted as a sound global bank. We know from Karl Polanyi that this commercial system existed within a political envelope in terms of the BoE's rock-solid, Bagehot-inspired commitment to raise interest rates to protect parity with gold. Polanyi understood the politics of this commitment. To commit to raise rates in this fashion was tantamount *to committing to crash the economy* to preserve gold parity, a commitment that only the absence of democracy could countenance (Polanyi, 2001 [1944]; Eichengreen, 1998). Thus, many of the 'givens' of the gold standard system were only given thanks to particularly undemocratic domestic political settlement.

The same is true in spades of the external political settlement, namely empire. As it happens, the very ability of the city to run as a global bank depended quite centrally on the political condition of empire: India was forced to keep its export surpluses in sterling in order to pay for 'Home Charges', representing the ownership rights of empire won through conquest, rather than convert surpluses into gold. These Indian reserves, records Marcello de Cecco, were critical to the whole operation:

> The reserves on which the Indian monetary system was based provided a large *masse de manoeuvre* which British monetary authorities could use to supplement their own reserves and to keep London the centre of the international monetary system. (de Cecco, 1975, p. 62, emphasis original)

As per Polanyi's story, this system collapsed as the political ground shifted, in part because technocrats operating the system did not have their lenses adjusted for politics. In reading the period of post-war reconstruction, Mehrling reframes the debate between Keynes and Harry Dexter White as one about different versions of the 'shared goal' of re-establishing a multilateral trading system rather than the now stereotyped debate between laissez-faire versus managed *dirigisme* (Mehrling, 2016).

The debate over Keynes' International Clearing Union (ICU) versus White's International Monetary Fund (IMF) is, for Mehrling, more usefully seen as one between elasticity and discipline in the global credit system. The ICU would be a clearing house which could expand its balance sheet to accommodate, among other things, a tricky monetary transition from sterling to the dollar. While the IMF could in principle do the same by lending to the UK, its very nature as a finite pool of foreign exchange (FX) would limit its ability for elasticity, delay the transition back to full multilateralism and over all represent more discipline than elasticity. This, of course, was why the Americans liked it.

While Mehrling acknowledges that the vexed issue of 'sterling balances' was 'simply the legacy of empire' and that 'India's accumulation of sterling balances had financed Britain's deficit with the rest of the world', he does not appreciate that the ability for India to do so was actually a requirement based quite centrally on, using his terms, 'political principles' rather than 'commercial principles' (ibid., p. 29). Thus,

> As World War II came to a close, the financially globalised world of 1913 seemed a much more distant goal than it had in 1923; indeed, in 1944 there were no functioning private markets that Keynes could use as part of any international monetary reform plan. As a consequence of depression and war, economic relations between nation- states proceeded not on a commercial basis but on a political basis, and that state of affairs seemed likely to continue for some time during the reconstruction that would follow the war. (Ibid., p. 26)

Again, this view is only possible by downplaying the fact that the 'financially globalised world' was in fact a world of empire, not incidentally but essentially. Gold covered over its political rudiments. This is not to make the Chartalist point writ large that India was held down by sheer force for that is only partially true; as we have said, the balance of coercion and legitimacy in empires is different than in a democratic state, but no state, even an imperial one, survives on force alone. It is, however, to make the link between the nature of the political settlement and the nature of the resultant money: an imperial political settlement enabled the operation of imperial money.

We therefore need to rethink how to apply the distinction between political and commercial principles. What in fact is being pointed to by Mehrling is again a distinct level of abstraction: commerce operates *within* a given political settlement and can be studied as such without continual reference to that settlement so long as it remains *settled*.

However, when that settlement begins to crack as it was in the post-war period, 'commerce' starts to look 'political'. Just so, the problem of 'sterling balances', when seen from the point of view of political economy rather than financial technique, is a problem of state sovereignty plain and simple. A free India would do as it liked with its surpluses. The threat of a mass conversion of sterling balances into gold or dollars would potentially lead to conversion restrictions by other nations and badly damage the reconstruction of the multilateral trading system. This is how emerging sovereignty expressed itself in the financial argot of the crumbling imperial monetary system, as the problem of conversion of 'sterling balances' by those in the 'sterling area'.

We saw earlier that Mehrling read the emergence of the post-Bretton Woods system as a flattening of the hierarchy of money as payments ended with national monies. Yet this situation only points to a flattening of hierarchy *if* we ignore the hierarchy of state power itself, namely empire. The international rise of the dollar is of course unthinkable without the global hegemony of the US. This is not to reduce the former to the latter, only to point to the consistency between the idea of a global hierarchy and that of 'the pervasive role of the state'. This consistency is simply another expression of a political theory of money: global 'acceptance' of gold, sterling and the dollar was and is predicated on an imperial political contract de facto or de jure. The dollar's empire is less formal and therefore has to encode a different balance between coercion and consent.

A Financial Theory of the State

In working out a conception of hierarchy, Mehrling renders the distinction between currency and credit differently than the Banking School—not as an absolute binary but as a spectrum along which an inherently unstable credit system fluctuates (Mehrling, 2012a, p. 398). The Currency School, in Mehrling's reading, gets its name by narrowly focusing on one end of that spectrum—the moment of final settlement or money as a means of payment. As we have seen, the logic of settlement requires an *outside* asset. Hence, the Currency School's other name, Metallism; gold after all was a means of final settlement. But 'currency' only points to the end of a chain of credits—*final* settlement. A transaction can be completed in other means of settlement that are not final if the debtor is happy to accept some entity's IOU as a means of 'temporary' or customary settlement. This acceptance makes this kind of IOU a form of money: near money. Here we have the other end of the spectrum, the credit end which the Banking School points to.

'Currency' therefore indicates the *discipline* of final settlement—payment *today*—whereas 'credit' points to *elasticity* in the system, the ability to *delay* final settlement by paying off a debt with another debt or rolling over a debt when it comes due. Once again, we can see that the credit system is essentially about managing the temporal dimension of economic life.

For Mehrling, the debate between the Banking School (with its residual Chartalism) and the Currency School is a bit wrong-headed because it is absolutist: money is either a commodity currency or credit bank money (with fiat national money). Rather, it depends on *where in the hierarchy* the analysis is taking place as well as the state of play in the balance between elasticity and discipline in the credit system. We have seen that to down-hierarchy balance sheets, higher-level IOUs may as well be a commodity as they represent a hard constraint and have to be acquired in the same way. There is therefore some residual truth to the Currency School conception though not at all in the way the School perceives it.

When Mehrling hears the debate between the Banking School and the Currency School, therefore, he reads it as a debate between those advocating either elasticity or discipline in a credit system. One can therefore be a 'practical Metallist'—that is, favouring discipline in the credit system, thanks to the prevalence of risk-taking banks, profligate governments, and/or the inherent instability of credit even while being a 'theoretical Chartalist', to use Joseph Schumpeter's terminology (Mehrling, 2003).

Why then, for Mehrling, does the state have the best money? In answering this question, Mehrling gestures towards a political theory of money by outlining the logic of robustness at scale for the state. In Chapter 1, we extended this logic to banks while observing the qualitative difference between the kinds of contracting operative at each level. Mehrling himself does not account for bank money in this way. Scale however remains critical:

> It is the *universality* of our dealings with the government that gives government credit its currency. The point is that the public 'pay community', to use an apt phrase from Knapp ... is *larger* than most any private pay community, not that the state is more powerful than any other private entity. Consequently, the state is ideally placed to be the issuer of the ultimate domestic money.... Liabilities that are default-free may make good investments for the risk-averse, but they do not make very good money *unless a large number of people* need to make regular payments to the issuer of the liabilities. (Mehrling, 2000b, p. 403, emphasis added)

It is not state power qua coercion but the sheer ubiquity of the state that generates the largest user base, a large-scale asset that is literally bankable—hence Mehrling's dissatisfaction with the term 'fiat' when used to describe state money. The superior creditworthiness of the state is not derived from the power of declaration but the power of confederation. 'Strong' Chartalism is wrong because it mischaracterises the very nature of the modern state. The state *does* have the best money domestically, but not for the reasons the fiat-money Chartalists think:

> Indeed, it's hard to find anyone who traces the value of currency to its metallic backing. If anything we are all cartalists [*sic*] now, but in a sense broader than that encompassed by the special dictates of war finance or of state-directed economic development, which is to say broader than the classic conception outlined in Knapp's *State Theory of Money* (1905). We

are not fiat money cartalists but rather credit money cartalists. Today the value
of national currency derives in most cases not from the raw power of the
state, but from its creditworthiness in commercial terms. National currency
is not a fiat currency but a promise to pay'. (Mehrling, 2003, pp. 33–34,
emphasis added)

'Credit money Chartalism' is, however, not meant to indicate any residual Chartalism
of the Banking School in the sense we outlined earlier. We read it alongside Mehrling's
gesture towards a political theory of money. Rather than seeing outside money as
legal tender in the manner of the rest of the Banking School, it is more useful, says
Mehrling, to view government-issued money not as a kind of paper gold but a promise
to pay—that is, a credit note. This means credit in both form and content.

In form, modern money is the liability of a central bank: it is literally an IOU. In
content, it is a promise to pay future tax revenues of the state: that is its source of
value. We just have to look through the balance sheets. The main asset that the central
bank holds is government debt which in turn is backed by taxation powers backed by
potential output: 'The principle asset on the government's balance sheet is its taxing
authority' (Mehrling, 2000b, n. 4, p. 402). Invoking the government in this context
is not, again, to invoke coercive power but the power of the political contract:

> The significant point is that our government is our creation. It is only able
> to tax us to the extent that we allow it to do so. Its taxing authority arises not
> from its raw power but from its legitimate authority. (Ibid.)

This is the nub of a political theory of money: legitimate authority is what gives the
state's cash flow both robustness and scale. If the robustness comes from the coercive
edge of the tax authority, this is legitimate coercion because we are being reminded
to undertake a duty we have solemnly and collectively taken on. The presence of the
political contract is what gives the state's liquidity 'pool' (both potential/futural and
actual) disproportionate scale and robustness domestically: the political contract
is the source of the universality of the state. What Mehrling observes about the US
Social Security system can therefore be applied to the state as such:

> Another way to think about Social Security is that it is a more or less fully
> funded *social mutual fund* holding ownership claims in the productive
> capacity of the economy through claims on wages and salaries. In this view,
> the FICA tax [Federal Insurance Contributions Act] ... is permanent, and the
> capitalised present value of the tax is the asset that backs benefit promises.
> **In this view, the state is a kind of trust into which we place collective assets,**

and it is also a trustee whom we engage to oversee management of the trust. *The state owns some part of each one of us, but we also own some part of it and, through its intermediation, some part of one another.* (Mehrling, 2000a, p. 367, emphasis added)

Such a view might be summarised as a financial theory of the state. The 'social mutual fund' is a political contract—'mutual' in both the financial and political senses of the term. The logic of finance is clear: the value of a capital asset is seen as the net present value of all future streams of income discounted back to the present. This future-determines-present temporal structure is recognisably that of modern financial theory as distinct from the 'dead-labour', 'savings-drives-investment' or 'past-determines-present' temporality of classical economics (Mehrling, 2006b). Just so, future tax flows are of such a magnitude and certainty that the state's tax-based assets swamp private assets. Political bonding between people and the state enables this scale as the institutional logic of banking coupled with a political contract turns a national economy into a bankable, leviathan-scale asset.

Mehrling does not render his account of hierarchy in terms of political mutualisation at scale; nor does he think of a bank's balance sheet in terms of a 'pay community' representing an economic mutualisation of liquidity. In Chapter 1, we applied the Chartalist term 'pay community' back to the bank in order to compare and contrast the nature of the contracting or mutualisation represented by banks' and states' balance sheets respectively (in Chapter 8 we make the comparison to even weaker mutualisation in shadow banks). While both banks and states represent commitments of liquidity mutualised together, the nature of the mutualisation is qualitatively different—one political and the other economic. This, in the end, is what accounts for the qualitative differences in the levels of the hierarchy of money. Robustness at scale drives hierarchy.

Banks Make Markets Make Banks

In form, central-bank money is indeed an IOU or 'inside money'. But functionally, Mehrling asserts a *qualitative* superiority for central-bank money compared to plain vanilla bank money. Monetary systems are hierarchical but not self-ordering. The institutional links between qualitatively distinct credit notes at the different layers of hierarchy are market makers: 'The key is to appreciate the institutions that, at each level of the hierarchy, act as market makers exchanging credit for money and money for credit' (Mehrling, 2012a, p. 400). This is how the operation of economic mutualisation proceeds, turning qualitative differences into quantitative ones.

The logic of operations, for Mehrling, is *market making*: security dealers, banks and central banks are all seen through the lens of this elemental financial function. This is a powerful insight because it allows us to stop fetishising institutional form and focus on institutional function. The function of credit institutions is to be *dealers* in credit liquidity, buying and selling liquidity on their own account across the temporal and risk spectrum, exposing themselves to the risk of spanning instruments of inherently different quality and garnering rewards for doing so.

As such, what we observe as different prices in the money market are actually the result of these market-making activities turning qualitative differences along the liquidity spectrum into quantitative differences—prices:

> [T]here is a simple hierarchy of market makers to go along with the hierarchy of instruments. And for each market maker, there is an associated price of money. There are three prices in the simple hierarchy: the exchange rate (the price of currency in terms of gold), par (the price of deposits in terms of currency), and the rate of interest (the price of securities in terms of deposits or currency). *These prices are the quantitative link between layers of qualitatively differentiated assets.* The market makers who quote these prices in effect straddle the layers of the hierarchy, using their own balance sheets to knit those differentiated layers into a coherent whole. (Ibid., emphasis added)

Through the lens of balance sheets, banks can be read as specific kinds of market makers, making a market between their own liabilities (deposits) and those of the central bank. Theirs is a particularly harsh survival constraint because as part of their business model, they have pledged to keep the 'exchange rate' between their own liabilities and the central bank's at 1, namely 'par'. They do this so effectively that we take bank deposits and money to be the same *thing*. Yet as we have seen, bank accounts are not money but *promises* to pay central-bank money at par on demand.

This par constraint is a harsh form of discipline, enabling banks to create liabilities that are nearer to money but also driving them to mutualise with each other and ultimately with the central bank to ensure the smooth availability of central-bank money—national money—when asked for settlement; it takes an entire system to produce a liability that looks like 'money'. Without any ability to move the price of their liabilities in terms of money, all the fluctuations in demand for liquidity have to take place on the collective balance sheet on the credit system and through 'internal' prices of money such as the interbank borrowing rate. Users are only aware of this operation when it breaks down, further enabling the appearance of equivocation between bank money and national money.

The target audience for Mehrling is economists for whom the institutional logic of the economy in general and money markets in particular are so much plumbing to be abstracted away:

> If the market makers do their job well, we will observe continuous markets at the various prices of money. In other words, the qualitatively differentiated hierarchy will appear as merely a quantitative differentiation between the prices of various financial assets. It is this transformation from quality to quantity that makes it possible to construct theories of economics and finance that abstract from the hierarchical character of the system (as most do). (Ibid., pp. 400–401)

In a well-functioning credit system, qualitative differences in the hierarchy can only be read as quantitative ones between the different prices of money. What is *not* explained, indeed what is taken entirely for granted in this demonstration of hierarchy, is the good old Banking School distinction between money (currency) and credit: 'The problem is that, in a liquidity crisis, everyone wants money and no one wants credit' (ibid.). What we have therefore, in true Bagehot style, is a '*description* of the money market' in terms of a qualitatively differentiated hierarchy rather than a theoretical accounting of the source of differential quality of money market instruments. '[P]ractically, and for the purposes of their daily life, [bankers] have no need to think, and never do think, on theories of currency' (Bagehot 1920 [1873]).

Mehrling is operating for the most part at a level of abstraction distinct from theories of money per se. He is also talking to a very particular audience for whom his explanation of hierarchy is plenty for them to be getting on with.

At the level of accounting for system dynamics, Mehrling wants to focus minds on the qualitative differences between levels of hierarchy because it explains something extremely critical about how the money market works—namely what Minsky called the 'survival constraint'. This is basically a settlement constraint: settling up your debts means providing some instrument that a creditor will accept as settlement. This is to focus on the means-of-payment function of money. A creditor will logically accept its own IOU as settlement and control over the issuance of that IOU rests with net creditors.

This is why the hierarchy of credit is a hierarchy of creditworthiness capped by the state. But between the distant-future arrival of taxes (or the finished product, the final delivery of goods, and so on) and the moment-by-moment endogenous metabolism of credit through transactions of all kinds, there is a huge liquidity spectrum to be filled. Banks and other dealers enter with their own liabilities as bridging devices, making a profit that is definitionally sensitive to the demand for better-than-bank IOUs. In a crisis, everyone wants money and not credit, but 'normal' shifts in preferences for different kinds of liabilities occur through the cycle. Banks and other near-money dealers are bound by this survival constraint, living and sometimes dying by how tightly it binds.

This of course is what gives the central bank leverage over the system both ex post and ex ante. The central bank is a dealer in liquidity only with a much deeper balance sheet thanks to its backing (in terms of political assets, namely bonds locked to value by fiscal anchoring, and not mere coercion) by the state. It therefore has the freedom to operate without constraints such as making a profit and can control the money markets 'on banking principles'. It also produces the best money, the final settlement instrument domestically.

Here we find the critical importance of asserting *qualitative* differences between central-bank money, bank money, repos, and so on down the line. What counts as money and credit respectively might change over time, but at any given moment qualitative differences must operate in order to give the survival constraint its bite. We therefore need to understand what drives these qualitative differences if we are to understand the nature of the survival constraint and how it evolves over time.

Settling Up

The survival constraint is now the centrepiece of Mehrling's thinking on money markets and the economy in general—what he calls the 'money view'—as it is what provides 'coherence' to the system (Chapter 7). From the standpoint of an economic unit, coherence is about how matched up promises to pay cash are with prospects of cash inflow. An avowedly Minskian term, Minsky's own schema of balance sheets—hedged, speculative and ponzi—is defined by degrees of coherence of inflows to outflows. A proliferation of incoherent balance sheets in the system leads to severe systemic distress, but even in normal times coherence needs to be managed by the matching engine that is the hierarchical credit system.

We are a world away from seeing money and its system as so many pipes sloshing around physicalist 'liquidity'. We are in Morris Copeland's world of batteries and wires which is just another physicalist analogy for the two sides of Mehrling's interlocking balance sheets (Copeland, 1952). But money is not a logistics problem. We can only use physicalist metaphors by immediately qualifying them with magical terms like 'alchemy'. Thus, if money is a logistics problem, it is the kind where the central node in the network can magic up packages only to take them away again as required. Since precisely this kind of magic is needed to make complex payments work, only social relations of credit hierarchically mutualised are up to the task.

The way that hierarchy is operationalised in Mehrling's description of the money market is by invoking the survival constraint. Yet the survival constraint only works by asserting a qualitative difference between different kinds of credit—'qualitatively differentiated assets'. An entire spectrum of difference between various inside and outside monies replaces the classical Banking School distinction between currency and credit. To a borrower (a household or firm), bank money is outside money, but it is inside money to the bank. To the bank, in turn, central-bank money is outside money while it is inside money to the central bank. To the central bank, its own liabilities are of course inside money but those of other central banks are outside money.

Hierarchy shows up in the system as an asymmetric settlement constraint. Surplus agents in whatever counts as outside money are in a position to dictate to deficit agents the instrument that will satisfy their debts; naturally, surplus agents will accept their own liabilities. This is not true for deficit agents: they need to source surplus-agent liabilities or some other acceptable outside asset to ensure final settlement, or else convince surplus agents to accept their own, inside liabilities. Applying this logic to the apex of the credit system, banks require central-bank money in order to settle up with each other. This might be encoded in the law, but it does not have its origin in law. We have to go beyond the law if we are to understand the creditary logic behind this settlement practice. Why do banks settle in central-bank money?

The special nature of central-bank money is that it is the outermost inside money in a particular economy—'outside' relative to the banking system since banks cannot create central-bank liabilities but 'inside' in the sense of being a liability of some bank. Settling implies ending a chain of debts, but a bank account is nothing but an IOU of a bank. As settlement, a creditor bank requires an instrument that is not simply an IOU of another bank in the system. Accepting final settlement in an IOU is a contradiction in terms: accepting an IOU *means* lending to the issuer of the IOU, while settlement means a termination of a debt and not its continuance.

The creditor bank therefore requires an outside asset to settle interbank debts, something that is by definition of greater quality than all bank liabilities since the creditor bank should be able to exchange it for bank liabilities or borrow against it. Domestically, the only outside asset that answers to this description is the liability of the state's bank, the central bank.

The logic of (interbank) settlement therefore requires a high-quality, outside instrument. This logic then sets in train the survival constraint: banks clamour for central bank or national money in order to settle up debts between them at the end of the trading day. A market in central-bank liabilities is set up to ration the settlement instrument between banks; the price therein is the interbank borrowing rate. The borrowing or lending plans of an entire economy are summarised in this market, given that banks themselves modulate liquidity demands further down the hierarchy between firms and households. The balance between elasticity and discipline for the entire economy, macro-coherence, is set here, the most upstream market in which the central bank operates to change the credit climate. The interbank market is the market where the settlement constraint is defined and with it the coherence of the entire economy.

Whether by banks deciding their own club rules or by the state imposing itself on banks, the *logic of settlement* itself dictates that a qualitatively distinct, *outside* instrument be used for interbank settlement. This qualitative distinction ought to have two elements: the instrument ought to be *outside* the circle of bank debt and of *higher quality* than bank debt.

This of course is why gold could perform this function in the last instance. As a commodity, it was an asset that was no one's liability; it was thereby outside the circle of debt. But there is nothing essential about gold or, indeed, any commodity performing the functions of outside money. The minimal attributes required are that it be both *outside* and of *higher quality* than the IOUs within the relevant circuit of debt. As per Hawtrey, the demand for this outside asset is a function of the internal requirement for settling debts in a credit system rather than some 'intrinsic value'.

The state might designate a commodity or fiat token to perform the functions of final settlement ('legal tender'), but an economy restrained by over-rigid money issuance will fail to be robustly capitalist, certainly not under conditions of democracy (Chapter 12). This is the key missing element in Mehrling—a recognition that the credit system is not simply composed of the operation of profit-seeking banks, but that banks are in turn driven by the requirements of a driving democratic capitalism. It is easy to forget this in a world of mature capitalism where in some precincts finance seems to be utterly disconnected from production. But to believe this is once again to buy into the fetishised forms in which the system appears.

A commodity anchor is over-rigid by construction because there is an arbitrary amount of the commodity in bullion form. This induces the system to invent its own means of elasticity. Since discipline is also required, it is better to control credit 'on banking principles' rather than through a draconian commodity anchor: this is the hard-won lesson of the Banking School. But it is also one of the requisites of democracy and capitalism alike that they will not accept the austerity of severe credit-system discipline unless they are themselves suppressed.

Thus, even prior to what we now recognise as democracy, Peel's Act of 1844 only worked because it disciplined the system up to a point and was then made elastic by its frequent suspension once a critical threshold was breached (Chapter 4). Discipline is required, but imposing discipline rigidly beyond a point will simply tear the fabric of interlocking payments, leading to cascading defaults.

Mehrling does not meditate on these qualities required of a means of final settlement. As catalogued in the following extracts, Mehrling has consistently *asserted* the qualitative difference between central-bank money and bank money as the lever that the central bank has over the credit system. Thus,

> [t]he reason that the government is able to prevent a cascade of defaults is that its cash commitments are qualitatively different from those issued by the private sector, for the simple reason that cash is the government's own liability. There can be no question of the government meeting its own cash commitments.... Of course, at a deeper level, its ability to do so rests on the continued acceptance of its liabilities as cash, which means that the government must look after the balance of its own inflows and outflows over time. So long as the 'full faith and credit' of government means something, but only so long as it does, the mobilisation of that credit can forestall crisis. (Mehrling, 1999, p. 142)

> ... state money is the best money because the central bank undertakes to make the market in currency terms of the even better international money, *and* because it undertakes to provide lender of last resort refinance for individual banks who undertake to make the market in deposit liabilities in terms of currency. (Mehrling, 2000a, p. 366, emphasis original)

> [t]he fact that state money is the ultimate means of payment does seem to give the state some leverage over the economy, leverage that shows up as a measure of control over the money rate of interest. (Mehrling, 2000b, p. 403)

> [w]hat gives the central bank its leverage is the fact that it is the supplier of Federal Funds, so that it can in principle expand its balance sheet with impunity. (Mehrling, 2005, p. 12)

> ... unlike other dealers, central bankers are dealers in a commodity that they themselves uniquely create (and destroy).... Bank deposits are thus derivative securities, the open interest in the commodity supplied uniquely

by the central bank. For all these reasons, the central bank enjoys a special position in the economy. (Mehrling, 2006a, p. 169)

[w]hy does the dealer loan rate key off of Fed Funds? Because the Fed Funds rate is the marginal cost of funds for the banking system as a whole. (Mehrling, 2010, p. 219)

[t]he Fed's monopoly supply of bank reserves gives it considerable control over the federal funds market, but there is quite a bit of slippage between conditions in the federal funds market and funding liquidity more generally. (Mehrling, 2011, p. 25)

... the central bank exploits its position at the top of the hierarchy, that is, the fact that its own liabilities are more money-like than the liabilities of anyone below it. (Mehrling, 2012a, p. 402)

... the settlement constraint in the payments mechanism [is] a constraint that the central bank can relax because the ultimate means of payment is its own liability. Even in a world of developed financial markets, this feature is the key source of central-bank leverage over the overnight interest rate, since the overnight rate is simply the price of putting off settlement for a single day. (Mehrling, 2014, p. 116)

[a] key disciplining element faced by everyone is the constraint to settle their debts as they come due. Debts are promises to pay money, and money is the means of settling debts. This settlement constraint is asymmetric, requiring deficit agents ... to find means of payment that surplus agents ... are willing to accept. In most modern economies, a basic form of money is the issue of the state. (Mehrling, n.d., pp. 2–3)

The State as Endogenous to Society

Thus, Mehrling both starts us off on a political theory of money and, as the earlier quotes show, partakes in the residual Chartalism of the Banking School. If he has seen the credit system as 'essentially hybrid', there remains a sense that the state is exogenous to the logic of the system: 'States quite typically *arrogate* to themselves the right of money issue; taxes are denominated and payable in state money' (Mehrling, 2013, p. 362, emphasis added). The same line can be found a decade earlier: 'States have always arrogated to themselves the right to designate legal tender' (Mehrling, 2003, p. 34).

As with Chartalism, the state is seen as epiphenomenal to the social system we call capitalism rather than a constitutive part of it. Yet, as we have argued earlier, the state, the state's bank and indeed all banks are institutions formed out of congealed politics and represented by balance sheets. The ontology of the state and banks is sociopolitical; political mutualisation binds this social matter harder, but this institutionalisation is made of the same social stuff, a fact that is all too apparent in so-called developing nations.

In the language of the money view, surplus agents (creditors) call the shots since they determine the instrument of settlement: credit or currency. Can we then conclude that the state has the best money because it is the ultimate surplus agent? Yes, but we have to look beyond explicit government balances to appreciate this.

The state, as Mehrling notes earlier, is legitimised as being our creation, a managing agent for our collective affairs. The state is just as endogenous to society as credit. Following Mehrling, we can see that the state as a social mutual fund makes up the very warp and weft of economic life. Recall Hawtrey's observation that '[p]roduction may be regarded as making society the debtor of the producer' (Hawtrey, 1919, p. 186). The ultimate creditor is the producers, the working members of society. By means of a political contract, the state becomes their agent.

While there might not have been, in most cases, an actual historical social contract, the state is retrospectively legitimised as such (see Chapter 12). Working citizens and residents contract together at a scale that far exceeds any private corporation to give each other ownership claims on their collective surplus by means of pledging part of their surplus to a state that they all part-own. This is how the state becomes the ultimate creditor with the best credit, the ultimate surplus agent.

The state is merely the institutional expression of a fundamental social fact: human beings exist in a division of labour whereby we depend on each other for the most basic material and spiritual needs. This dependence is mediated through different degrees of 'solidarity', some of which are systematically unequal. Despite inequalities, mutual dependence is the deep condition. The political bonds of the state both express this deeper, socio-material bond and enable it to function. This foundational socio-materiality is precisely why the political bonds of the state generate a credit note that is backed by 'real' value.

If we all owe a foundational debt to society for the deep interdependence of the division of labour, then the state is the institutional repository of that debt under modern conditions. As the institutional expression of our constitutive sociality, the state carries society's debt to itself. As the surplus agent par excellence constructed at society-scale and made robust by qualitatively distinct, *political* mutualisation, the state has the best money. Money becomes an index of our collective material and political co-dependence, with its value varying along those dimensions. It is in this sense that money is founded in politics and legitimacy. As Michel Aglietta notes, 'Public debt is honoured in the flow of taxes, whose legitimacy depends on the recognition of the common good' (Aglietta, 2018, p. 74).

Netting it all out, Mehrling retains the difference between currency and credit, rejects the residual Chartalism of the Banking School by undermining the 'legal tender' or 'fiat money' accounts of outside money, gestures briefly towards a political theory of money as an account of the same, and then proceeds to operationalise the Banking School's key distinction between currency and credit within the contemporary institutional space of American and international money markets by means of the unique entry point of 'market making'. 'Credit' is defined variously and institutionally; this is entirely appropriate, given the fact that while there is only one 'money' at any given moment, a credit system invents all manner of near monies. To paraphrase Minsky, anyone can issue near money; the problem is to get it accepted. This issuing and acceptance happen in concrete times and places and therefore have to be studied historically. We undertake some studies of this nature in Part II.

6 | THERE IS NO SUCH THING AS FIAT MONEY

Sovereignty is misconstrued by Chartalism. A state theory of money implies a theory of politics, yet Chartalism lacks one. The politics of money, as we have seen, operates at two levels: the broad 'social contract' and the granular, institutional instantiation of the political settlement.

While both are missing from mainstream Chartalism, Ingham addresses the latter. While his Weberian or conflictual account of politics is central to his theory, Ingham ultimately downgrades politics to *datum*, something that sits oddly with his invocation of Weber. This ambiguous position omits *legitimacy* as foundational to states, provincialises capitalist money despite its technical superiority and world-historical dominance and ignores the material nature of the state's survival constraint.

Having learned so much from Ingham, we presume to invert him in this chapter. His contingent *datum* we read as universal—namely the conflictual politics that define the ontology of all institutions including money. This gives us a richer account of sovereignty and supplies the missing explanation of variety and hierarchy in money.

Clearly, the state has a central role in monies both past and present, but nailing down the exact nature of the state's role in money has been a troublesome task. This chapter seeks to do this through a critique of the State Theory of Money as outlined by Ingham. A 'state' theory of money necessitates at least an outline of a theory of *politics*: this distinguishes a political theory of money from a state theory of money. Again, we see politics operating at two levels: the agglomerative level of the 'social contract' and the institutional level instantiating a particular political settlement.

While both these understandings of politics are missing in Chartalism, Ingham is extremely attentive to the second understanding, showing how the rise of capitalism in early modern England was precipitated by a balance of power between capital and state forces leading to a new, hybrid form of sovereignty and a consequent mutualisation of public and private credit. He therefore has an account of politics only to suppress it as contingent history rather than fundamental logic. Ingham suppresses or downgrades his Weber-inspired conflictual account of politics, we argue, in order to foreground the salience of coercive power in the establishment of money as a unit of account, itself a move in his case against the neoclassical position.

Yet the theoretical cost of this downgrading of politics is to slide Ingham back to a more traditional and therefore inadequate Chartalist position. A political theory of money seeks to overcome this suppression by bringing politics in the two senses mentioned earlier front and centre.

We begin by outlining an ambiguity regarding the nature of monetary power at the heart of Ingham's account of money, the most developed social theory of money we have bar none. In outlining the logical priority of the money of account, Ingham is at pains to stress the coercive power of the state as determinative. However, when discussing the historical rise of capitalist credit money in early modern Britain, Ingham traces a braiding of coercion and consent in the ontology of a new kind of sovereignty: King-in-Parliament (Crown-in-Parliament). He reconciles this ambiguity—which is an operative, coercion or a coercion–consent hybrid?—by downgrading capitalist credit money to a 'historical' phenomenon, while 'logically' money as a unit of account and therefore power as coercion drive a basically Chartalist ontology of money.

Ingham's reconciliation presents four challenges that we try to build on. First, to take legitimacy out of the equation of state coercion is to eliminate the difference between the state and an organised criminal gang. In other words, brute coercion is never by itself a device of the state by definition: such coercion is always accompanied by more or less legitimacy however configured. And legitimacy, in turn, encodes a more complicated relationship between coercion and consent; in many ways, Weber's legitimacy foreshadows Antonio Gramsci's hegemony. In short, even before the rise of capitalism, money as a device of the state is an artefact of a political equilibrium because the state itself is such an artefact.

Second, the downgrading of capitalist money to a contingent formation ought not distract us from the fact of its world-conquering sway. Since all historical formations are fundamentally contingent, by what criteria is capitalist money *less* world-historical or ideal-typical than ancient Sumerian money? Surely that institution that has 'technical superiority' (Weber, 1978) ought to form its ideal type? Capitalism is the universal, not the particular, at least until it is replaced by a new universal.

Third, Ingham and the Chartalists consider the survival constraint as solely an ideological fetter rather than a material one. This is by no means to downplay the determinative nature of belief systems or their role in configuring the political settlement and its money. But to ignore the state's material need for liquidity or, equivalently, the problem of the acceptability of state IOUs is to misspecify the problem. As creatures of the political settlement, states face the limit of the acceptability of their IOUs, either bonds or money. The politics of liquidity is the politics of acceptability: to have one's IOU widely accepted is to be liquid. Since all states before and after capitalism face this limit, they are subject to a very material survival constraint. This constraint is configured more or less elastically given the nature of outside money (commodity or credit) and where one sits in the international hierarchy of money, but this is a question of degree. Setting the limit on the state's liquidity-raising capacity exclusively at the level of ideology therefore misses these dynamics. For all nations other than the global hegemon, there is always a better outside money that mediates their access to the global division of labour.

Finally, by foregrounding the unit-of-account function of money and the role of coercion in securing this function, Ingham does not do enough to distinguish the measurement of value from the production of value. Debts, both political and economic, create value to different degrees; these qualitatively distinct relations can then be measured to be commensurate. The creditary relation with the state is distinct from the state's necessarily monopolistic regulation of weights and measures of all kinds: the former creates value; the latter measures it.

Further, Ingham somewhat underplays the material dimension to value. He builds again on Weber to mark the difference between formal and substantive value of money—the former arising from nominalist power but the latter emerging almost entirely from a political equilibrium. Yet debt always has two elements, the promise and that which is being promised, and the latter points decisively to the material dimension. As we have seen, this is true of the state's debt or money as well. Without these dimensions, it is hard to fully account for monetary variation.

While a modern credit system obviously exists within the envelope of a monopoly of violence, tracing the state's operational power over money to brute coercion challenges us to better specify the nature of monetary sovereignty. The state has the best money on *commercial calculation* because it has the highest-quality (politically mutualised at scale) assets. Political scale anchors the state in the real economy. Before the rise of capitalism and after, political mutualisation gives the state its power; overlooking this, Ingham cedes more ground to the strong Chartalist position than his own theory and history perhaps warrant.

While Ingham follows Weber in seeing money as a weapon in 'the struggle of man against man', and he deploys his understanding to great effect while explaining the rise of capitalist credit money, he does not view political struggle per se as being part of money's ontology. Rather, inspired by Georg Simmel, Ingham claims that 'money is a socially constructed tautology.... In a monetary system, debt and credit are mutually and indivisibly determined by the money of account' (Ingham, 2018, p. 848).

Ingham is of course entirely correct to point to the logical priority of 'the money of account', but he risks theoretically overweighting the role of coercion at the cost of hegemony, on the one hand, and nominalism at the cost of materialism, on the other (see Chapter 7). Coercion might well be required to establish a monopolistic money of account. But unlike debt, measurement itself creates no value. *Money is not a tautology*: like all debts, it points to that which is promised, namely national money itself in the case of bank money and a fiscally secured share of GDP in the case of national money.

As such, Ingham's reconciliation of his ambiguity around power and money produces an odd contrast effect: political struggles over money are framed as historical, contingent and entirely exogenous fetters on the nominalist power of the state over money—that is, the state's power to define the unit of account (the power to 'write the dictionary'). By the same token, it casts a key material predicate of money, the medium of exchange dimension that foregrounds acceptance, into a completely derivative position. By contrast, we will place the struggle over payment and acceptance at every level of society, but especially between the state and key power brokers in society, at the very centre in order to drive an argument for the political ontology of money rooted in the society-wide political settlement.

Money's value is not 'tautological' because the power of the state is intrinsically *defined*—not merely externally circumscribed—by the nature of the political settlement that undergirds it, and this settlement lays claim to the future national product of a *demos* politically contracted together. Once we have a fix on the ontology of national money, we get a more realistic sense of the possibilities and limits of monetary power.

In Chapter 3, we introduced the idea of 'the survival constraint' drawn from Minsky and developed by Mehrling to show that the hegemonic monetary authority domestically and internationally functions according to the provision and withholding of liquidity to market operators. The state inhabits the commercial logic of banking; thanks to political mutualisation at scale, it can occupy the apex of a hierarchical credit system and takes its place at its domestic apex. As such, the state's bank is in a position to modulate the credit system: this is its 'infrastructural power'. This techno-power is tightly indexed to the degree to which the state expresses democratic sovereignty: 'acceptance' is both a political and banking operation.

This line from democratic sovereignty outlines an alternative to the state theory as to why the state's money is at the top of the hierarchy of money. A political theory of money sees the state, amongst other things, as a very special kind of *financial intermediary* that can differentially solve the liquidity survival constraint of other balance sheets, thanks to the strength of the contracts that bind together balance sheets at unmatched scale. This differential ability puts the state at the top of the hierarchy of capitalist money rather than coercion per se. Coercive state power operates within the limits of a legitimate political settlement, else the state and its money diminish. The politics of state debt enables the state to play the banking game at greater robustness and scale than private banks, enabling it to issue a liability that is at once stable and flexible.

We argued that the source of this power is not just the Weberian notion of the state having a legitimate monopoly on coercion, but the still-Weberian but also Marxist and pragmatist trope of equilibrium emerging from political struggle. Ingham himself is the arch exponent of this trope in articulating his social theory of money and value—hence the peculiarity of his ceding so much to coercion. As such, we try and set the equilibrium between coercion and consent in a different relationship than Ingham has, emphasising how the social-contractual element of politics generates *commercial* reasons for the state having the best money and thus unmatched monetary power. The central bank's power is non-sovereign and commercial in its operation rather than purely coercive. There is of course coercion in commerce as well, but to quote Kindleberger (1967) again, this is the force of circumstance rather than the force of arms.

Unmatched power is not unlimited power. By generalising what Ingham takes to be a merely historical fact, we see the state's power over money as *constitutively* limited by the political contract from which it emerges, not contingently but essentially. If we forget this limit, we will fail to correctly assess plans for democratic monetary (re)construction.

Ingham's Ambiguous Monetary Power

Ingham takes the Chartalist view, on the one hand, that money is a creature of sovereign power and combines it with the enhancement of this view by the Innes–Keynes line, on the other, that money is a form of state credit (the 'Neo-Chartalist' position) and develops it in two directions.

First, he recognises that money is by definition contested in capitalist modernity and that state credit money is itself a creature of that struggle. Given that modern money is a form of credit or debt, it is a dyadic institution that brings together debtors and creditors in a potentially conflictual relationship. This struggle is writ large onto state structures of money. Seemingly economic variables like inflation and creditworthiness are thus shown to be fundamentally political and social all the way down; Ingham's is a social theory of *value* as well as money. In this political struggle over money, agonists attempt to naturalise extant monetary arrangements using authoritative discourses that have varied historically from the intrinsic value of metal to those emerging from the discipline of economics.

Second, as a result of this struggle, modern credit money is a hybrid, a contingent institutional compromise resulting originally from an internecine political struggle in early modern England. This struggle pitted the king-sovereign against mercantile interests to create what amounted to a new state formation personified by the hybrid structure of the King-in-Parliament. The modus vivendi between rising capital and established sovereign power made a set of financial techniques and institutions, summarised under the heading of 'Dutch finance', available to a rising commercial power. By sharing sovereignty, the state won hitherto unreached heights of credibility and legitimacy, especially in the money interest, which broadened and deepened the fiscal catchment area in which it could operate. It also secured for itself the (literally) world-beating social technology of private credit money that was now put on firmer and broader footing by its association with the public fisc. These developments provided a distinct competitive advantage to the early modern 'fiscal-military state' (Brewer, 1990).

Notwithstanding these signal innovations, the role of power sits uneasily in Ingham's analysis. On the one hand, he seems to toe the (neo-)Chartalist line when outlining the role of coercion in underpinning money, especially but not exclusively when discussing the historical development of money as a *unit of account*. In a sense, much of the ambiguity that we diagnose in Ingham's theory arises from his prioritising the money-of-account function over the medium-of-exchange and means-of-payment functions of money.

Ingham resorts to the 'authority' story when disputing the Metallists and classical economists regarding the irrationality of the idea of money spontaneously emerging from markets. An authority is required to establish a single unit of account. Coercion therefore has a fundamental role in the historical development of money:

> Money is a form of sovereignty, and as such it cannot be understood without reference to an authority. (Ingham, 2004, p. 12)

> Establishing the promise requires 'authority', which ultimately rests on coercion.... The monopolistic imposition of a money of account, and a refusal to accept any other than the approved credit tokens of the issuer, go hand in hand with monopolisation of physical force. (Ibid., p. 76)

... the standardisation of the unit of account in relation to any standard of value has to be established by an authority. (Ibid., p. 179)

Money is essentially rooted in the money of account and the final means of settlement that is, of necessity, established by an authority. (Ibid., p. 181)

Ingham's main theoretical target is classical and neoclassical economists who want to reduce money to their preferred non-monetary theory of value. For such theorists, convention or the process of exchange throws up one commodity as the standard-bearer of value. Hence, Ingham frames his theory thus:

[T]he *fundamental* question for an ontology of money—regardless of the adequacy of historical evidence—is whether a money of account could possibly emerge from the mere tradability of things. (Ingham, 2018, p. 841, emphasis added)

Yet in seeking to undermine the notion that money emerges from exchange, a salutary move, Ingham ends up giving the entire medium-of-exchange element of money and thus the entire politics of acceptability, the survival constraint, short shrift.

Standing against the logical argument from coercion is Ingham's historical argument from hegemony. Here he is careful and quite superb in his historical analysis of the development of 'capitalist credit money' in the early modern period in Europe. This is the story of how the techniques of Italian and Dutch merchants around the floating, accepting, and circulating of bills of exchange came to insinuate themselves into the state apparatus so that credit came to be national currency. When summarising the developments subsequent to Charles II's default on his debt in the Stop of the Exchequer of 1672, namely a debtor revolt that ultimately led to the Glorious Revolution and a new state formation, Ingham consistently tells us that monetary sovereignty now had a 'dual', 'shared', 'disputed', 'balanced', 'hybridised' nature:

Underpinning this transformation in the social production of money was the change in the balance of power that was expressed in the equally 'hybridised' concept of sovereignty of the 'King-in-Parliament'. (Ingham, 2004, p. 128)

For most of its history, money in capitalism was produced in a dual or hybrid system in which public metal coinage and private credit were integrated and transformed. (Ibid., p. 132)

The state and the market share in the production of capitalist credit-money, and, as I have stressed, it is the balance of power between these two major participants in the capitalist process that produces stable money. (Ibid., p. 144)

In capitalism, monetary sovereignty is shared and disputed. (Ingham, 2013, p. 301)

The mutual dependence of money-capital and the modern state is capitalism's axial relation. (Ibid., p. 315)

How then does Ingham square the circle between the requirement, on the one hand, for what ought to be a standard, Weberian sovereignty, namely the monopoly of violence (albeit missing the crucial element of legitimacy) and, on the other, this altered, hybridised, contractual form of sovereignty that gave rise to our capitalist present?

He seems to make two moves in trying to settle this ambiguity on the nature of power that undergirds money, both of which are aimed at marking off the necessary from contingent elements in the dynamic between money and power.

Coercive Standards and Contingent Credit

First, Ingham claims that while the evolution of *capitalist* credit money into national currency was entirely contingent, the role of a central authority in generating a monopolist unit of account is both logically necessary and an historically uncontroversial fact for all forms of money across all historical social formations. The logic and history of the unit-of-account function is not a contingent feature of the nature of money; for Ingham it is an essential feature. Many things have answered to the description of money over time—from stones to metal to tally sticks to paper credit and electronic IOUs—but the very function of money does not make sense if there is no unit of account that tells us what these money-things are measures of. The metric logic of money, telling us when something has more or less value, demands that money be expressed as a unit of measure.

Measurement standards by their nature cannot be plural, else they lose their abstract ability to render disparate things commensurate. Ingham shows that the idea that such a singular standard could emerge spontaneously from a near-infinity of individual comparisons in regular market exchange—the Metallist origin myth of money—to be logically inconsistent and historically unfounded. The natural-monopoly logic of measurement—money being a measure of value—*combines* with the monopolistic tendency regarding means of violence to make a central state the obvious institution to define the unit of account in which several money-things can be denominated.

So the establishment of a central unit of account is a key enabling condition for money itself in its other functions as a medium of exchange and a store of value; a coercive authority is required for the establishment of such a unit. Thus, coercion is critical to the development of money as such.

The development of merchant's private credit money into a national currency in early modern England, on the other hand, was an entirely contingent political outcome that could have gone otherwise:

> [T]here should be no presumption of the inevitability of a hybridised form of money.... As ever, events proved decisive in tilting the balance away from the sovereign's monopolistic control of the supply of money. (Ingham, 2004, p. 127)

The story Ingham tells of this historical development is of the securing and broadening of monetary space by English sovereigns in progressive steps from the late mediaeval period onwards—one that occurs through firmer control and extension over metallic currency and its minting. This securing of monetary space by coercive force creates the conditions within which private forms of contract, including credit contracts, can flourish:

> The maintenance of the (metallic) standard encouraged a steady supply of long-term creditors for the state, and in this way provided a secure basis for the eventual adoption and expansion of the credit-money system. England eventually achieved what Venice and others had been unable to secure, and reaped the benefits. (Ibid., p. 123)

Again, this was an entirely contingent development. The solidity of monarchical power in this period was such that it might have crushed incipient hybridisation of credit and metal, given the common-sense equivocation of strong metallic currencies and strong states:

> In the absence of further events and conditions, credit-money's development into public currency could just as readily have been inhibited by monarchical monetary policy—as it had been in France, for example. (Ibid., p. 125)

Now, according to the Chartalist position, the state does not need creditors and indeed does not even face a budget constraint in the normal sense. Taxes drive money, and thus all the state has to do is issue an IOU that it will accept in return as payment for tax liability it imposes on its constituents. Extra spending can be cancelled out of the system by imposing more taxation. The early modern state or any state for that matter does not need creditors to survive, goes the argument.

What then did capitalists bring to the Chartalist state, for Ingham? Simply put, robustness at scale. An overmighty sovereign (France) would have crushed the incipient credit system, but a sub-scale sovereign (Venice) would have been robust but too small militarily and lost on the battlefield. England got it just right. But for this merger of public and private interests to succeed, there would have to be a balance of power between the contending sides to achieve both robustness and scale. Out of this political equilibrium comes a historically specific form of money, that of capitalist credit money.

Of course, this political equilibrium between capital and the state takes the form of a constitution that *limits* the degree of coercive power that can be deployed by the sovereign in its national monetary space. So while for money per se to exist, we need a centralisation of violence in a state, there is a further condition imposed by Ingham for the successful creation of *specifically* capitalist credit money—namely that violence be *both monopolised and limited* by countervailing forces. This of course echoes the prominent line regarding the conditions for the rise of capitalism in the 'West' espoused by the new institutionalist economics (North, 1989; North and Weingast, 1989).

Here then is our first example of how Ingham attempts to resolve his ambiguity, namely money and power. Is money backed by the centralisation of coercive force in the state or by a political balance of forces between the state and its creditors? Does it depend on which money function we are talking about? Is coercion necessary for a unit of account but insufficient for specifically capitalist money?

The elision being made here is to posit historically specific forms of money, each with their own structure of social relations and therefore with their own conditions of possibility. For money per se, in all its forms going back to ancient Sumer, we need a coercive state to get a monopolistic unit of account. This is a *logical* necessity. But for modern, capitalist credit money, one of many *historical* monies, we need a balance of power: sovereign power underwrites infrastructural power, quite literally.

There is a problem with this line of argument. It is not sufficient to cite historical examples wherein states were able to control money in a Chartalist sense—namely in the absence of a modus vivendi with its creditors, capitalist or otherwise—because such a historical comparison ignores the fact that capitalist credit money has what Weber would call a *technical superiority* over pre-capitalist forms of money. Ingham's own invocation of early modern England's victorious battles with patrimonial France indicates as much. Capitalist money is 'superior' in the sense that it has underwritten state formations that have politically dominated those with non-capitalist money. Capitalist money has won Weber's battle for the time being.

Money is a set of functions. A specific historical form of money will emerge out of a local political matrix to perform these money functions. That historically coercion was critical in the development of money as a unit of account need not distract us from the fact that capitalist credit money underwritten by a balanced political settlement won the day in terms of which form of money had technical superiority in terms of underwriting dominant state formations down to the present. This is precisely why the apparatus of capitalist credit money was mimicked the world over.

As we know, the transmission mechanism for this mimicry was war: capitalist credit money enabled the war machine as no other form of money before it. Patrimonial systems based on mere coercive power were swept away, transforming themselves into ones defined by balance rather than force, blending coercion and consent in different proportions than previous social formations. Those state formations that failed to achieve the balance that Ingham so trenchantly describes were cast into colonial subjugation from which they only recently emerged and often in merely formal terms.

Competitive political struggles are one proving ground to test which form of money might be most fruitfully used as an ideal type. If money is fit to the type of social formation, and robustly configured social formations dominate others, these forms of money are prime candidates for ideal types. If hegemony produces better money than coercion, why is hegemony (coercion and consent) not definitional of money rather than mere coercion?

The Technical and the Political

The second way Ingham deals with the tension between coercion and consent in the ontology of money is to make a distinction between the in-principle capacities of the state and the actual historical fetters on monetary sovereignty. Here again we see a downgrading of capitalist money along with the material dimension.

If coercive power is both necessary and sufficient for the functioning of money even as a metallic medium, and English political space was being consolidated by rising early modern sovereigns, why did these sovereigns feel the need to make any alliances with their lowly creditor-subjects to begin with? Were they merely in the thrall of a fetishised commodity theory of money? Was it simply that they failed to come around to a properly Chartalist thinking on money? Ingham sounds like he is saying something like this when he claims:

> In capitalism, taxation is also a part of the settlement with the state's creditors— the rentiers, whose dividends are *believed* to be secured by taxes. Concepts of 'sound finance' comprise the 'fiscal norms' that govern struggles surrounding this exchange of goods, services and money between the state and the major economic interest groups. (Ingham, 2004, p. 79, emphasis original)

Yet the fact is that Charles II went bust; technically, he ran out of means of payment. Ingham and the Neo-Chartalists would argue that he only went bust according to the narrow rules of the capitalist game: there ought to have been no *in-principle* reason for the default if we buy the Neo-Chartalist theory. Or was there something more material going on: did Charles II's military ambition not run ahead of his access to liquid funds?

There is also an international constraint here: unless we assume pure autarky, a state will require imports of some nature for daily use and for war. In the early modern period, international money was gold. Did a state have access to international means of payment?

The very fact that a sovereign could actually get into this situation means that there might be, even in principle, a 'technical' limit to monetary sovereignty per se and, by extension, the ability of pure coercion to undergird money's ontology (not merely its value). Ingham is clearly placing the limit on monetary sovereignty at the level of *ideology* or belief systems that work to naturalise money, perhaps something akin to a commodity fetish. No doubt this was and remains operative. But is ideology the whole story?

Of course, Ingham is far too sensitive a reader of monetary history to pass over this. He is only too aware of Minsky's dictum that anyone can issue credit money; the problem is to get it accepted:

> In simple terms, the rules ... by which money is produced in the capitalist system depend, ultimately, on the willingness with which a state's debt will be accepted by an independent class of rentiers. Taxation and state securities are two essential elements, or social bonds, in the capitalist state. (Ibid., p. 144)

Here is Ingham's ambiguity about coercive power laid bare. The early modern sovereign is already bound down by rules of capitalist debt—namely the 'willingness' of its creditors— notwithstanding a monopoly on legitimate violence and all the highlighting of coercive authority cited earlier. There appears to be another form of power operating against brute coercive power, negating its potentiality. What power is this?

The fact that he sees a limit at all to sovereign power qua coercion means that Ingham does not totally agree with the Neo-Chartalists who see no in-principle limit to a sovereign's monetary power other than vaguely defined 'political will'. In marking his point of difference with this school of thought, now operating under 'modern monetary theory', Ingham notes in a more recent piece:

> 'Modern monetary theory' *is right to insist* that a monetary sovereign state that issues its own currency does not *technically* need money market credit to finance its deficits. But these are the terms of the existing relationship between the state and money-capital in which the latter is sustained as an element of modern capitalism. Regardless of what might be possible, *it is widely held* that credibility and creditworthiness are required to appease the anxieties of the capital markets—the so-called 'bond vigilantes'. They insist that prudent fiscal rules should be obeyed to avoid default or inflation induced devaluation by accidental or deliberate currency debasement. This *structural relationship* is not easily overcome by right thinking and political will. Is 'euthanasia' an option? (Ingham, 2013, p. 315, emphasis added)

Ingham seems to be suggesting that the 'technicalities' the Neo-Chartalists see as possible might exist but only *outside* really existing capitalist social relations. In other words, these technicalities are those of a utopia.

These technicalities are, for the Neo-Chartalists, derived from an intense reading of the historical literature, especially that of ancient history but of also American civil war history. Indeed, so strong is this reading of history that, paradoxical as it may sound, Neo-Chartalists seem to have committed the sin of ahistoricism.

The historical origins of a social institution do not necessarily dictate its present functionality, a point that social theorists since Durkheim have made. The entire ensemble of sociopolitical relationships congealing around such an institution changes over time. The specificities of capitalist relations of production are hardly universal in their presentation and dynamics: they themselves are particular to context.

Ingham's agreement with the Neo-Chartalists is only partial. The Neo-Chartalists are right in principle, 'technically', or as he says somewhat less generously in *The*

Nature of Money, in 'bookkeeping terms. [But] bookkeeping, like money, is not neutral' (Ingham, 2004, p. 79). Whatever might be possible technically, says Ingham, capitalist relationships cannot simply be wished away. Monetary sovereignty is limited to the extent of creditworthiness, and creditworthiness is *a market fact*. 'Confidence is required on both sides of the money relation' (ibid., p. 77).

Why create a technical carve-out that amounts to utopianism when real political conditions suggest a serious limitation on monetary sovereignty? Why downgrade *political struggle and balance* to a kind of exceptional, contingent force rather than that which defines money all the way down? Why particularise capitalist structural relationships rather than generalise them as world-historical? Why downplay the material process of exchange as epiphenomenal in favour of the nominalist predicate when one can have both at their appropriate levels?

Importantly, what Ingham ends up doing by conceding that institutionally the state does not really need its creditors is to place *ideology* as that which operationalises the balance between capital and the state and thus sets the limit to monetary sovereignty. By counterpoising a technically broad institutional capability against an operationally narrow, constraining ideology, Ingham simply misspecifies the nature of monetary sovereignty and its constraints.

However, there is in fact a *material institutional constraint* on the state, namely money, not merely an ideologico-political one (though there is undoubtedly that too). This constraint is the material and political requirement for liquid funds, namely the survival constraint, which for the state plays out as the requirement for acceptance of its IOUs. The survival constraint is relaxed by undertaking a financial or non-financial transaction ('production'); we deal with the former here and the latter in the following chapter.

Staying Alive

Ingham argues that once a political settlement between state and capital is achieved, the state has access to borrowing like never before. But what exactly is this borrowing power that capitalist creditors withheld from the state leading to Charles II's default? It is the command over instantaneous—that is, *liquid*—funds.

As we saw in Chapter 3, the constraint of acquiring liquid funds binds all economic units to a greater or lesser extent, even the state. The sovereign's privilege is to bend the survival constraint further than any other economic unit, not to break it. As Ingham fully recognises, access to liquidity is mediated by the politico-economic relation of *acceptance*. For a unit's IOUs to function as money, the unit's solvency needs to be accepted by its creditors. With the state, these creditors are simultaneously a payment community and a political community. Imposing a taxation burden denominated in the state's IOU on this community might drive demand for this debt instrument up to a point, but that only defers the question of acceptability to the tax settlement itself, arguably the most foundational element of any political settlement.

As such, the balance of power between the state as a semi-autonomous actor and organised political interests *is* one of the key forms the survival constraint takes when applied to the state. This balance of power is the survival constraint's most general form, encompassing all forms of money from commodity to state credit. The particular configuration or gearing of this constraint can be radically different. Thus, in contexts where metallic liquidity is required because that is what is accepted as 'cash' either domestically or internationally, the sovereign has to either tax in the metal or borrow it, with both operations entailing acceptance in direct or indirect ways.

In a sense, this comes down to seeing the process of exchange as a kind of political process even with the state. There is a politics to obtaining liquid cash, a politics that is all the more apparent when one is attempting the functional equivalent of obtaining liquid cash—namely to have one's own IOU accepted as money. In seeking to undermine the notion that money emerges autochthonously from exchange, a salutary move, Ingham ends up giving the entire medium-of-exchange element of money and thus the *politics* of obtaining liquid cash short shrift. By going back to Babylonia, Ingham and colleagues miss the historical specificity of capitalism as a cash nexus and downgrade its social relations in their theorisation of money.

The survival constraint is the financial expression of Marx's terrible double freedom. Under capitalist social relations, most economic units have nothing to sell but their labour. This freedom from owning the means of one's own reproduction, which could be a source for positive cash flow, generates a demand for money. Even more fundamental than the state's taxation liability which, for the Neo-Chartalists, drives demand for liquid cash is the demand for cash that capitalism imposes for sheer survival. Capitalism is a tougher taskmaster than the state.

Minsky brings Marx's notion to modern capitalism. For Minsky, capitalism is essentially a financial system because of the irreducibility of the liquidity dimension. We have seen that this liquidity dimension itself emerges from the temporal nature of all economic life, exchange and production alike. Positive cash flow can be secured by a unit either by selling something or borrowing, either by a 'real' or financial transaction. It is easy to imagine this for a non-state economic unit, and we have seen how this might be extended to the state as a two-sided balance sheet.

Ingham is of course aware that the dyadic relationship of debt–credit creates the potential for power on both sides and therefore struggle. But following the Neo-Chartalists, he argues that because the state will always be in a position to impose a debt on society, it will technically *always have the upper hand* subject to ideologies of confidence and creditworthiness. Increased spending today can always be met by increased taxation tomorrow, and the state can always get people to accept the new tax.

As we outlined earlier, here the Neo-Chartalists have confused solvency with liquidity. Taxation power means the state never has a solvency problem: it will always have (taxation) assets that outstrip its (IOU's) liabilities in some final accounting. But just because the state can issue IOUs today and tax them away tomorrow, it does not escape the survival constraint. Taxation takes time, but the state needs the cash today. It therefore needs acceptability today.

It is precisely because there is a finite period of time between the efflux of IOUs and the influx of tax receipts that the state is constrained by the acceptability of its IOUs in the first instance: spending must precede future debt-cancellation. Assuming the state signals an increased tax burden in the future as it spends, in doing so it basically places taxpayers into a kind of forward-looking contract that connects the first period of spending to the second of taxing. What ensures that this forward-looking contract would be adhered to? What kind of bargain is able to sustain a money-today for money-tomorrow exchange with a state?

Note further that when any unit, including the state, is facing a liquidity crunch, it is no longer in a strong bargaining position: it needs the cash *now*. If state spending is merely the issuance of its IOUs against future tax, the state still needs the acceptance of its IOUs *immediately*. That is the meaning of having access to liquidity to bend the survival constraint.

Once subject to the survival constraint, to the need for instant liquidity, the state will have to accede to the terms of an organised body of creditors, either those with access to whatever counts as liquidity or those in control of the means of trade and/or production. This does not depend on whether cash is metal or IOUs, outside money or inside money, although the constraint will bind more or less tightly depending, amongst other things, on whether credit money or a commodity functions as outside money.

It is precisely because functional capitalism has been, so far, the ultimate generator of material goods that states seeking to escape the survival constraint decided to seed it as a social formation; states were even willing to share sovereignty in order to partake in capitalism's bounty. Indeed, war compelled European states to make such a compromise. All pre-modern monetary forms must be seen against the frighteningly productive machine that is functioning capitalism.

Commensurately, in a world of a *commodity* outside money, the demand on the state to share sovereignty in order to overcome the survival constraint is all the more intense. Unable to conjure up more metallic cash out of nothing, the state would have had to compromise even sooner with those non-state balance sheets that, because they were plugged in to first merchant and then industrial capitalism, had managed to secure a substantially positive cash flow of metallic money.

This is one way of thinking through Ingham's paradox of the early modern world where a strong and 'sound' metallic currency lays the foundation for its apparent opposite, namely a world of credit money: 'paradoxically, the first step in the creation of stable monetary spaces that could sustain credit money was the strengthening of metallic monetary sovereignty' (ibid., p. 122).

The more credible the state made a commodity outside asset function as money, the sooner it would have to create a settlement with those whose economic activities generated positive *metallic* cash flow, namely the merchants and bankers engaged in incipient global capitalism complete with its entire credit apparatus. Credit systems require a stable anchor, one now provided to variable degrees by national money anchored to a growing economy.

As we moved in the post-Second World War period to a world of credit money functioning as the outside asset, the money interest had to work much harder to control the state because the state's own money liability was the final means of settlement both domestically and, for globally hegemonic powers, internationally. Our world creates more demands on the money interest to capture the state as the latter becomes an even more potent, autonomous source of liquidity and therefore monetary power.

States face the survival constraint just as non-state actors do. The Chartalist assumption that states can always spend ahead of securing liquid cash and thereby escape the survival constraint does not account for the dimension of time. Because spending ahead of taxes is an operation occurring in distinct time periods, and the state's need for liquidity occurs immediately whereas its ability to tax expresses itself over time, the state finds itself in a somewhat weak bargaining position at the instant it needs liquid cash. This is the survival constraint binding on the state, requiring it to contract politically with substantial elements of any durable political settlement and secure their acceptance of the state's liability.

The State as the Best Financial Intermediary

In a world of fully developed capitalist relations, why do non-state actors accept and indeed demand state credit money, according to Ingham? Under capitalism, what makes state credit money the best money, giving the state differential monetary power? What is Ingham's account of hierarchy in money?

For Ingham, even under a fully developed capitalist system, state sovereignty continues to drive the differential creditworthiness of state credit money:

> [R]estricted monetary networks and circuits are organised in *hierarchy* [*sic*] that is structured by the degree of acceptability in terms of the fungibility of these restricted 'moneys' with those of the most powerful and legitimate issuer. This is almost always the state's money.... Again, it must be stressed that this is a question of sovereignty. (Ibid., pp. 76–77)

By 'sovereignty', Ingham means the classic Weberian definition of a state with a monopoly on violence, *even under capitalist relations*. Continuing immediately from the previous passage, he goes on to note:

> For example, all attempts to create a modern currency under central bank control in early twenty-first-century Afghanistan are compromised by the ability of local warlords to print their own money for the payment of their soldiers and the collection of local tribute. (Ibid., pp. 76–77)

Further, when discussing the production of capitalist credit money, he notes:

> The credibility of the promises forms a hierarchy of moneys that have degrees of acceptability. The state's sovereign issue of liabilities usually occupies the top place, as these are accepted in payment of taxes. (Ibid., p. 198)

Put together, Ingham's claim is that the state occupies the apex of a capitalist credit system for non-capitalist reasons, that is, because it has the violent means to *impose the acceptability* of its IOUs given that tax liabilities are denominated in them.

Here again is Ingham's ambiguity about power and money. If capitalism is defined by a balance of power between the state and capital, the bargain is that capitalist interests accept taxation so long as they share sovereignty. These interests are no longer coerced by an external state; the state along with its feudal, coercive power has become a managing committee for the affairs of the bourgeoisie. Sovereignty itself has morphed into something that over several iterations would become democratic sovereignty.

And yet Ingham acknowledges that the state faces a survival constraint *under capitalism*. The money market has a voice on the base interest rate, the rate at which the state borrows. It is only by comparing this base rate to any potential return on capital that investment decisions are made. As such, says Ingham following Schumpeter, the money market is the 'headquarters' of capitalism (ibid., p. 202), its 'inner sanctum' (ibid., p. 82).

Where is this power coming from? As a matter of daily operation, the money markets are clearly not calculating the likelihood of the state using violence to enforce the taxation settlement with the money interest. The very definition of a *legitimate* monopoly of violence means that such a daily flexing of coercive muscle to ensure the social peace would simply be a contradiction in terms. If that happens daily, we are in a failed state, or what Ingham refers to as 'Afghanistan'.

If violence is not a daily part of the money market's calculus as to the state's superior creditworthiness, what is? Must not there be some *everyday commercial logic* to the state's creditworthiness even if the deep enabler of this logic is a settled social space with legitimately monopolised violence?

This brings us back to the survival constraint. After the capitalist settlement, the combination of bank-like mutualisation of liquidity at the national scale is achieved by political rather than commercial contracting creating a balance sheet like no other. With access to liquidity that no other economic unit, public or private, has over a horizon that is assumed to be perpetual, the state can stretch the survival constraint further than any other unit. It can ration this elasticity for a price by lending to other units and in this way control the entire credit system. This interplay between elasticity and discipline is of course what goes by 'monetary policy', what we have called monetary sovereignty.

The state's ability to relax or tighten the survival constraint—the terms on which its own liability that functions as a means of payment is available to economic units— gives the state commercial and financial power. It is in daily reference to *this* kind of monetary power that money markets, the inner sanctum of capitalism, operate. The tug-of-war between the state and money interest over elasticity and discipline then determines credit conditions in the entire economy.

The view from the survival constraint, from liquidity as opposed to only solvency, gives us a story about why state credit is at the top of the hierarchy of money that *does not depend on coercion* in any operational sense.

To be sure, in extreme, end-of-the-world scenarios all bets are off, literally. As such, capitalism absolutely does exist within the envelope of a *legitimately* coercive Weberian state. Yet saying that is very different from saying that the state technically does not need creditors and only refers to them for political or ideological reasons, but ultimately has the best money because when the world ends, it has all the guns.

Daily adjudication on the fidelity of the state's monopoly of violence could hardly produce stable money markets, leave alone robust capitalism.

What is referred to by money markets, instead, is that the state has better liquidity because its IOUs are accepted as money in a commercial calculus rather than an explicitly political one. This illustrates that the *contractual element* is more operative in the normal course of events than the *coercive element* in the ontology of money. The politics that undergirds money, *in all but the very last instance,* is that of a bargain.

This bargain can be configured on radically different terms and at radically different economic scales. A historical political economy of the varieties of this structure of state finance can tell us why some state monies are better than others—that is, why state monies themselves exist in a hierarchy of international money. By foregrounding coercion even in capitalist money, Ingham leaves us with no account of the vast space of monetary variation between mature capitalist formations and a failed state.

Cash Is King

By borrowing through deposits—that is, mutualising units with surplus national money—banks are differentially able to relax the survival constraint of non-bank economic units. The central bank's market power over national money—the power to move the price that represents the survival constraint—comes from the most durable mutualisation at scale, which in turn comes from political contracting. Politics enables overwhelming commercial power, but this is politics qua contract rather than brute coercion. Money as credit is inherently hierarchical because the survival constraint applies differentially to differently mutualised or scaled balance sheets.

As such, we can see that, pace Ingham and the Neo-Chartalists, the state does not even have the technical ability to free itself from its creditors because the state's power over money is itself derived from a political contract with those creditors to begin with, even citizen-creditors. The state is endogenous to society. This political contract sets the bounds of what is technically feasible rather than the other way around. A widespread, democratic political contract in a highly productive nation sets the bound very wide indeed, but there remain bounds. Politics determines the ontology of national money because it determines the ontology of the state.

We have attempted to redraw the relationship between coercion and consensual contracting that generate money. Rather than seeing violence as enabling monetary power in principle but ideologically restricting this power in practice, we argue that political contracting enables state power in money markets and violence only operates at extreme moments to maintain the overall social peace. The sovereign does indeed call the state of exception, but it is not *this* quality of sovereignty alone that drives money. Rather, it is the element of the political bargain that anchors money to the value- or liquidity-generating machine par excellence, capitalism. If we read the ontology of (state) institutions as political all the way down, the generalisation and development of capitalist relations merely brings the inherent politics-qua-settlement essence of sovereignty to the fore once the system sloughs off the fetish of commodity money. Reading acceptance as political allows us to see the survival constraint itself as a creditary form of the political ontology of institutions.

The presence of a survival constraint that binds even the state is met by the fact of political contracting at scale, giving the state differential market power and thus differential degrees of freedom to overcome this constraint. The bounds of discipline and elasticity differ between different states because of the different strengths of political contract and the scale of the capitalist economy within which the state operates; this drives monetary variation between capitalist states. But on home turf these bounds are wider than any non-state actor.

Learning from Ingham, we have been presumptuous enough to invert him. What he takes to be contingent we take to be universal—namely the centrality of the politics in defining the ontology of all institutions, including money. We can agree with the logical priority of the unit of account function even while subordinating the role of coercion to the legitimate political settlement. This also gives us a more balanced view of the nominalist and materialist dimensions of money.

Violence operates at the extremes of social formations and also at a day-to-day level in terms of enforcing the criminal law. Ideologies of sound money, technocratic independence, and so on, also play a daily role in configuring the system between elasticity and discipline. But in terms of what Minsky called the daily coherence of the capitalist system, the state's power over money operates as market power derived from, and therefore limited by, political contracting—acceptance in both political and creditary senses. It is infrastructural in its operation and consensual, and thus legitimate, in its underwriting.

The flip side of a political theory of money is a financial theory of the state. While this is a more societal and political reading of the state than that of the Chartalists, it is inspired by the kind of history that Ingham recounts, coupled with Mehrling's idea of the state as a social mutual fund. Ironically, the State Theory of Money falls short by having a thin theory of the state and sovereignty.

Ingham moves far beyond this limitation only to then limit himself by downgrading capitalist credit money as insufficiently ideal-typical. In doing so, he also sets the limit of monetary sovereignty at relations of credit which are read as purely ideational.

What pushes Ingham in this direction is a commitment to defeating the Mengerian account of money as emerging from exchange.

As we will see in the next chapter, this in turn is based on his commitment to a philosophical *nominalism*—hence the foregrounding coercive power in establishing the unit of account. Over-prioritising the state's nominalist power gives us the fiction of 'fiat money'. Once we read 'fiat' as the outcome of a bargain, and once we anchor money's value in the wealth of nations, we can dispense with the term once and for all and replace it with 'credit'. There is no such a thing as fiat money.

7 | COHERENCE
Why Money Is Not Value

The entire system is like an archetypical Escher print, where stairs and pillars mutually buttress an elaborate interconnected edifice, but no part of the edifice ever touches the ground.

—Mirowski (1990, p. 717)

Production, consumption, and trade, are nothing more than flows of money in and out and between different economic units. The most real thing is money, but money is nothing more than a form of debt, which is to say a commitment to pay money at some time in the future. The whole system is therefore fundamentally circular and self-referential. There is nothing underneath, as it were, holding it up.

—Mehrling (1999, p. 138)

Forms of money represent an abstract conception of value which is measured by itself—that is to say, a tautological but efficacious social construct.

—Ingham (2018, p. 844)

There have only ever been various monies of differing quality. Our contemporary world is now a world of national monies tied to bank money backstage. Money's variability is part of its ontology. A theory of money has to account for this variation: why do some monies have more value than others? This question points to the material power of money, but not necessarily only through the question of how much of the world of goods and services a particular money can command.

Our theory of money takes the material dimension of money to be irreducible, but it does so via the financial or contractual route rather than the purchasing power or exchange route. This is not to say that the command of wealth is not a key driver of money's 'substantive value', to use Weber's term; it obviously is. Yet money remains a liability that promises to pay what is on the asset side of the issuing balance sheet. If credit or debt is part of money's very ontology, then so too is this asset or liability structure that contractually anchors money's value in the material dimension. The nature and extent of this anchoring vary with the form of mutualisation of the issuing balance sheet, economic or political, but both forms point to something *external* to the credit–debt relationship. There is something holding up money after all.

Nominalists (such as Simmel and Ingham) read money as a tautological social construct—value itself. While it is argued that this refers mainly to the abstract money of account, we will argue in this chapter that there is a distinct downplaying of money's material dimension even when it comes to the *substantive* value of money. Salutary at the level of money of account, nominalism might have corrected too far.

Perhaps what has been overlooked is that the debt that the money of account measures is at once political and material. The sovereign's imposition of a tax debt derives from politically mutualised sovereign power to be sure, the debt relation itself (*without* any material referent) imbuing the debt-cancelling instrument—money—with value. But balance sheets are not a mere accounting device; money as credit or debt is ontologically two-sided. And the balance sheets indicate an irreducibly material referent for money, both national money and bank money. Money is always the liability of a mutualised institution and, as such, has a corresponding material asset: the national economy itself for central-bank money and individual or collective labour powers for bank money. Money actually is a promise to pay something, namely prospective value anchored in a real economy.

Classical economists were certainly overly reductionist and required correction. An adequate materialism must indeed go beyond the physical monetary medium. The balance-sheet view allows us to read money's material dimension as simultaneously sociopolitical and futural or probabilistic, opening up a non-tautological, non-deterministic reading of the relationship between money and value.

A given money's value varies with the fidelity of the credit-promise, the development of the credit system and economic scale. Putting variation almost entirely down to the balance of creditor or debtor power, as Ingham does, is insufficient to account both for money's ontology and monetary heterogeneity. Like all credit, national money is a compound—a sovereign or collective contract locked more or less firmly into a more or less productive economy. Money is therefore not tautological. Money is anchored in the material dimension.

But because money's anchoring is achieved by inherently variable politico-institutional bonds, its value is not simply reducible to the material dimension in some deterministic way. Moreover, mutualisation anchors money to the future of a productive economy, and the future is inherently probabilistic. This is 'coherence': the non-linear, unstable, political relationship between money and value run through an inherently hierarchical and inherently politicised credit system.

Everyone likes to talk their disciplinary book and those who focus on money are no different. Yet the thinkers who have been most inspirational for this work—Mehrling, Ingham, Mirowski—are sui generis in that they have eschewed disciplinary nationalism and, true to their subject matter, roamed across sociology, history, political theory, history of science and political economy to attempt to come to grips with our troublesome social fact. Their work is unique, and it could not be achieved within the confines of any one discipline.

Yet as we can see from the epigraph, one thread ties these diverse, post-disciplinary thinkers of money together: their nominalism. They have a tendency to think of money-as-credit purely as a self-referential social construct. This might also be a reflection of the fact that the period of neoliberalism did in fact see a hypertrophy of financial claims that seemed to be far in excess of 'the real economy' however measured.

But this hypertrophy is a conjunctural fact. A credit system can remain highly elastic for a substantial period if the relevant pay community is highly accepting, and it can find new sources of material value to plug into along the way. Of course, once the music stops, substantial incoherence and crisis will result. Yet most discussions of 'financialisation' are deeply parochial as they do not account for the simultaneous *industrialisation* of economies representing a substantial chunk of humanity on the other side of the planet. We cannot in this day and age be methodological nationalists.

The 'social' in social construct is often construed as lacking in 'material' qualities, most especially those having to do with human provisioning. This dematerialised worlding generates a very odd ontology of the social. Marx's definition of capital, at once social and material, concrete and abstract, worked against a Manichean framing of the social versus the material. Perhaps foolishly, we will attempt something analogous in this chapter by trying to piece together the relationship between the 'social construct' of money and some material fact called 'value'.

Given the tyranny of 'theories of value' of either the utilitarian or crudely materialist kind, our champions' nominalism embodies a badly needed anti-foundational impulse. However, while useful as a means of ground-clearing and critical in helping us understand the metric functions of money, an excessive nominalism can produce the irony of an almost entirely non-materialist account of that core materialist impulse—money.

As we outlined earlier, money as a liability of a national bank is a claim on the future national product, a secure claim on the wealth of a nation. The claim itself might be merely contractual, but its 'economic' or 'substantive' value is derived at least in part from the politico-legal locking of the money instrument to future material wealth. A money-claim with equal contractual fidelity but less material potentiality is simply less valuable. To suggest, as Ingham might, that differences in purchasing power are almost entirely a result of the balance of competing interests in various locales is to give a wholly 'internal' or 'social' account of how money gets its value—that is, by exclusive reference to a set of countervailing sociopolitical relations and not at all to the productive capacity of human beings conjoined together in social, commercial and political bonds.

This is all the more ironic since Ingham is a powerful advocate for overcoming the pernicious effects of the 'Methodenstreit'. Yet when Weber spans the divide with his own brand of materialism, he is seen by Ingham as falling into error by following economic orthodoxy. Such, perhaps, is the cost of a determinist nominalism: it generates a 'pure' *social* theory of value that eschews the material dimension, as if the material has to be fully subsumed in a non-material 'social'. This undermines the creditary ontology of money as a promise to pay and comes at the cost of explaining critical empirical questions like why different monies have different values. As Ingham has taught us, getting over the 'Methodenstreit' means incorporating the material dimension and liberating it from the ill-fated monopoly of the economists. But we cannot by the same token disappear the material dimension in the social.

This treatment of the material dimension perhaps comes down to the fact that the Currency School, Ingham's main theoretical enemy, erroneously conflates the valuableness, or formal value of money, and its substantive value with money stuff—that is, the physical attributes of monetary media. Nominalism is absolutely the correct response to *this* error, but it need not come at the cost of restricting the deployment of the material dimension to the question of the physical composition of monetary media.

'Valueless' book entries have substantive value not merely because they are socially constructed, which all contracts patently are, but also because they represent a property-right claim over a portion of the national product (or a part of the social product for bank money). National money is a contract with a particular set of properties, politically linking the future national product to the hierarchical national credit system through the interlocking balance sheets of the fisc and the central bank.

The national economy itself is the reserve asset of the central bank whose liabilities are money. Bank money is an economic claim on a particular set of activities within a division of labour. Ignoring these facts, the result of a downgrading of the material dimension of money, leaves us unable to fully answer why different national monies have different values. We are thereby left unable to appreciate a fundamental fact of capitalism, namely its wretched unevenness.

The Limits of Nominalism

Why do some monies have more purchasing power than others? This is another way of inquiring into the value of money, but invoking the vexed concept of 'value' immediately implicates us in theories of value—namely that set of answers to the question, what drives the value of all goods and services? Articulating the question this way already presupposes that there is something called 'value' that is autonomous from its monetary expression—price.

This of course *sounds* like the classical formulation of value that reduces money to a neutral veil and points to a 'real' economy 'out there' upon which money is thrust. But it is perhaps more fruitful to read the 'classical dichotomy' from Marx to Knut Wicksell as merely one way to deal with the simultaneously social or abstract and material or concrete nature of value. The spirit of the Currency School therefore contained a necessary but poorly deployed materialism. Yet its ontological errors do not exhaust the possibilities of understanding the material dimension of money's value.

In short, we need not succumb to the reductionism of classical economics in order to acknowledge that there are 'relatively autonomous' material forces of production. Ingham acknowledges the relative autonomy of the material at several junctures, if only in passing. What a theory of *money* demands is an adequate understanding of the relationship between the monetary and the material dimension. We attempt an outline of such a relationship by submitting the material dimension to two operations: reading it as simultaneously social (political) and futural (probabilistic). To say this still falls well short of outlining a distinct theory of *value* even though it delimits the set of theories of value that might be compatible with the present theory of money.

Thus, without committing to a theory of value which is beyond the scope of this work, we make room for such a theory that is compatible with the present theory of money. It is our contention that any theory of money that does not provide space for a materialist theory of value runs the risk of conflating money with 'substantive value' per se, a risk elevated by the nominalist predicates of some of the leading theorists of money.

Different national monies are (more or less better) promises covering economic catchment areas of differing magnitudes (of which GDP is a rough and ready measure). Following balance-sheet logic, national money's value in fact has three independent dimensions to it: the political fidelity of the credit-promise in one dimension, the state of development of its credit system in another and the size of the economic catchment area in a third dimension are all critical to understanding the variability in the value of different monies. One can after all have a highly developed credit system with a well-balanced equilibrium of power between social forces that will result in a highly stable money and yet the resulting credit system might preside over a relatively small economy. Think Switzerland.

The Swiss franc has at times been stronger than the dollar in terms of its market price. Should we conclude from this that the Swiss franc can challenge the dollar as world money? The Swiss franc's stability is thanks to its contained scale in terms of the liquidity float over the economic catchment area overseen by the Swiss government, a scale generated by the balance of political forces bearing down on its well-articulated credit system. If the Swiss tried to provide global liquidity on the scale of the dollar, however, its limits would quickly be reached.

The limit of a bank's loan book is the size of its capital base combined with how elastic its creditors are willing to be: solvency is to a large extent in the eye of the counterparty. Acceptability and capital combine in non-linear ways to produce bank solvency and liquidity, but these forces pivot around a well-defined capital base so that particular leverage ratios conventionally come to be seen as safe or not.

So too is the case with nations and their IOU money. The taxed fraction of a nation's economy is the 'capital' anchoring the central bank's money issuance, but this is mediated through the fisc. There is no direct analogy between the share capital of Citibank and the share capital in the US. Yet the debt of the government of the US provides a rough analogy: it is based on the underlying productivity of the nation and can be used as capital-ballast for (central) bank leverage.

We cannot reduce money or credit to the 'prior' value of monetary media, but nor can we reduce it entirely to the balance of social forces, trust and other social norms. The complex, thoroughly politicised nature of the relationship between money and value qua (national) productivity defines the nature of (national) money itself.

As we outlined earlier, national money is nothing but a special kind of state debt. All IOUs are probabilistic claims on some future material production process; money, the IOU of a state's bank armed with treasury-bill assets, is a claim on the wealth of the nation, 'value'. For the financial claim of money to have substantive value, these claims need to be 'validated' (Minsky's term) by a future, non-financial 'production process'.

This is not a deterministic relationship by any means, whence the *relative* autonomy of the financial from the material; further, the relationship between these two dimensions is shot through with the politics of money which is also essentially non-linear. It is precisely within the (definitionally) blurry-edged space of variation outlined by this relative autonomy of the financial and material that we find monies with differential purchasing power. Such variation is constitutive of the nature of money and therefore must be accounted for theoretically.

The social theory of money's value outlined by Ingham seems to account for this variation almost entirely by pointing to the relative balance of power of creditors and debtors within different monetary spaces—that is, *without* recourse to a semi-autonomous domain of material value. It appears that, for Ingham, such recourse to the material can *only* be done along the lines of substance theories of 'anterior' or 'prior' value. Yet anchoring money-as-credit to *prospective*, future value would make its value no less materially mediated. Ingham defends the tautological attributes of money's value thus: 'In a monetary *system* [*sic*]', he asserts, 'the value of credit and debt is mutually and *internally* determined' (Ingham, 2018, p. 844, emphasis added).

There can be no argument with the nominalism of Ingham's position— namely the creation of a money of account which can only be the work of a central coordinating authority, public or private. Further, the state can and does nominate the instrument that will pay off the tax debt. Yet this argument lacks a material or 'external' dimension that is required if one wants to adequately account for relative variations in the value of different monies. An account of the value of money that relies entirely on the equilibrium of political forces and not at all on the relation of those forces to an underlying economy cannot account for the material difference between the US dollar and the Swiss franc, both characterised as they are by stable political equilibria undergirding their respective credit systems.

For Ingham, acceptability of the credit note that is money appears to turn *entirely* on a combination of accepted norms of creditworthiness ('sound money', the treasury view, the commodity fetish [namely metallic money], the performativity of economics, and so on) operating through a balance of power of organised social forces. Yet he also points in passing to the material dimension.

Thus, while outlining the production of capitalist credit money, Ingham observes that the central bank's performance of the norms of creditworthiness is directed at *'labour, productive capital ...* and the *money markets*' (Ingham, 2004, p. 148, emphasis original). Ultimately, '[h]igh-powered money is the result of the struggle between debtors' demand for money and creditors' belief that the state can service its debt, which in turn depends on tax revenues. And it is the need to work for a *taxable* income that gives it value' (ibid., p. 150). The first part of this quote is the standard Chartalist formula of taxes driving monetary value—that is, a purely political and social account of money's value. Money is valuable *only* because you need it to pay taxes. As we have seen in Chapter 6, Ingham allows only for the social norms that govern the balance of power to operate as a fetter on state spending: '... the neo-chartalists are correct to say that the state doesn't actually need the taxpayers' money' (ibid., p. 79). And yet Ingham points in the end to the material by acknowledging that people have to work for national money and that gives it its value. But working for money means generating material value that will validate the money earned. Money's material dimension bleeds through his otherwise rigorous nominalism.

Ingham is entirely right to point to the irreducible level of social relations of credit and social norms as embodied in the varied institutional means of credit production as pivotal for determining the relative value of money, but to turn a determining variable into a determinative one is to commit the sin of ... determinism. At times Ingham seems to leave a crack in the door for materialism but, especially in his more recent interventions, he defends a robustly nominalist position. Thus,

> [e]conomic theories which focus on the substance or utility of 'material' things fail to provide an adequate conceptual framework for grasping money's nature. A more appropriate model, e.g., would be Durkheim's social ontology of religion which the anthropologist Mauss applied to money and likened it to the magico-religious power of *mana*, as brilliantly explicated by Orléan. (Ingham, 2018, pp. 843–844)

Again, we do not wish to eliminate this sui generis level of the social: bringing it to the centre of the study of money's nature is Ingham's signal contribution. And we must also agree that economic theories of value focused either on utility or congealed abstract labour fall far short as he says. They arguably do so because they adopt the erroneous temporality of classical economics (past determines present) rather than that of finance theory (future determines present). They also miss the institutionalist dimension of robust contracting.

Put in Minsky's language as explicated by Mehrling, the past is relevant because the pattern of past creditary promises constrains (*not* determines) the domain of possible future action: once we take on debts, their burden delimits our future course of action, individually and collectively. This path dependency can evolve in complex ways, more so to the extent that our past promises are validated by still more financial promises rather than non-financial productivity. But to say this is quite different from saying that future investment must come out of past saving; money is always based on an 'intrinsically' valuable commodity or some such physicalist notion.

The 'coherence' between the promises of the past and the open horizon of future productivity is managed by the money markets *today* by mapping cash outflows to cash inflows. Coherence is a fragile achievement, a dynamic balancing act watched over daily by market operators and monetary technocrats alike. The political balance between the money interest and the public interest is most definitely expressed in the configuration of these markets as we will see in some detail in Part II. But to say that *only* the political balance coupled with norms of creditworthiness or good economic management are salient for the coherence of an economy is to write out the material dimension to an untenable extent.

Put differently, the M-M' or financial course of action can only proceed so far and no further before it hits the limits of the M-C-M' course of action (Ingham, 2004, p. 151). The fact that this crisis point is completely unknowable in advance, even in principle, says nothing about its existence. Surely the existence of such a threshold is material to understanding the nature of money, to say nothing of contemporary capitalism.

Therefore, even as Ingham points to the material facts of productive labour and capital as operative in the production of *capitalist* credit money, this is for him merely a temporally localised historical fact confined to the capitalist mode of production and one that is driven by the belief structures of the wielders of power rather than the transhistorical significance of the material dimension. For Ingham, all that is required is a Weberian monopoly on the means of coercion (legitimacy, so key for Weber, shows up in Ingham in the relatively weaker form of norms of creditworthiness) in order to institute a money of account. This, for him, is where the possibility of monetary values qua a unit of account *and* the substantive value of particular monies come from.

Formal and Substantive Value of Money

As we have alluded to, a theoretical commitment to an almost 'pure' sociopolitical account of money's nature and value sells the creditary nature of money short even while leaving critical monetary phenomena partially explained. Ingham's particular solution to the problem of money's value no doubt has much to do with his salutary drive to take down the Mengerian fable of money emerging autochthonously from exchange. That fable had to be put to rest once and for all, and Ingham, with the help of money's historians, does so decisively.

Yet in the process, he unintentionally narrows the terms of a theoretically legitimate materialism to the wooden version deployed by the classicals and neoclassicals. Thus we are repeatedly told that the *fundamental* question for an ontology of money—regardless of the adequacy of historical evidence—is whether a money of account could possibly emerge from the mere tradability of things ... the *fundamental* analytical question is whether the existence of a unit of account, which denominates debts and the means of their payment, can be derived from the barter commodity-exchange model. (Ingham, 2018, pp. 841–842, emphasis added)

This clearly points to Carl Menger and the 'Methodenstreit'; yet what makes that 'fundamental' to the question of the ontology of money tout court remains obscure. The money of account, after all, measures debt, and this debt has two *irreducible* elements: the political element of the state's sovereign imposition on citizens or subjects and the economic element of its material anchoring, via taxation, to the real economy. Thus, if the money of account is fundamental to money's ontology, so too is money-as-debt's anchoring in the real economy.

The somewhat crude materialist ontology of Menger and the Currency School makes no distinction between the value of money and its valuableness, or what Weber calls 'formal validity', its capacity to bear economic value. Derived from classical economics, the Currency School sees a commodity's value as inhering in its material substance which is reduced to past or dead labour time. Marx's distinction between concrete or particular and abstract or social labour makes him only a partial exception. Menger's utilitarianism has an altogether different value 'substance' undergirding commodity values but is homologous with classical economics in deploying 'conservation principles' cribbed from nineteenth-century physics to describe the operations of production and exchange, namely utility (Mirowski, 1989). Therefore, for both classicals and neoclassicals (for different reasons), money's valuableness was simply reducible to the value or utility of the money commodity, and value then accounted for in their respective ways. This of course is why non-commodity or non-material monies were such an abomination for the Currency School or 'fictitious' in the vernacular of traditional Marxism.

Following Georg Friedrich Knapp and Weber, Ingham locates the valuableness of money in the relations of credit and debt between state and subjects or citizens, relations that subtend a particular monetary space governed by a state-imposed unit of account. The primordial debt, wherein the 'social' encapsulates the 'material', is that of the subjects to the crown in the form of a tax liability. The sheer universality (within national space) of this debt denominated in the state-imposed unit of account then sets the scene for other, downstream economic debts to similarly be denominated in this unit of account. This ability to measure debt stemming from the primordial relation of debt to the state is what lies behind the valuableness of money. Money can cancel all debts (that is, serve as a means of payment) because it can cancel the ur-debt to the state.

Ingham goes further though and locates the actual or 'substantive' value of a particular money within this matrix of conflictual social relations. The sheer pressure of this social relationship of debt is enough to give real economic value to otherwise valueless material items or indeed mere (electronic) book entries:

> Money's value is *ontologically* grounded in its debt settling and purchasing power not from any pre-existing tradable—but unspecified—value. Money's power of objectively (inter-subjective) given 'valuableness' derives from the existence of a socially constructed monetary space delineated by the common unit of account by which all prices and debts are denominated. Money is a credit in the sense that there exist *actual* and *potential* debts, denominated in precisely the same way, awaiting cancellation. If this ceases to be the case, then money loses its power. This is an emergent social property in which particular social arrangements confer attributes which are qualitatively different from the mere tradability of commodities, based on any 'substance' value or utility. (Ingham, 2018, p. 841, emphasis original)

In our political theory of money, our materialism has very little to say about the tradability of commodities as the root of money's historical or logical origins: the financial or contractual prediction of money is institutional and does not run through its purchasing power. Nor is it based on a notion of money emerging as a convenient means of exchange although exchange qua command over goods and services is critical for the substantive value of money.

Rather than relying entirely on mutually constituting, inter-subjective relations of credit and debt, the theory of money outlined here operates from the financial fact of money being an IOU of some issuing entity and therefore being a very particular kind of financial asset to the holder. Like all debt instruments, money as an IOU is only as good as the creditworthiness of the issuer which, in turn, is based on the issuer's actual assets. The imbrication of the fisc and the central bank turn (the future productivity of) the national economy itself into the reserve asset of the state's bank. The same is true of the asset base of banks at a lower scale with particular branches of the division of labour. Differential asset bases *qua* the size of the national economy will, all things being equal, generate monies of different qualities and therefore value.

The national economy		The state		The central bank	
Assets	Liabilities	Assets	Liabilities	Assets	Liabilities
'Value'	Tax	Tax	Bonds	Bonds (Gold)	'Money'

Borrowers		Commercial bank	
Assets	Liabilities	Assets	Liabilities
'Value':			
Labour power	Loans	Loans	'Bank money'
Businesses			

Figure 7.1   The political or economic institutionalisation of money's value

In other words, this reading of the value of money finds an irreducible place for the material dimension (mutualised future productivity) without succumbing either to the reductive materialism of the classicals or a creeping sociological determinism (see Figure 7.1). To invoke the material dimension as irreducible to the nature of money is very different from reducing money to that dimension. Money's materiality comes in part from robust creditary claims of the issuing balance sheets on the real economy.

This reading of money as a kind of financial asset is less rarified than it may seem. Recalling our reading of Commons from Chapter 1, what we trade in the market are not in fact commodities but rather *rights* to various goods and services. From the institutionalist standpoint, *it is contracts (and therefore politics) all the way down*. National money is merely a special contract as it is coextensive with the social contract itself and thereby undergirded by the social product.

An irreducible part of money's *substantive* value therefore goes beyond the balance of power between creditors and debtors, beyond its purchasing power in the market to the (political or economic) contractual anchoring in a material economy which occurs through the asset side of the balance sheet. Money is some institution's *liability*; its material anchoring comes, irreducibly but not exclusively, from the nature of that institution's future-oriented *assets*.

Measures Are Tautological

Committed as he is to a largely 'internal' account, Ingham has to resort to a tautological scheme in order to account for money's valuableness. There are two elements to this, one theoretically essential and the other tending to a deterministic extra. First, it is important to note that tautology is almost definitional of mensurating or metric activity per se. Metric conventions of all kinds are at once abstract (you cannot touch or smell them), social (they are human constructs) and tautological in that they refer only to themselves: therein lies their ability to be the measure of *other* things. What else does a 'metre' refer to other than the self-same metre's length? Further, Marx noted that the *material* properties of objects can still be *abstract*: 'A sugar-loaf being a body, is heavy, and therefore has weight: but we can neither see nor touch this weight' (Marx, 1992 [1867], pp. 148). So too with value.

Perhaps the tautology internal to the logic of mensuration is what Ingham refers to—namely the ontology of money. He quotes Simmel in saying that money is 'the value of things without the things themselves' (Ingham, 2018, p. 844). Money qua a unit of account *is abstract value itself*: 'Money is abstract value *sui generis*, existing in a monetary space defined and circumscribed by the money of account which is sought by all participants' (ibid.). But we can see how such inherent, metric self-referentiality can bleed into substantive value.

Value, following Philip Mirowski (1991), is a scoring system: it allows actors within a market system to keep track of who is winning and who is losing. In order for this to work, all economic actions must be made commensurate with each other by means of some method of quantification. Value theory enters the fray to provide various accounts of what makes this quantitative commensuration possible. For this to work, in order to understand gain or loss, one element in the system must operate as a stable benchmark against which change is measured. Some quantitative 'invariant' has to be postulated. However factually inaccurate such a move might be, we need a benchmark invariant for economic life for commensuration to get off the ground. Such is 'value'—a necessary but provisional invariant.

These value invariants are both enabling of economic life but commonsensically false in that 'nothing in human experience is perfectly invariant, perfectly identical, or perfectly reversible (Mirowski, 1990, p. 694). This basically fictional nature of value, covering all theories of value, has therefore impelled human culture to ground its constructed, essentially false economic invariants in naturalistic 'conservation principles' in order to give them moral and political authority, a point that both Mirowski and Ingham owe to anthropologist Mary Douglas.

With characteristic brio, Mirwoski urges us to grow up and acknowledge the fact that our economic invariants are essentially false but eminently useful for the business of conducting business. We need our invariants, so we must cultivate an ironic distance from the fact that they are 'working fictions' (Mirowski, 1991, p. 581). Mirowski says:

> What is required is a transpersonal index of gain and loss, which will serve as the identity element in the algebra of exchange. Money, by its very nature a socially constructed institution, performs this function.... Hence, in a very narrowly defined sense, in a social theory of value *money is the embodiment of value*; but precisely because it is socially instituted, its invariance cannot be predicated on any 'natural' ground, and must continually be shored up and reconstituted by further social institutions, such as accountants and banks and governments. (Mirowski 1990, pp. 711–712, emphasis added)

Money is the provisional invariant of economic life, the 'transpersonal index of gain and loss' that enables commensurate and therefore market calculation. Consistent with this proposition that money *is* value, Mirowski proposes that in such a social theory of value, the main locus of the expansion of value is the expansion of the monetary unit itself through the creation of debt. Only the creation of money breaks the symmetry of the invariant standard, allowing actors to get something for nothing. The limit point to this is the compromising of the invariant standard and a breakdown of the economic order: 'there is a trade-off between the expansion of value through debt creation and the breakdown of the value invariant through inflation' (Mirowski, 1991, p. 580). Here is the postmodern, anti-foundationalist, tautological proposition at its clearest: money is value and 'growth' comes from sustainable expansions of money.

Yet if money *is* value, money's value inheres in its issuance as debt, that debt is itself denominated in the money of account, and value can expand by the mere issuance of debt, then why is economic growth so hard? How do we even begin to explain vast divergences in the wealth and poverty of nations if we can expand value by expanding money?

While a full specification of the substantive value of particular monies is of course beyond the scope of any theory of money, such a theory can offer some sense of the ontological space of substantive value. Yet Ingham only parenthetically indicates that the *substantive* value of money is anything other than its derivation from the debt liability imposed by the state.

Indeed, he regretfully notes that Weber himself succumbed to orthodoxy regarding the substantive value of money (Ingham, 2004, p. 67). For Ingham, the state has to establish money's valuableness, namely the unit of account, abstract value itself, since that cannot emerge from 'the mere tradability of things'. But further, money's substantive value is *also* reduced to the equilibrium that emerges from the tax liability imposed by the state:

> In Weber's terms, the 'substantive' value of money (purchasing power) at any moment in time *is the result* of the economic 'battle of man with man' in which money is a weapon. (Ibid., p. 71, emphasis added)

> The state not only establishes the valuableness of money by its declaration of what it will accept in payment of taxation; it also *determines* its substantive value by influencing what must be done in the economy in order to earn the income to pay the tax. (Ibid, p. 84, emphasis added)

Weber did not do it himself, but his work 'contains the germs of a sociological recasting of a substantive theory of money' (ibid., p. 67). Such a recasting sets both the valuableness *and* the substantive value of money almost entirely in terms of social relations with the force of debt intersubjectively recognised and thus holding the entire system up. For Ingham, money *is* value, and it is 'social', by which he means something antithetical to the 'material', more Maussian mana than Marxian M.

In short, while Ingham does not collapse the distinction between value and valuableness (substantive and formal value, in Weber's terms) as with classical economists, both elements find their source in the same place—the balance of social forces between state and society, or what we are calling the political settlement. Valuableness qua the abstract unit of account cannot in principle come from anywhere other than a central coordinating authority like the state, while substantive value comes from the (balance of) sociopolitical pressure the ur-debt of tax liabilities owed to the state. While we heartily agree with the first (nominalist) premise, the second one is only partially true. All states have tax owed to them, all states express a balance of power between competing interests, but not all state monies have the same material anchoring. Ingham's sociological account of substantive value cannot explain this phenomenon as it lacks a fully worked out material dimension.

In more recent interventions, Ingham seems to dial back from a purist nominalism. Thus, when discussing the sources of monetary disorder, namely inflation, he recently stated:

> In an expanding economy, *operating at full capacity*, demands from households, businesses, governments, and foreign buyers compete for the finite supply of goods and services, bidding up prices and causing inflation. (Ingham, 2020, p. 50, emphasis added)

There are also many possible *external* sources of monetary instability: for example, inflation triggered by a narrowly economic event such as a falling exchange rate and a consequent rise in the price of imports might lead to discontent and a loss of government legitimacy. (Ibid., p. 54, emphasis original)

Or again, when discussing the state's role as regards the substantive value of money, he states:

States can declare and impose what is to be accepted as payment—money's *formal* [*sic*] validity ('valuableness') but they cannot *directly* determine its *substantive validity* [*sic*] (purchasing/debt settling value).... Of course, as major participants in Weber's 'struggle for economic existence', states have a considerable impact on the purchasing power of money, but they *do not determine it*. (Ingham, 2021, p. 495, emphasis added)

The 'internalist', conflict theory account of monetary value is obviously not incompatible with a more balanced account, but we are not merely quibbling over a degree of emphasis. Contractual anchoring of substantive value goes to money's very ontology as an IOU. It is also a variable material channel sui generis, one that Ingham largely downplays.

Exchange as a Socio-Material Process

As we noted earlier, Ingham's reading of the material dimension is perhaps coloured by his engagement with the Mengerian account of the rise of money. Seeing money, in part, as a kind of financial asset fortified by political promises and backed by the wealth of a nation provides us with a non-Mengerian yet substantially material account of money's value.

But further, following the logic of the survival constraint, we can read exchange itself in a materialist register. Weber is also impugned by Ingham when the former invokes the means of exchange dimension of money in trying to account for its purchasing power. Here is the full Weber quote that Ingham amends (in Ingham, 2004, p. 67):

However, it is not merely a matter of dealing with existing debts, but also with exchange in the present and the contraction of new debts to be paid in the future. But in this connection the orientation of the parties is primarily to the status of money *as a means of exchange* and thus to the probability that it will be at some future time *acceptable* in exchange for specified or unspecified goods in price relationships which are capable of approximate estimate. (Weber, 1978, p. 169, emphasis added)

Given the somewhat narrowed definition of materialism that Ingham is operating with, he reads the aforementioned move as Weber 'following economic orthodoxy' (Ingham, 2004, p. 67)—that is, resorting to exchange or the market as the source of money's value rather than reading Weber as invoking the material and political attributes of acceptance (Chapter 3).

Recall that in *both* the valuableness and substantive value dimensions, it is money as *a means of payment*, a means of final (debt) settlement, that is determinative for Ingham (2018). Weber fully agrees with Knapp and by extension Ingham that 'formal validity' or valuableness is indeed nominalist in its essence. 'But,' cautions Weber, 'naturally this formal power implies nothing as to the *substantive* [*sic*] validity of money; that is, the rate at which it will be *accepted in exchange* for commodities' (Weber, 1978, p. 178, emphasis added). Invoking exchange is where Weber lapses into orthodoxy, as per Ingham.

In a sense, this revolves around the theoretical status of 'exchange'. To admit to the importance of exchange, namely money's value, would, for Ingham, let the Mengerians into the gate. Yet this is to throw the material baby out with the Mengerian bathwater as it denies the fact that exchange itself is an eminently material process: this is the very basis of the survival constraint.

The exchange of rights over goods and services is after all *the* alternative to violence: we can either exchange things with each other or violently appropriate them (or, capitalism's genius per Marx, appropriate through superficially equal yet structurally violent exchange). Exchange indexes acceptability and is therefore the obverse of violence which of course implies the absence of acceptance.

Following Durkheim (2014 [1893]), we might read our very material existence as definitionally incomplete and fragile monads coming together in a socio-material division of labour. Exchange, whether mediated by the market or by social relations more directly, is a critical element of the materiality of social life. To abandon the exchange to the Mengerians is to cede too much ground.

Some Chartalists take on this Durkheimian–material dimension explicitly. Thus, Aglietta's (2018) particular version of Chartalism might be given this reading since the primordial debt we all have is 'social debt'—that is, debt to the social division of labour of which tax is merely a fiscal expression. But again, rather than taking the somewhat metaphysical rendering it does in Aglietta, we can see that the material and the social are two sides of the same phenomenon: the *social* division of labour with 'social' now given a fully materialist predication.

Our real historical division of labour has never quite hewed to the image of autarky that lurks beneath the surface of much Chartalism: exchange, often over long distances, has been the anthropological universal. This sense of autarky is surprising since for both Knapp and Weber, a critical element in establishing the substantive value of any particular money is its policy-driven fixing to the value of *foreign* exchange.

The international domain marks the limit point of the nominalist power of the state where, by definition, violence (actual or formal) breaks out of its domestically institutionalised amber. This is an example of a more general point: the state's autonomous power is limited both internally and externally, albeit to different degrees. Where state violence finds its limit, as it must at some point, exchange is required, either of the (internal) political kind or of the (external) economic kind or various combinations thereof. 'Acceptability' can and must be read as both a political and economic variable.

As such, Weber's invocation of the link between the substantive value of money and its stabilisation with FX is by no means a resort to economic orthodoxy but again to struggle between various groups. It is entirely of a piece with his view that battles of competing interests drive monetary policy and thus the value (price) of money:

> Among the interests determining such policy [pegging domestic money to foreign money] are those of prestige and political power. But on the economic side, the decisive ones are financial interest, with particular reference to future foreign loans, and other very powerful business interests, notably of importers and of industries which have to use raw materials from abroad. Finally, the interests as consumers of those elements in the population which purchase imported goods are involved. Today there can be no doubt that 'lytric' policy is in fact primarily concerned with regulation of the foreign exchanges. (Weber, 1978, p. 179)

Ingham's austere nominalism, as with all Chartalists, including its latest 'MMT' incarnation, always has an autarkic sensibility: the international field is rarely mentioned, a luxury perhaps for those sitting at the current and former centres of empire. Yet the economy, any economy, is a complex division of labour which *always* has branches extending beyond political frontiers. Certain domestic interest groups take up positions in those branches and are therefore keen to ensure the acceptability of their nation's money abroad. This, for Weber, is how the gold standard was established: England went on it somewhat arbitrarily, but once it did its location at the imperial centre of a global division of labour impelled other nations to adopt the barbarous relic, not out of any fidelity to 'the real economy' (pace its ideologues) but out of the material requirement, imposed by the fact of exchange, of hierarchically arranged acceptability.

In the end, it comes down to which set of interests control which set of real resources. In order to prise those resources away from those who control them, either force or exchange (political or economic) is required. While this fact shows up most explicitly at the boundaries of nations, it applies equally in form and to a lesser extent in substance domestically in institutionalised political and economic contracts. To say this is merely to extend Ingham's own work which is unmatched in its telling of this story as it played out in the rise of capitalism in early modern England.

Ingham might well retort that this is precisely what is meant by a sociological understanding of 'the battle of man with man' as determining the value of money: the political balance of power always already mediates the material control of things. Quite so, but then this should include the social process of exchange. The creeping subsumption of the sociopolitical dimension over the material is unwarranted. The way is open to combine the political, nominal and material dimensions in an account of the ontology of money along with the variable value of different monies.

Coherence with Output

The institutionalist predicate means that each economy has its own 'laws' of social physics: the view from nowhere sees precious little. We ought to perhaps read the classical economists as propounding provincial theories for their types of economies—theories we continue to learn from methodologically. The historical and probabilistic nature of its 'laws' is what makes political economy a distinct kind of science. 'Economic systems are not natural systems' (Minsky, 1986, p. 7).

Minsky was an arch-proponent of such a science, able to see both the historical and the abstract in equal measure. Given his institutionalist background, Minsky came up with regularities for 'our type of economy', namely an economy in which extremely expensive capital assets are privately owned and advanced production takes a long time and must be financed during that period. Such a system would be inherently, not incidentally, unstable: 'Paradoxically, capitalism is flawed precisely because it cannot readily assimilate production processes that use large-scale capital assets' (ibid., p. 6).

A quick glance at Minsky's ideas can help us think about the relationship between the money and the material dimension. Minsky's understanding of instability is predicated on two interacting dimensions: finance and production. Being inspired by institutionalism, his vision has more than enough bandwidth to accommodate the political ontology of institutions with all their dynamism even while maintaining that the material has its own dynamic attributes: 'Institutions are both legislated and the result of evolutionary processes. Once legislated, institutions take on a life of their own and evolve in response to market processes' (ibid., p. 7).

For our purposes here, whether we agree or not with Minsky's particular conclusions is secondary. What is critical is that Minsky provides methodological inspiration for an integrative social science, political economy, wherein each dimension of social reality is brought to bear on an understanding of complex social phenomena. In particular, he points to an integration of 'money' and 'value' that respects the sociopolitical ontology of institutions even while enabling us to account for the material dimension.

Minsky starts with the straightforward premise that capitalism entails people investing in capital assets used in production processes because they expect a future return. This might sound like a simple rendition of M-C-M', but unlike with Marx and the classicals, the futural element is absolutely central and not merely 'fictitious'. M-C happens now; C-M' happens later, maybe. In this sense, all economic life is literally 'speculative', a description that now loses its pejorative connotations and merely means 'futural'. This does not make it any less materialist. We can be materialists without being dead-labour-time essentialists.

Futurity is why the financial dimension is inextricable from 'real' investment: 'An investment is like a bond; it is a money-now-for-money-later exchange' (ibid., p. 192). Capitalism is 'financial' in its inner logic because that logic is temporal, making 'real' investment logically congruent with the financial transaction of buying a bond. Identifying this financial logic of real investment does not mean escaping the reality of material productivity or invoking financialisation qua dematerialisation. But it does mean that notions of neutrality, of money being merely a veil, of credit being definitionally fictitious are dispensed with.

Investment in production takes time to yield its fruits, and while it is 'gestating', owners, suppliers and workers need to be paid in liquid means of payment. Our initial M therefore has to be either accumulated over time (savings) or raised by some means (borrowing), and it has to be of sufficient magnitude to see us through to the end of the production and subsequent sale (C-M'). Typically, we find some combination of savings and borrowing fuelling investment, so all investment plans will perforce generate relations of credit and debt.

Marx found a way around this requirement for substantial upfront M by pointing to the original sin of primitive accumulation. His point stands, of course, both historically and as applied to the expanding boundaries of the current system. But that should not distract us from the system's daily metabolism, especially when financing production processes with long gestation periods. Once the system is up and running, the necessary obverse of 'real' investment is a financial contract. As Minsky says, 'A decision to invest—to acquire capital assets—is always a decision about a liability structure' (ibid.).

Breaking with ideas of functional circularity or efficacious tautologies, Minsky makes clear that while debits and credits might be two sides of the same coin within a financial system, the interlocking complexity of such a system cannot be stable unless financial flows are 'validated' by returns from non-financial investment. At bottom:

> [a]n owner of capital assets has a special contingent contract with nature or the economy, a contract stating that money (profits) will be forthcoming to the capital assets depending upon how well the firm does, which in turn depends upon how well the industry and the economy do. (Ibid., emphasis added)

This is not to say that *only* flows from 'nature' can validate the liability structures of the past—far from it. But it is to say that there is a gearing or 'coherence' of the financial and real output that is mediated by the credit system:

> Thus, a complex network of cash flows due to contractual relations exists side by side and intertwined with the network of cash flows resulting from the production and distribution of current output. (Ibid., p. 195)

Uncovering the nature of this evolving complexity in different, nested global–local weather systems is the ongoing work of political economy. In the Anglo-American context of the mid-twentieth century, Minsky documented how the behaviour of firms requiring long-term external finance and portfolio managers providing that finance would interact to produce an endogenously unstable economy.

Whether we agree with his account or not, Minsky shows us that one does not have to be reductive or orthodox to invoke material output as one amongst several key factors determining the value of monetary flows and monetary (dis)order more generally.

The only way to really escape the survival constraint for society at large is more material production. Recall the survival constraint: in order to survive, all economic units under capitalism must be able to force a positive cash flow in their direction. As we have seen, a capital asset is nothing but a set of property rights to a stream of such future flows. Reading Minsky, and updating the classical dichotomy, Mehrling notes:

Capital assets come in two types, financial and non-financial. Financial assets are two-sided, the sense that they represent future cash outflows to the debtor and future cash inflows to the creditor. *Non-financial assets are one-sided since the 'debtor' who commits to pay cash flows is not any other economic unit, but rather nature, or the production process, or some such.*

[U]nits issue financial assets to trade future cash flows, but, and this is the crucial point for Minsky, such borrowing does *not* [*sic*] relax the survival constraint for society as a whole. Because of their two-sided character, financial assets can only transfer the constraint from one economic unit to another. *The only way for society as a whole to relax the survival constraint is to create new non-financial assets by means of investment.* (Mehrling, 2000c, p. 82, emphasis added)

A decision to invest is a decision about a liability structure: this is true for both individuals and society as a whole. Some bets pay off while others fail; if too many fail, then the system's coherence is undone and we have a financial crisis. While collectively engaging in credit allows us to reach beyond the limits set by past accumulation, the collective credit-reaching sets some constraints on economic life in the direction of the complex pattern of credit commitments. As Mehrling memorably writes, 'the veil of money is the very fabric of the modern economy' (Mehrling, 1999, p. 138).

A hierarchical credit system, formatted as a money market in contemporary Anglo-American economies, is the place where competing visions of the future are ultimately tested and priced. If too many errors accumulate in the system, the system has a 'heart attack', namely a credit crisis. All complex systems are subject to entropy, all require an occasional 'reboot' or bailout. How this technical requirement is executed is a matter of political balance.

This is coherence—the complex, unstable, political relationship between the monetary and the material. Read through the prism of the political ontology of institutions—implicit in both American Institutionalists Minsky and Mehrling—coherence can be amplified or dampened depending on how the balance of political forces plays out in the design and construction of the monetary system. The dimension of political ontology is sui generis but not foundational. Indeed, foundationalism of any kind is an error.

'Happy' consilience of forces, political and economic, leads to capitalism of rude health expressed as a monetary unit of robust substantive value; an unhappy conjuncture of forces leads to poverty and imperialist subjugation.

Political struggles can either amplify or dampen these inherent, entropic tendencies. But whether we buy this account or not, note that there is a source of monetary (dis)order that is relatively autonomous from political conflict per se. This source, the relative coherence of the financial and non-financial balance sheets, is not reducible to an 'internal' political conflict.

Institutions Bind the Future (or Not)

'Money' as a legal contract is a compound of two elements: the first is the sovereign or collective promise locked into the second element, namely a productive, value-creating economy. Both elements are necessary, and neither by itself is sufficient to generate high-quality money. Variation on both dimensions gives us money of varying value.

A thick set of legal institutions are required to bind money to value, but these institutions develop in uneven and discontinuous ways over time and space. In the meantime, actual skeins of 'value' had to make an appearance along with the money contract itself in order to achieve coherence with the real economy. This is one way to read the history of metallic money—namely as the inverse of thick institutional development.

Keynes famously called the Indian rupee 'a note printed on silver'. The divergence between the value of the metallic content and the substantive value of the money instrument referenced both the accumulated value dimension represented by the metallic collateral along with the anticipated value with the nominalist element folded in as well.

The presence or absence of metallic collateral in the money instrument was therefore an index of the intensiveness of the institutional binding of money to value. The more effective that binding or 'security' is, the less material collateral was required to be carried around with the credit note and vice versa. At the boundaries of nations where the domestic institutional development was the thinnest, the balance between the contractual or the futural and the metallic or the anterior lent decidedly to the latter. As transnational, imperial relations encircled the globe, the institutions of empire themselves anchored credit expansion across borders, enabling, for example, British pensioners in the nineteenth century to invest in railway bonds in faraway India and Latin America. The best way to deal with 'sovereign risk' is to eliminate the sovereign.

The denser and more extensive the institutional binding to value, securely anchoring the money contract in the future, the freer money was to operate apart from its brute-metallic collateral companion. This institutional binding is the functional equivalent of metallic content qua collateral because it enables the national economy itself to function as the reserve asset of the economy rather than gold reserves. Gold was the liquid tip of the GDP iceberg; political and economic contracts reach much further with greater flexibility than gold.

Most of the time, however, this operation *fails*: robustly institutionalised capitalism is far from evenly spread across the globe, even though the entire globe is unevenly integrated in its brutal division of labour. Mapping politics onto production to devastating effect, the early modern fiscal-military state saw one corner of the planet subsume the rest. This imperial effort took more than the mere issuance of credit notes, but it would have been unthinkable without it.

Credit is *pharmakon*, both remedy and poison. It is the remedy that allows a collective to give form to the future void but poison when we collectively abuse its alchemical potentiality. We need to grasp both these aspects of money if we are to appreciate its relative and probabilistic relationship to value.

PART II

8 | NATIONAL MONEY VERSUS SHADOW BANKING

Contradictions of a Public–Private Credit System

National money is a credit instrument issued by the state's bank, the central bank: money has everywhere been nationalised. However, in rich nations, the institutions that actually issue day-to-day credit remain private, for-profit banks. This contingent nesting of *private* banking within *national* money creates hybrid and potentially contradictory phenomena as public credit and private interest clash. This hybrid hierarchy is contingent, expressing a local political settlement. A conflict between private profit and public good is baked into such hybrid systems, the political settlement modulating the antagonists.

This chapter outlines some of the dynamics and contradictions of a hybrid credit system in the abstract and then illustrates how this logic has played out in the development of the post-war American system. In America, hybridity and marketisation combine to amplify the inherent instability of credit. While banks share the exorbitant privilege of 'issuing money', they are disciplined by the par constraint. Qualitative differences in public–private robustness are papered over by central-bank control mechanisms: bank regulation, deposit insurance, LOLR and bailouts.

The political settlement determines whether the central bank sets these mechanisms for elasticity or discipline. We read the development of American shadow banking as an instantiation of neoliberalism, the prevailing political settlement. Shadow banking developed through a contingent conjuncture of long-term marketisation processes, first of liabilities (*c.* 1960) and then assets (*c.* 1980). This confluence metastasised private money markets which dangerously amplified the inherent instability of the hybrid system.

There is nothing 'essential' about this hybrid nature of modern money and its attendant institutions (pace Mehrling, 2013). Hybridity between public and private banking is a contingent historical and political fact. It only appears essential, arguably because this particular formation, having grown up with capitalism itself in early modern Europe (Ingham, 2004), is now globally hegemonic and therefore naturalised.

India and China, between them half the world's population, have nationalised both money and banking. These systems have their own specific set of contradictions. They are themselves hybrids of political and economic mutualisation, a form of hybridity that is in fact essential and compatible with different formal ownership structures (see Chapter 1).

All credit systems are inherently unstable, but the profit motive amplifies instability because it incentivises banks into 'procyclical' behaviour, making both booms and busts bigger than they would otherwise be. Yet money is also inherently hierarchical. A combination of hierarchy and instability leads to a constitutive tension within public–private hybrid systems: the tendency for unstable private expansion at the capillaries is pitted against the attempt at public control of unstable expansion at the system's apex.

This tension between expansion and control coincides with a contradiction between the public interest and the money interest given that the apex of the system is formed by national money. Control or discipline therefore becomes a function of the political equilibrium between the money interest and the public interest. Stability in credit comes from a balanced political equilibrium, whereas an unstable expansion in credit is the result of an equilibrium in favour of the money interest. Given that this was occurring in the world's largest economy and issuer of world money, local political settlements had global implications.

In the inherent struggle between control and expansion, the American system evolved in a particular direction. The logic of private credit creation within a nationalised shell remained, but public-minded control was undermined by a particular form of marketisation. With control no longer suppressing the system's in-built contradictions, they stood exposed. In the absence of robust control, a hybrid credit system becomes an engine for moral hazard: private banking takes the gains of expansion, but the state picks up the pieces when the bubble bursts. The perverse incentives of bailouts and 'too big to fail' were not novelties; the Credit Crisis of 2007 merely saw an older tendency raised to a new scale.

The first section of this chapter considers the hybrid nature of these systems as a structural matter. The two historical sections trace the development of the post-war US financial system through the lens of the system's contradictions. The shadow banking system was the result of a two-stage revolution, one on each side of the balance sheet. The revolution on the liabilities side of the system's balance sheet gets special attention as this relatively early development is under-appreciated in the literature on the crisis. The confluence of developments on both sides of the balance sheet meant that the inherently fragile nature of any credit system and the specifically fragile nature of hybrid credit systems were amplified out of all proportion.

Hybrid Credit Systems: Instability, Hierarchy, Control

Building on the Banking School and informed by American institutionalism, Minsky evolved a hypermodern vision of interacting balance sheets of economic units contracting together to project credit into an inherently uncertain future. This projection of credit generates an interlocking network of financial claims and counterclaims stretching into the future, both alleviating insecurity and constraining micro and macro behaviour in the direction of the structure of these claims (Mehrling, 1999). Mehrling built on this to outline how such credit systems are inherently hierarchical, how specific institutions emerge between layers of hierarchy to make qualitatively different credit instruments commensurable and how the logic of these market-making institutions can be used for system control (Mehrling, 2012a). We have accounted for the sources of hierarchy earlier. Hierarchy affords opportunities for control.

Instability, hierarchy and control are abstract features of all credit systems. Politics 'chooses' the actual from this space of the possible, giving abstract features concrete shape at any conjuncture. But the constitutive power of politics is constrained by the abstract properties of credit systems; the political settlement can configure the properties but not eliminate them.

Private banks have an incentive to expand credit, the source of their profit. Credit is extended into an inherently uncertain future, so some portion of all credit decisions will definitely fail. However, the claims these bad loans generate do not evaporate; they form part of the interlocking credit structures that bind an economy together. As such errors accumulate, the system evolves from robust to fragile if the cash commitments of a large enough number of units outstrip their cash inflow—Minsky's now-famous financial instability hypothesis (Minsky, 1992).

Private Money and the Par Constraint

In hybrid systems, private banking is the capillary level while state banking forms the mainline trunk. But even though users interact with the capillary level more, the fetish of fiat money makes them experience banks as fiat-money intermediaries rather than bank-money creators (Chapter 2). The hypertrophy of the bank-money level *was* the shadow banking system.

As we saw in Chapter 2, we can understand such a system by imagining a situation where purely private banks each issue their own credit money alongside a central bank. We would have Citibank dollars, JPMorgan Chase dollars, and so on, alongside Federal Reserve dollars. An 'exchange rate' would emerge between public and private dollars reflecting the relative creditworthiness of the issuing banks much like the market for international currencies today. The relative degrees of risk in each IOU would be fully visible as these exchange rates bounced around.

Hybrid credit systems are very much like this hypothetical system with one critical difference: the 'exchange rate' between private and public dollars is fixed by law at 1, 'par' (Mehrling, 2000a). Volatility and relative creditworthiness are not therefore reflected in the exchange rate but on the bank's fluctuating balance-sheet value. Banks can go ahead and issue their own money (create checking accounts when making loans) subject to the constraint that their private money trades *at par* with the public dollar at all times.

Again, it takes a system to achieve this equivocation; it can be so successful that the private element can disappear behind the fetish of fiat. Private-bank money is both denominated and measured in the state's unit of account and a promise to pay public dollars at par. This concealment of the settlement instrument that liquidates the bank-money promise and the par constraint together paper over the public–private hybrid nature of such credit systems.

In a hybrid system, a freshly created private dollar can be exchanged at par on demand with public dollars by the loan recipient when they seek to make a cash withdrawal. Central banks can choose the price at which they accommodate this expansion of private or inside money since bank IOUs are promises to pay outside or central-bank money.

In our hypothetical private system, central-bank money would have a fair value higher than commercial-bank money; the ratio of the latter to the former would be less than 1 reflecting the greater creditworthiness of central-bank money. Fixing the 'exchange rate' price at 1 therefore over-values commercial bank money and thereby places pressure on banks to act in risk-averse ways in order to achieve a higher than politically mutualised creditworthiness for its IOU. On the other hand, banks like the ability to borrow money at cheaper rates given that their liabilities are conflated with that of the central bank. As such, this fixing also generates incentives for banks to expand on the back of the state's liability.

In the hybrid system, we cannot directly observe fluctuation in price between private and public dollars, but we can calculate a kind of shadow private dollar price by observing any particular bank's balance sheet. The value of such shadow private dollars would fluctuate on the balance sheet of the bank rather than in a directly observable exchange rate. This fluctuation becomes observable in extreme cases when a bank goes out of business: depositors of an insolvent bank might get only a few cents per dollar deposited.

A similar logic operates with money market mutual funds in the shadow banking system that offer investors 'deposits' at a USD 1 NAV, equivocating between units in the fund and the means of payment, national money; fund holders can write a limited number of cheques against their account, furthering the equivocation. The flowering of money market mutual funds can be read as the hypertrophy of private banking in hybrid systems.

Control Mechanisms and Their Politics

In a hybrid system, private, profit-driven entities have been given the qualified right to coin money: banks' short-term, highly liquid liabilities are freely exchangeable at par for the coin of the realm. They are as a result subject to a rigorous survival constraint, but their embedding in a hierarchical system of liquidity provisioning enables them to meet it.

There is a deep and obvious conflict here between the money interest and public interest that sets expansion against control. Control mechanisms emerge to deal with this conflict, and their configuration is naturally the subject of a political struggle. Political struggle determines how the system is configured, and system configuration drives system dynamics: stability, growth, crisis.

Competition drives private banks to seek the illiquid edge and to try and slip out of their state-imposed constraints that are costs on their businesses. Private banks therefore face perverse incentives. While their liabilities can be exchanged for those of the state's bank, their profits are their shareholders' alone. Further, a risk to one bank might create a panic that could spread to the whole payment system, creating externalities and systemic risks. Banks pool together in hierarchical systems for payments scale and to ensure access to liquidity, but this very act of pooling creates a system that, because it endogenously creates the very lifeblood of the economy, is a public utility.

Given such conflicts, it is a wonder that banks can be privately owned at all. Nationalisation would hardly be a panacea, but it would generate a smaller set of problems (see Chapter 12). That banks can still be private is testament to the nature of the balance of power between the money interest and public interest in rich nations.

To contain inherent conflicts of interest as well as inherent instability, a system of controls has evolved over a series of crises to contain the private element. Broadly, there are price-based controls (monetary policy), non-price-based controls (banking regulation) and emergency refinance controls (LOLR).

Each of these control mechanisms can be calibrated for elasticity or discipline in the issuance of credit. Each of these controls is therefore subject to substantial political heat. This never-ending game of cat and mouse between the money interest and the public interest might be run through the arcane details of banking technocracy, but it is a political game of the highest stakes. The balance between public and private is by no means given in advance. It is constantly fought over, creating cycles of 'financial innovation' and advances in controls, whether market or non-market based.

In the US context, while the balance of power favours the money interest, the public interest imposed a kind of indirect, structural pressure on credit-system control that perversely leads to instability. This is especially true of an enforced gradualism in raising interest rates to cool off an expanded credit system. The central bank has to raise rates only gradually, else it risks crashing the economy—something populist democracy cannot sustain. Thus, certain of the central bank's gradualism, private money markets with access to liquid funds, often global, can continue to expand their balance sheets so long as their rates of return are above the central bank's cost of borrowing. A central bank committed to gradualism in rate hikes thereby accentuates a bubble, the opposite of its intention. We take up the implications of this dynamic for finance and democracy in Chapter 12.

The next section attempts to understand how the post-war political equilibrium in the US expressed itself through the evolution of its credit system. We run through alternating revolutions on the asset and liabilities sides of the balance sheet that changed the balance of public and private power in the monetary system and thereby substantially altered system dynamics.

The Liabilities-Side Revolution: From War Finance to the Market, c. 1945–1980

A credit system configured for financing war could not sustain the post-war boom, but balance of politics ensured that the transformation took the form of a money-interest friendly marketisation—that is, replacing institutional relationships with market-based ones configured over time for elasticity. These were asynchronous revolutions, the liabilities side transforming well before the asset side: all instruments used to borrow money in the 2007–2008 Credit Crisis were in place by the end of the 1960s. Securitisation of assets, uses of funds, took longer even though they got a start in the 1970s.

A prelude to the marketisation battles started immediately after the war. During the world wars, the entire credit system was directed towards funding war (Mehrling, 2011; Konings, 2011). While the liability side remained deposit based, the asset side was dominated by government paper; treasuries flooded the books of banks and thrift institutions that had concentrated on mortgage lending. The Fed sacrificed its independence to support the secondary market for Victory and Liberty bonds. Interest rates across the board were controlled.

Ironically, the sheer homogeneity in terms of credit risk of the system's asset base meant that the Fed's collateral policy (what quality of paper it accepted from banks at the discount window) no longer had traction. It therefore started to undertake direct open *market* operations (Mehrling, 2010). Control under conditions of asset homogeneity meant market-based control. War had shifted an intimate relationship between the Fed and its member banks to one based on market interactions involving only arm's-length dealings in government paper (Minsky, 1986, pp. 46–48).

To exit this wartime arrangement, the Fed sought to develop the private-dealer system in government paper. Thus, while market-based control was initially geared to democratic ends, it was gradually turned in another direction. The 'bills only' policy of Fed chairman William McChesney Martin Jr sought to tie the Fed's hands by limiting its operations to the short end of the maturity spectrum; this was designed to make space for the money interest.

There is nothing inherently undemocratic in market-based controls. Yet this process of configuring market-based control was explicitly politicised: Martin expressed a resurgent view that the government had no business in operating across the yield curve; it should limit its operations to the bare minimum short end, leaving the private market to handle the rest. His opponent at the Federal Reserve Bank of New York, Allan Sproul, railed against the establishment of a 'constitution' that would artificially tie the hands of the Fed and cede control to the money interest. The locus of monetary control was shifting to the money interest along the marketised tracks laid down by the Fed itself. Sproul was clear on where the neoliberal ideas were coming from:

> This is a legacy, perhaps, of a fundamentalist religious slant as bent and twisted by the University of Chicago, but it is also a consequence of his having had no experience in a money market. (Sproul in Hetzel and Leach, 2001b, p. 61)

Martin won: today, the Fed deals with the primary dealers in the treasury repo market at the short end, and dealers transmit these prices throughout the system. With direct access to the Fed, the primary dealers form the ultimate liquidity backstop for the dealer system as a whole. These primary dealers were used in Fed rescue operations during the Credit Crisis, but they had to violate the Chicago-inspired constitution to do so by operating across the credit structure rather than bills only. The Fed then became the 'dealer of last resort' and implicitly (and partially) harked back to pre-war practice by diversifying the kind of instruments it would lend against in the crisis (Mehrling, 2011).

The Liabilities-Side Revolution

Back to the post-war period, just as the Fed was creating a private-dealer system for treasuries, a revolution was occurring on the liabilities side. Participating in the post-war boom had pushed banks up against controls on their sources of funds. Banks innovated around these to whittle away restrictions and source their liabilities from increasingly wholesale, and more febrile, markets. These wholesale liability innovations were certificates of deposit (CDs), the Eurodollar market, short-term commercial paper and repurchase orders or repos. Rather than contain this movement, the Fed accommodated it for fear of bank disintermediation.

Given the high level of their holdings in government securities, however, the banks faced a problem. Moving out of government paper would depress bond prices, leading to capital losses for the banks themselves. But the incentive was enough for the banks to take these losses. Between 1952 and 1960, government securities as a share of commercial banks' financial assets declined from 40 per cent to 26 per cent (Rodrigues, 1993, p. 40). Between 1960 and 1974, the share dropped to 11 per cent before starting to climb again. The figure was 15 per cent in 2018; today it stands at around 20 per cent (Federal Reserve, 2023).

Banks were locked into local deposit bases, and no time-deposit market had yet evolved at scale, so they had no other marginal source of funds. Indeed, as the boom of the 1950s proceeded and interest rates started to rise up to the limits set by law (Regulation Q), depositors started fleeing banks for direct investments in higher-yielding treasury paper in a process dubbed 'disintermediation' (Wojnilower, 1980).

This spurred the banks into an innovation that would signal the beginning of the structural shift on the liabilities side. In 1962, the first negotiable CD was created by the predecessor of today's Citibank. This was a large denomination liability that the banks used to borrow funds wholesale from large corporate clients. No longer constrained by small local deposit bases, banks could now begin to operate at a scale that their corporate clients, who were beginning to flower into multinationals, required. Another source of wholesale funds was the Eurodollar market, an offshore market for dollar deposits that had sprung up, with the blessing of the local authorities, in the City of London (Helleiner, 1996). Banks began to find funds in the wholesale dollar markets *outside* the jurisdiction of the Fed.

Added to the CD and the Eurodollar market, the repo—a loan structured as a market transaction, namely the simultaneous sale and repurchase ('repo') thus equivalent to a loan against collateral—became a major instrument of 'liability management' in the late 1960s. The Fed exempted such borrowing from reserve requirements (Stigum and Crescenzi, 2007, p. 536). Increasing interest rates led corporate treasurers to repos. Repos run directly to the Credit Crisis of 2007: money-market mutual funds would be big lenders in the repo market, holding over half a trillion dollars' worth by the time the financial crisis of 2008 hit (Gorton and Metrick, 2012; Tooze, 2018).

From Control to Mopping Up: The Emergence of 'Too Big to Fail'

If the Fed decided to make the fed funds more costly, banks would still have access to wholesale money and would accept higher interest rates if their expected profit margins remained. The seeds of 'upward instability' were sown much before any of the high-tech innovations we take to be definitional of contemporary finance occurred.

Short-term commercial paper was another innovation, bonds issued for shorter durations of 30 or 90 days. They were used by 'fringe banks', as Minsky called the shadow banks of his day, to finance themselves and move into evermore risky territory. Facilitating commercial paper, banks would offer these fringe-bank finance companies lines of credit as emergency backstops. So if the fringe bank could not roll over its commercial paper, it had an emergency line of credit with a Fed-regulated bank. This 'liquidity put' given to shadow banks by commercial banks persisted into the contemporary period and was critical in transmitting the Credit Crisis to the heart of the system.

As in the Credit Crisis, banks themselves functioned as LOLRs to this shadowy penumbra. This put the Fed on the hook. 'In effect, the Federal Reserve is the indirect lender of last resort to fringe banking institutions' (Minsky, 1986, p. 86). Banks encouraged thrifts, finance companies, real-estate investment trusts and insurance companies to purchase loans that the banks themselves could not or would not (Wojnilower, 1980, p. 286). Banks were pushing the shadow system to take on more risk while being hooked up to the ultimate source of emergency liquidity, the Fed. Yet the public interest was already losing its handle on the system. Heads—the banks win; tails—the Fed loses.

Demand-driven credit expansion pushed the economy upwards, often spilling over into inflation, with the Fed unable to adequately curtail the system. The unremitting populist political demand to keep the economy from anything but the slightest recession meant that macroeconomic control was increasingly a one-way bet, and the banks knew it.

As high as the Fed set rates, credit would continue to expand so long as Fed-controlled borrowing costs were below prospective gains. The smallest spread could be leveraged up with more borrowing. Rather than cooling the system down, raising rates *gradually* only drove the system to greater instability. The only way to control the system was to crash it with extreme rate hikes: 'There is no kill except overkill' (Wojnilower, 1980, p. 291, also pp. 323–324). This was ruled out politically, so an unstable gradualism was the net result of the prevailing democratic political settlement.

As inflation started to become an issue in the late 1960s, the Fed sought to tighten things up in the money market. But the system was so overexpanded that it was bound to crack somewhere. The weak link was the Penn Central Transport Company, which defaulted on its commercial paper in 1970. The Fed arranged for a lifeboat operation, and lines of credit were now formalised, but no substantial reform of the system took place. A precedent was set, solidified by the bailout of the Franklin National Bank, the twentieth largest bank at the time, in 1974.

The Fed was not only implicitly backstopping the CD market but the offshore Eurodollar market in London as well given Franklin National's operations there. When risky loans to developing nations exploded in 1982 with the Mexican default, the debt workout was also tantamount to a bailout, given the degree of US bank exposure to Mexican state debt. The trick was repeated with the huge Continental Illinois National Bank in 1984. 'Too big to fail' was becoming the Fed doctrine (Minsky, 1986, p. 59).

With control slipping, the Fed was moving from controlling bubbles ex ante to minimising the fallout ex post, an approach that was taken to new heights by Alan Greenspan and his infamous 'Greenspan put'. According to Greenspan, 'the Fed's declared policy prior to the subprime crisis was to "clean up the mess", that is, to mitigate the consequences of bursting bubbles rather than try to detect and prevent asset price bubbles' (Brunnermeier and Schnabel, 2016). This configuration of credit control only reflected growing financial power.

The deregulatory fervour of the 1980s meant that just as regulations needed to be beefed up and reconfigured thanks to growing system entropy, they were wound down. The thrift industry, faced with largely fixed-rate mortgages and escalating interest costs, had started its long, slow bleed and was the subject of several covert, overt and highly politicised bailouts, while banks started to fail at an alarming rate at the beginning of the decade. Allen Berger and colleagues estimate that, in the period between 1979 and 1994, the number of independent banks fell from 12,463 to 7,926, a decline of 36.4 per cent even while the assets of the industry grew at 23.4 per cent in that period (Berger et al., 1995, p. 67).

The banks' own inventions had come back to haunt them as marketised competition and deregulation of interstate banking laws, critical firewalls for system robustness, began to erode their depositor base (ibid., p. 179). As rates on treasury paper rose and disintermediation of both banks and thrifts proceeded, a new private shadow bank emerged, one that would play a central role on the Credit Crisis by synthesising both asset- and liability-side revolutions: the money-market mutual fund (Stigum and Crescenzi, 2007, p. 1099).

The Asset-Side Revolution: Securitisation and Shadow Banking, c. 1970–2007

The asset-side revolution started in the 1970s, although it only exploded once it went private and combined with the liabilities-side revolution outlined earlier. It started by marketing bank assets—loans.

To generate a loan, a regular bank ideally undertakes a long series of checks to ascertain the creditworthiness of the would-be borrower. The value of this asset is substantially based on the idiosyncratic information that the bank has privileged access to. Selling that loan asset to a third party is therefore difficult; no one other than the banker knows what it is really worth. Typical bank loans are therefore highly illegible assets and tend to sit on the books of the bank till they mature, with the secondary market for them being thin and illiquid.

All this changed with securitisation, which, starting in the early 1970s, began to homogenise the idiosyncrasies of mortgage loans in particular by putting borrowers through a standardised screening process. The output was a set of seemingly generic loan assets made legible by quantification through FICO credit scores (named after the Fair Isaac Corporation). Individually varied, these assets were thought to have actuarial properties when massed together in a way that lent themselves to pricing like any other fixed-income instrument.

The purpose was to give the qualified retail borrower access to the much larger pool of liquidity in the capital markets and therefore lower interest rates. For this to work, capital markets had to have an instrument asset that looked and felt like a bond. Small-ticket, idiosyncratic risks are not legible to global capital market operators, many of whom were, it eventually turned out, based in Europe (Tooze, 2018). Homogenisation was not a seamless process, and investors needed some assurance to get them to bite. So the Federal government wrapped the entire programme in a government guarantee, making qualified mortgage securities nearly as good as treasuries.

The government invented its own off-balance-sheet shadow bank for this purpose. The Federal National Mortgage Association, created in 1938, was converted into a private company in 1968. The market understood that Fannie Mae remained a government entity in all but name as reflected in the price of its bonds which traded at a small spread above treasury bonds (Hancock and Passmore, 2011).

Individual loans could now travel far from the originating bank. By the end of the 1990s, these techniques were applied to all kinds of loans, not just mortgages (Tett, 2009). This was securitisation: turning local, idiosyncratic bank assets into globally tradable securities.

Central to the 'minting process' (Carruthers and Stinchcombe, 1999) of formatting these idiosyncratic assets for broad circulation was the government insurance wrap. As with money, mortgage securitisation saw the state implicitly backing private liabilities. Being far more legible to investors than an individual's guarantee, the state's insurance enabled the mortgage securitisation process to expand to scale.

Like all subsequent securitisations, government securitisation worked by pooling 'prime' mortgages together on Fannie's asset side, funding the purchase of mortgages by issuing securities (bonds) that carried an implicit public insurance option. Since these mortgages were 'prime', this was considered a reasonable risk to make with taxpayer money.

A revolutionary technique had been invented and was quickly adapted by the private sector with two critical modifications: the securitisation apparatus expanded to 'sub-prime' mortgages and even further to all manner of receivables (credit cards, student loans, corporate debt), and *private* balance sheets supplied the insurance. Monoline insurers expanded from municipal bonds, and the world's largest insurer, the American International Group (AIG), entered the bond-insurance business. In a market-based credit system, insurance is a vital enabler of the commodification of idiosyncratic assets, but which balance sheet and on what terms insurance is provided determine system dynamics.

Where regular banks took on liquidity risk, interest rate risk and default risk as a bundle in the loan asset, shadow banks (outside but linked up to commercial banks) could peel off these risks as financial engineering had apparently made these risks priceable and thus commodifiable (Mehrling, 2012c). Innovations in financial engineering were thus a critical enabling condition of this market-based revolution. The commodification of these kinds of risk was critical in moving to a market-based credit system. Bond insurance took care of credit risk; interest rate swaps dealt with price risk.

The hardest thing to commodify was liquidity risk since that comes from acceptability of a balance sheet's IOUs: the private dealer system could manage this only up to a point at which the Fed had to become the 'dealer of last resort' (Mehrling, 2011). Where commodification found its limit, politics stepped in by compromising the LOLR by providing liquidity risk insurance was cheap enough for marketisation to grow unabated.

Confluence in the Shadows

These two revolutions came together when the banks, in their effort to compete with the money-market mutual funds, created off-balance-sheet (hence 'shadow') banks that used market-based funding to finance their securitised loan portfolios. Because they issued commercial paper, shadow banks had to have lines of credit from banks, their own liquidity backstops. This would come back to haunt banks: Citibank had to bail out its Special Investment Vehicles to the tune of USD 49 billion (Wighton, 2007).

Being a bank, a shadow bank borrows short with money-like liabilities and lends long. The difference is the *form* of the borrowing or lending and therefore its greater fragility (see Table 8.1). Shadow banks have only wholesale 'deposits', large amounts lent for very short periods, often overnight. While commercial banks did both retail and wholesale business, shadow banks were pure wholesale entities with 'liquidity put' links to commercial banks that sponsored them. These 'liquidity puts' meant that when the shadow system collapsed, it fell back onto the formal system which was now swamped (Pozsar et al., 2010).

The shadow banks depend on rolling over this debt just like a normal bank. With a normal bank, this rollover corresponds to a depositor's spending and saving. A shadow bank borrows from corporations, pension funds, sovereign wealth funds, and so on. Unlike retail depositors, these savers have no transactions motive to keep their money in shadow banks; they are merely looking for security and a steady return coupled with high liquidity (Pozsar, 2015). Their lending has to be explicitly rolled over in every period rather than the implicit rollover of depositors leaving their cash in the bank. As wholesale overnight loans come due, shadow banks have to borrow the money again for the entire duration of their long-term asset holdings.

Table 8.1 Parallel structures, transformed content

	Regular banks	Shadow banks
Liabilities (short-term borrowing)	**Retail deposits** Sticky checking and savings accounts	**Wholesale money market** Volatile repo, certificate of deposit (CD), Eurodollar, (AB*) commercial paper
Assets (long-term lending)	**Individual loans** Decommodified home, auto loans and business working capital	**Securitized loans** Commodified Mortgage-backed Securities and other ABS†

Sources of instability

	Regular banks	Shadow banks
Liquidity risk	**Depositor runs** Simultaneous call on all short-term deposit borrowing	**Failed borrowing rollover** Inability to borrow in the short-term money market
Solvency risk	**Non-performing loans** Loss accumulation gradually eroding capital	**Decreasing spread** No capital buffer, losses quickly threatening funding
Interest rate risk	**Increasing borrowing cost** Reigns in lending in a world of fixed lending rates	**Decreasing spread** Ramps up lending in a world of leveraged margins and populism

Note: *AB stands for asset-backed; †ABS stands for asset-backed security.

This is much more volatile than the already fragile retail bank. When depositors start to question a regular bank, they rush to withdraw: a bank run means depositors stop rolling over their loans. Similarly, when a shadow bank's repo or commercial paper counterparties start to question shadow banks, they will only roll over their loans at ever-increasing 'haircuts' or discounts to the value of the collateral, tantamount to a rate of interest. A spike in haircuts in the wholesale credit markets is the shadow banking system's version of a run (McCulley, 2007).

Marketisation and foreign competition undercut domestic banks, leading to the consolidation of a few diversified, interstate giants. Banks with assets over USD 100 billion dollars doubled their share of all banking industry assets between 1979 and 1994, from 9.4 per cent to 18.8 per cent (Berger et al., 1995, p. 67). Diversification led to the undoing and ultimately repealing of the Glass–Steagall legislation and the re-emergence of the 'universal bank' that combined commercial and investment banking.

The Tax Reform Act of 1986 made mortgage interest tax deductible, and the adjustable-rate mortgage shifted interest rate risk onto the borrower: these made housing a hot sector (Hester, 2008, p. 159). As the decrepit thrifts finally vacated this space, banks climbed aboard the securitisation bandwagon.

Banks could not compete with their completely deregulated shadowy counterparts and therefore increasingly morphed into them. Capital adequacy regulations, sanctified by the transnational Basel Accord in 1988, sought to peg things back, but all they merely succeeded was in driving business to off-balance-sheet entities: collateralized debt obligations, structured investment vehicles and a whole host of alphabet-soup shadow banks that had the basic structure illustrated earlier. The 'Greenspan put' exaggerated the system's expansionary bias. Driven on by a new pool of savings from the booming part of the developing world, the credit machine blew up the housing market.

With both wholesale liabilities and securitised assets, the shadow banks and marketised commercial banks represented the culmination, over fifty years, of different streams of financial development. They were still banks in their logic, borrowing short with liquid liabilities and lending long, but the form that this operation took was totally different; so was the politics.

By design, very little capital was held in reserve as this cost the banks. Restricted to a fixed ratio of capital to loans, banks can only issue more credit money (make more loans) if they raise more capital, an expensive, time-consuming process that dilutes ownership. This of course is the entire point of regulatory capital adequacy ratios. By moving risks into the shadows, marketisation increased bank leverage (loans as a multiple of the capital base), thereby increasing the risk for the entire system.

Market Design as Politics

Shadow banking enabled banks to get out of restrictive capital regulations, do more loan business and issue more credit money even while remaining protected by the state. This issuance of new credit money led to inflation not in everyday items but in asset prices, specifically houses.

An extra-legal, private expansion of bank money had occurred, inflating the private element of the hybrid credit system and stretching the outer-shell public system in ways that were not immediately obvious given the off-balance-sheet, shadowy nature of the expansion.

Once the bubble burst, the two systems, public and private, had to be brought back into some coherence but only by a massive expansion of the central bank's balance sheet. Partial economic collapse and substantial bailouts achieved some of this. The authorities had little choice but to bail out a substantial part of the shadow system lest a substantial part of the economy burn away. But this only further illustrates the contradictions of the hybrid credit system wherein the money interest can hold the public hostage.

It is important to note that the shift from a bank-based to a market-based credit system is not by itself destabilising: like any banking system, a market-based banking system is hierarchical and can therefore be managed 'on banking principles' (see Table 8.2). The American story, however, was one of markets specifically designed to evade controls set up for a bank-based system. Marketisation and regulatory evasion came to be synonymous, but they need not have been; politics made them so.

Table 8.2   Control politics: interest and configuration

Control mechanisms in regular and shadow banking systems	Public interest	Money interest
Price Regular: Interest rates Shadow: AAA CDS spreads	**Hike to stem bubbles** 'Lean against the wind'	**Set too cheap, cut to fuel bubbles** AIG, 'Greenspan put'
Non-price Regular: Institution focus Shadow: Instrument focus	**Strict regulation** Detailed knowledge of idiosyncratic risks	**Lax regulation** Generic knowledge despite opaque, off-balance-sheet risks
Lender of last resort Regular: Money market Shadow: Credit-risk market	**Bagehot Rule** Only the solvent banks saved by lending freely against quality collateral	**Capture** Lax collateral quality monitoring leading to extreme moral hazard

A key feature of the world of securitised banking from the mid-1980s was the decoupling of real sector inflation from financial inflation. Once the empire of cheap, high-saving labour in the Global South was brought online to defeat the workforce of the North, wage-push inflation ended. Northern incomes stagnated even as people worked harder while cheap South-sourced goods held prices down. Dubbed 'the Great Moderation' by economists, this pairing of growth and low inflation was erroneously heralded as a 'golden age' of central banking (King, 1999). In fact, a reordering of the global political economy was expressing itself in the price of world money.

The bubble in asset prices helped fund what remained of the welfare system in the North that was charged with taking the edge off neoliberal capitalism, 'privatised Keynesianism' (Crouch, 2011). Inflated house prices were critical to maintaining rising living standards of living in the context of wage stagnation. Wedded to an incorrect neoclassical model, central banks looked at prices rather than the money markets and did not view the credit-fuelled asset bubble as something to be corrected. Intellectual error and empire combined to aid the money interest.

Conclusion: Control Mechanisms for a Market-Based Credit System

This chapter has charted the rise of the shadow banking system as an institutionalised expression of political dominance by what the US once called the money interest (Mehrling, 1998). Contradictions of public–private hybrid, national money systems played out as an unregulated expansion of private credit money implicitly backed by the state.

Yet public-minded control mechanisms for a market-based credit system can be fabricated (Mehrling, 2012c). Indeed, control of the American system must now be market-based, given the current structure of the credit system combined with the political strength of financial capital. Even if the political settlement could bear bank nationalisation, which would be consistent with the public utility nature of banking, American banks have leaned well into the dealer logic giving the system a particular shape. Either control is configured for the system as it is or burned down and built anew, something politically and economically unviable. Fortunately, market-based control in the public interest is entirely possible.

The rationale for regulating banking emerges from the very public–private nature of rich-nation credit systems. A jerry-built system that sees nationalisation of money coupled with the privatisation of banking creates all kinds of perverse incentives, amplifying the inherent instability of credit while leaving the public balance sheet on the hook. If hybrid systems are to remain, if the profit-motive is to continue to operate in banking, then institutional methods have to be found to contain the inherent contradictions of the hybrid system.

This means configuring the control mechanisms for the system at hand. Table 8.3 summarises a potential set of control mechanisms that analogise control between bank-based and market-based systems, highlighting the key roles for insurance and credit markets.

Table 8.3   Control mechanisms for a market-based credit system

	Regular banks	Shadow banks
Price	**Short-term interest rates** Discount window, interbank borrowing rate (fed funds)	**Benchmark insurance rates** Market-making in credit default swaps
Non-price	**Bank regulation** On-site supervision, lending norms, capital requirements	**Off-balance-sheet supervision** Liquidity stress tests, counter-cyclical capital requirements
Lender of last resort	**Bagehot Rule** Lend freely at a penalty rate against the best collateral Backstop liquidity in banking and payments systems	**Mehrling Rule** Insure best assets freely at a penalty premium Backstop liquidity in wholesale credit risk markets

Yet markets are now global, and market-based control would have to contend with the global division of labour that sees a perverse situation in which developing nations with export surpluses recycle these surpluses into the government debt of developed nations. This 'saving glut' or 'great wall of money' was of course a major source of liquidity in the American credit system over the most recent past as global cash pools sought the safe havens of dollar repo markets, driving down interest rates and offering bubble-forming elasticity to the shadow banking system (Bernanke, 2005; Helleiner and Kirshner, 2014). Controlling global liquidity will require a coordinated global solution that will have to include capital controls (Chapter 9).

The hybridity of national money systems is an institutional expression of the political settlement that has been central to mature capitalism since the early modern period—namely that between the public interest and the money interest. As the state democratised, state credit became the people's credit; in this context, the money interest had all the more reason to capture the state. And so it did under the auspices of neoliberal thought.

There is no in-principle reason for marketisation to operate like this. Markets as institutions are subject to design. Modern finance is often thought of as a highly quantitative sport played by rocket scientists and other demigods. Yet for all its mathematical sophistication, the basic logic of finance is institutional, namely that of banking and credit. This chapter has attempted to argue against our received wisdom that the roots of the Credit Crisis lay in some over-fancy, quantitative wizardry. That certainly contributed, but the institutional story is the centrepiece.

The wholesaling and marketisation of funding can in principle be controlled by central-bank operations either through price-based or non-price control mechanisms. The entire success of neoliberalism as a paradigm, however, was to conflate marketisation with *diminishing* public control. If neoliberalism is a method of doing things with markets, then perhaps in the American context at least we all ought to be neoliberals now—methodological neoliberals batting for the public interest.

9 | A WORLD WITHOUT WORLD MONEY

Instead of the Federal Open-Market Committee ... we need an Atlantic Open-Market Committee.

—Kindleberger (2000 [1967])

The US credit system saw banks break out of public-minded control mechanisms; the inherent instability of credit was thereby amplified and crisis ensued. Control mechanisms have evolved precisely to configure the collective's exposure to the inherent instability of the credit system. Without them, the system is incomplete, unstable and tends to be undemocratic.

Yet at the global level, we have precisely such an incomplete, public–private-like hybrid system but without the attendant public element. The global system is therefore even more subject to capture and instability. The US' national-economy–central-bank complex acts as a 'private bank' in the world economy but *without* a corresponding global central bank given the absence of a world state. There are therefore no global mechanisms to control global credit. Central banks issuing their own liabilities are to the global economy what Citibank issuing its own money would be to a national economy. The last attempt to erect such a private money system detached from central-bank control, namely American shadow banking, ended in disaster. Yet this is the very nature of the global credit system.

Non-state global institutions, either global markets or the IMF, fail at issuing world money because they lack robust mutualisation at scale. We therefore have a dilemma: if a sovereign provides world money, it is difficult to discipline, seeding global risk. If a non-sovereign provides world money, it will not be credible: only (some) sovereigns can do this. Following Charles Kindleberger, we argue that the international community needs to invent forms of global, non-state political mutualisation that could underwrite the rough equivalent of domestic control mechanisms, contain the 'private bank' that is the American Fed and contain the global system's contradictions. Permanent swap lines between core central banks already point in that direction, but they are mere fire engines at this point, lacking countercyclical pressure on the Fed.

How do we provide the global public good of monetary governance without a world state? There is no 'world money', no single instrument whose reserve asset is the entire world economy because without a world state, there is no fiscal means to tap into the entire world economy in one go. We have instead a small set of *national* monies tethered to substantial national economies functioning as global means of payment. Global public governance of these public goods is a geopolitical issue to be sure, but it also requires a particular institutional imagination.

Since we cannot have a world state, global monetary control mechanisms cannot look like their nation-state counterparts. The problem of global monetary reform is therefore similar to that facing the EU: how to come up with non-nation-state equivalents of international monetary institutions (see Chapter 11)? The logic of a world without world money, we argue following Kindleberger, requires the *internationalisation* of the governance of the *national* currency that serves as the global reserve currency.

The debate around the future of the global reserve system in the field of the IPE tends to focus on discrete sources of monetary power: what ingredients go into making a national currency hegemonic? This literature focuses on listing the constituents of monetary power in the abstract and then auditing a currency as to their presence or likelihood (for example, Frankel, 1995, 2012; Helleiner and Kirshner, 2009). Benjamin Cohen summarises this approach: 'The principal qualities required for competitive success are familiar to specialists and hardly controversial. Both economic and political factors appear to be involved' (Cohen, 2015, p. 11).

The problem with the ingredients approach is that it takes the hierarchical structure of the system for granted. It assumes that there must be a currency hierarchy and then goes out and looks for its component parts. Such accounts of monetary hegemony are also somewhat tautological: descriptions of monetary power are sometimes framed as determinants. Are deep and liquid markets in a given currency and debt, for instance, a description of monetary power or an explanation for its emergence?

While all accounts of power arguably run this risk, constructing lists of determinants of hegemonic currency status runs the further risk of a kind of methodological econometrics, decomposing a complex system into discrete, measurable 'independent variables' rather than providing an account of why the system is structured as it is.

Why is the global reserve system hierarchical to begin with? Why does its hierarchical logic call for *nation states* to occupy the apex of the system rather than other kinds of institutions such as an international fund or clearing union? Why do private global markets trust a sovereign state's money? What do the answers to these questions tell us about the future direction of the system and possibilities for monetary reform?

This chapter tries to get at these questions by applying a political theory of money to the global reserve system. Money is credit; monetary power is therefore the structural or infrastructural power of being creditworthy. States backed by substantial economies have much better credit than non-states because they have the most substantial and secure value flow (taxes), and tax inflows in turn are secured by political contracts (Part I). However, substantial economies and well-articulated fiscal systems are necessary but not sufficient conditions for being globally creditworthy. A state must also configure its credit system to achieve this. Such configuration turns on the balance of monetary politics domestically. Domestic political contracts interact with the inherent instability of credit to generate monetary control mechanisms (Chapter 8). Systemic instability (Borio and Disyatat, 2011) emerges from the absence of a world-spanning political contract and resulting absence of global control mechanisms. Post-crisis reform proposals for the global reserve system that ignore the centrality of political contracting to robust credit or money provision are therefore a dead end.

Unlike the IPE literature, we start from a definition of *what money is*. By foregrounding the ontology of money as credit, we open up an inquiry into the politics of credit-providing institutions. Because the most robust political contracts on the planet are state-based, we underline the centrality of domestic politics to international monetary power. We do not assume international hierarchy; we account for it with a theory of money.

Several reform proposals that centre on the IMF's Special Drawing Rights (SDRs) are doomed to failure because they ignore the centrality of political contracting to credit robustness. Operations to internationalise *control* over the dollar in the spirit outlined by Kindleberger are more in tune with the system's logic but need to be taken further.

Domestic systems in rich nations are peculiar public–private hybrids with *nationalised money but private banking* (Chapter 8). Money is national, but credit creation occurs in a highly regulated private sector. But since money is credit, private banks have what almost amounts to an exorbitant privilege to issue 'money'. They are mandated to maintain par between their own liabilities and that of the central-bank money, but they are given substantial privileges such as access to central-bank backstops to make sure they operate within that constraint. The upshot is that hybrid monetary systems have private, profit-oriented balance sheets—the part—issuing credit for the whole. As we saw in the previous chapter, this disjuncture is fraught with a moral hazard that amplifies the inherently unstable, procyclical dynamics of the credit.

The part issues credit for the whole, but an institutional agent for the whole controls the part in the public interest. Political bargains are expressed in the configuration of control.

The global reserve system has an analogous disjuncture of the part issuing credit for the whole, whereby one nation's credit money is the global reserve asset. As Kindleberger noted, the hegemon functions as the world's bank, complete with the privilege of having its own liabilities function as world money. Yet the absence of a formal global political contract means the absence of the corresponding control mechanisms to contain this disjuncture.

From the point of view of the domestic system therefore the international system is radically incomplete, a monetary anarchy that amplifies moral hazard and inherent instability. This incompleteness and instability are perhaps one source of the chronic 'declinism' in conversations about the global reserve system (Kirshner, 2014, p. 1012). The system periodically appears fragile because it lacks the stabilising institutions that have evolved over centuries of crisis-bred trial and error at the domestic level.

The particular gearing of the global hierarchy of money—more or less imperial— will depend on specific, conjunctural elements, but it will always be a more or less benign *hierarchy* unless credit itself is superseded as money. Credit systems are inherently hierarchical, but that does not make them inherently unaccountable.

After a short review of the IPE literature, the chapter addresses the following aspects of the global reserve system: the fact that it is a *system*, the nature of international monetary power, system dynamics, the impossibility of non-state world money, the incipient internationalisation of the dollar and, finally, the role of China and its rising currency.

Bringing the System Back In

The global reserve system is just that—a *system* of interlocking balance sheets, public and private. A hierarchy of international money sees private balance sheets issuing their own liabilities denominated in the unit of the account or liabilities of the central banks of financially hegemonic states.

The pyramid expands and contracts with the credit cycle: when the pyramid is expanded, the world can look flatter as the difference between high- and low-risk bets attenuates; this is a cyclical phenomenon. In expanded periods, we indulge in speculating about the death of the state, the rise of non-state actors, globalisation, and so on.

As the cycle turns and the hierarchy steepens again, we witness a 'flight to quality' as 'safe havens' are just as sought after as 'yield' was in the upswing. Only the biggest balance sheets, those of hegemonic states, provide safety in such periods. The method of war finance takes hold and the 'independent', arm's-length relationship between the treasury and the central bank is obliterated, revealed as the cycle-bound contingency it is.

In a downcycle, we are all reminded of the nature of the relationship between the system's private and public components: private balance sheets expand and contract on a foundation laid by public balance sheets. The pillars of the global credit system are particular states.

Cohen insists on a systemic view when he highlights the 'macrofoundations' of monetary power, pointing to the 'distribution of the burden of adjustment to external imbalance' as a key systemic constraint (Cohen, 2006). All states are 'inescapably linked' through their balance of payments, the financial expression of a global division of labour; all trade nets to zero. Interdependence means distributing the costs of adjustment to trade imbalances.

But trade and production have to be financed, and this can happen either domestically or internationally depending on where financial power sits globally (Borio, 2016). In Minsky's terms, adjustment for trade and financial balances is about shifting around a national survival constraint, and this is a banking function.

Cohen's focus on 'power to delay' adjustment costs of trade imbalances chimes with Mehrling's vocabulary of elasticity and discipline that financially hegemonic states, as world banks, can grant or impose on other states. The power to delay is based on 'financial variables', so liquidity and creditworthiness are key.

Creditworthiness is the asymmetric ability of an institution to set the terms of borrowing or lending from or to less creditworthy balance sheets. It is an asymmetrical, 'structural power' that imparts discipline or grants elasticity of credit to other less creditworthy balance sheets (Strange, 1996). Creditworthiness is a definitionally asymmetrical attribute that makes all monetary systems *inherently hierarchical*. States sit atop domestic hierarchies, and the states of the largest economies with highly articulated credit systems dominated by a domestic money interest sit atop the international hierarchy.

So domestic interest groups are vital. As Cohen notes, the focus on domestic politics has been comparative, looking at how interest group politics translate into policy through parties, regimes and the electoral system (Cohen, 2015; see also Helleiner, 2008). Such considerations of the domestic political settlement are vital, but a financial elite needs to be in control of a substantial and robustly mutualised national balance sheet for a national currency to operate as world money. Luxembourg is not the City of London, nor is it Shanghai.

Domestic legitimacy is addressed by Leonard Seabrooke, who notes how buy-in from low-income groups helps 'broadening and deepening the domestic pool of capital' from which the state can draw international financial power (Seabrooke, 2006, p. 2). Helleiner observes that China's lack of legitimacy with lower-income groups would limit its currency's international role (Helleiner, 2008, p. 361). Yet legitimacy can be more than purely formal and function differently across the globe (Chapter 12).

The IPE has several pieces of the elephant, especially elite control over central banks, domestic legitimacy and some globally systemic elements. But without a supporting theory of money, the IPE ends up with descriptions of monetary power rather than a theory of the system, its characteristics and its dynamics. This will occupy the balance of the chapter.

A World without World Money

From the point of view of the domestic system, the international system is radically incomplete—a monetary anarchy akin to 'free banking' (Dowd, 2000; Goodhart, 1988). Like private banks issuing their own money, state-backed central banks issue competing liabilities at the global level—no control mechanisms, no stability and unaccountable hierarchy.

Hence, there were recurring post-war fears about the behaviour of the monetary hegemon, inaugurated by Robert Triffin and his dilemma: would the hegemon's and the world economy's interest converge, as to the timing and extent of liquidity provision (Triffin, 1960)? In our terms, this maps onto the disjuncture between the money interest (the hegemon) and the (global) public interest, a contradiction between part and whole.

Under the pre-war gold standard, exit from the hegemon's currency to the outside asset of gold disciplined the hegemon in theory. In practice, a political settlement that prioritised the money interest within the domestic sphere of the hegemon and empire abroad ensured that the discipline of gold was maintained (Polanyi, 2001 [1944]; de Cecco, 1975; Eichengreen, 2008). A combination of market scale and domestic and global geopolitical contracting made the system tick.

Once the political settlement within the hegemon shifted, the threat of exit to gold was no longer sufficient to discipline the system even in theory. It collapsed, only to be reconstructed on a foundation that radically controlled and insulated national markets (Ruggie, 1982).

The discipline of gold in the post-war period was really a proxy for the balance of power between states as well as between states and their own people. Gold was politics all the way down, a credit system configured for discipline that ended up failing to discipline the hegemon. Nostalgia for gold is perhaps displaced hope for discipline in a world of finance run amok.

In our contemporary, unipolar, neoliberal world, all counterbalances to American (monetary) power are enfeebled. Its domestic space sees the dominance of the money interest, while global unipolarity means neither geopolitical nor economic counterbalances are sufficient. A lack of exit options keeps things networked in place. Dollar hegemony seems like a stable equilibrium—hence the hegemon's destabilising indiscipline.

Yet all these features—neoliberalism, unipolarity, no exit—are conjunctural: they send monetary hegemony into overdrive, amplifying the already hierarchical and unstable fundamentals of the system. Rebalancing therefore would take the form of paring the system down to the minimal degree of hierarchy possible and then turning hierarchy into accountable leadership, no matter which nation is hegemonic.

Without a non-credit-based outside asset like gold, the international monetary system is now overtly governed by the balance of power—hence American monetary imperialism. The US has leaned in, weaponising a force of hierarchical circumstance. This is not at all to advocate for gold but for *discipline* for which gold was an extreme solution. Democracy means we need something short of the draconian discipline of gold, but we do need to discipline the monetary hegemon because they are issuing a global public good.

The Impossible Esperanto of World Money

The two single largest economic entities in the world are the US economy and the EU economy, representing roughly a quarter of the global GDP each. Yet these entities are not equal in terms of their ability to issue world money. The dollar is of course backed by a single, coordinated sovereign whose assets are the juggernaut of the US economy. A (still) robust political contract of taxation welds together state and economy. The EU, by contrast, has no singular, coordinated fiscal mechanism to tie the currency to the economy (Chapter 11). Hence, the euro is not world money on par with the dollar.

The incompleteness of the global system gives rise to recurring schemes to invent a non-national world money as an outside asset from the bancor to a BRICS (Brazil, Russia, India, China and South Africa) currency, synthetic currencies that would discipline the hegemon by offering an exit strategy. The post-crisis scenario was no exception (Ocampo, 2014; Stiglitz and Greenwald, 2010; Xiaochuan, 2009).

Any technical design proposal worth its salt has to deal with the force of circumstance of monetary systems, the hierarchical force of political contracting at scale. Non-national solutions to world money appear to be non-starters, given their absence of both robust political mutualisation and scale. Even highly engineered non-national yet political solutions such as the euro are not up to the task.

In a crisis, an LOLR needs to be able to *immediately* create near-unlimited, widely acceptable liquidity for it to be credible. The euro itself only has the qualified ability for such expansion (Tooze, 2018). This is perhaps the reason that Mario Draghi waited for the southern European economy to burn for some time before declaring that he would do 'whatever it takes' to save the euro. The problem had to shrink to a manageable scale lest the ECB itself be exposed (Chapter 11). The post-crisis Fed had no such concerns; that was a problem of capture, cognitive or otherwise.

This leads to the following dilemma in the global reserve system: if a sovereign provides the global reserve, that sovereign's fiscal and monetary behaviour is difficult to discipline, leading to a dynamically unstable provision of the global reserve. But if a non-sovereign provides the global reserve, the instrument will not be credible: only sovereigns have assets of the scale required for currency provision, all sovereigns are not created equal, and pretenders to hegemony require an appropriately configured fiscal–monetary machine.

Global synthetic currencies will not work. If discipline is sought, better to seek it directly by rebalancing sovereign power both from within and beyond the hegemon.

Kindleberger was of the same opinion. Recognising the irreducibility of hierarchy, he understood that the best that could be achieved was a benign form of hierarchy, what he called 'leadership' (Kindleberger, 1981).

A good liberal internationalist, Kindleberger posited that the path to discipline in a world of inside money was the *internationalisation* of parochial monetary control rather than the creation of a new currency top-down: '[t]he futility of a synthetic, deliberately created international medium of exchange is suggested by the analogy with Esperanto' (Kindleberger, 1967, p. 10). World money, for Kindleberger, needs to be anchored in 'the day-to-day life of the markets'. But the markets have voted for a state's money, so this money has to be globally regulated. A political theory of money tells us why a state's money was picked by the markets—robust mutualisation at scale.

The centrality of political contracting to creditworthiness and the absence of a global political contract mean the impossibility of world money—no world sovereign; no world money in the sense of a credit note backed by global fiscality. If sovereigns are going to rule global money, then monetary discipline will in many ways be reduced to old-fashioned balance of power. You cannot shoot your way to monetary power. Even that can only alter the global political settlement. Operationalising global monetary control would require globalising control of the dollar.

Empire as a Public Good: Varieties of Hierarchy

Hierarchy and dominance are not the same thing. Many man-made systems are both hierarchical and democratic—the judiciary, for instance (Goodhart and Meade, 2003). A range of possible 'global financial orders' (Drezner and McNamara, 2013) are therefore conceivable from despotic to democratic; it depends on politics.

Both Kindleberger-style and political approaches highlight the force of circumstance rather than a force of arms lying at the heart of the international monetary hierarchy. States weaponise this force of circumstance to maximise their own interests, sometimes using the force of arms to do so. Yet states cannot summon currency hegemony into being with pure coercion (although they might rebalance matters that way). Military might cannot replace the hard graft of creating a leviathan-scale political contract and then building the credit-system architecture required on top of that. There is no synthetic world-money design that gets us out of this foundational condition.

Yet there are varieties of hierarchy. Following Kindleberger, we can distinguish between narrowly self-regarding hegemonic behaviour and the willingness to provide global public goods. The best we can hope for is leadership: non-hierarchical arrangements are not available. The fact of hierarchy under conditions of anarchy means that the solution to imperialism is responsible, accountable leadership. This of course is the 'rules-based order' beloved of liberal internationalists. But to be consistent, it has to apply to the hegemon as well.

The absence of outside money amplifies the imperial tendency. Market 'vigilantes' attack peripheral economies by exiting to safer rich-nation assets further up the hierarchy. Having reached the top, there is nowhere to go. Economies at the top are immune to market discipline. This of course is another face of the hegemon's exorbitant, indeed imperial privilege (Panitch and Konings, 2008). Where there is no global outside asset, an asset that is not simultaneously some unit's liability, system discipline is explicitly political.

Without discipline, we have imperialism, a malign, unaccountable configuration where the hegemon leverages the technical fact of hierarchy and externalises costs to the rest of the system. This has been the experience under Bretton Woods II, a monetary regime that is virtually coterminous with aggressive US military action (Dooley, Landau and Garber, 2009). As we saw in Chapter 8, the configuration of the control mechanisms under Bretton Woods II was that US monetary policy was excessively loose, its domestic regulation too lax and its LOLR facility priced far too cheaply. The crisis could only occur under a specific, highly undisciplined global reserve system.

In pitching for leadership, Kindleberger drew the analogy that inspired this chapter, namely to the domestic scene. He pointed to the American situation at the founding of the Fed. Just as the nationalisation of monetary policy under the Fed saw a coming together of sub-national reserve banks into the Federal Reserve Board, so the global system must see an *internationalisation* of dollar policy in the context of a globalising economy: 'Instead of the Federal Open-Market Committee ... we need an Atlantic Open-Market Committee' (Kindleberger, 1967, p. 7).

Whether or not Kindleberger's well-intentioned liberal internationalism is politically viable is beside the point. The logic of hierarchy lays out, in the abstract, the possible set of configurations for a global monetary system under conditions of anarchy. Non-sovereigns are not credible, but hegemonic sovereigns can be undisciplined; this was Triffin's concern as it was Keynes'. Crisis after crisis elicits more central-bank coordination. We are, willy-nilly, being pushed down Kindleberger's road. Disciplining hierarchy means that international currency leadership is constrained to take the form of an internationalisation of control of the part that issues money for the whole.

In another one of Kindleberger's famous formulations, the US economy functions like a world bank, borrowing short through treasury-bill sales abroad and 'lending' long through foreign investments (Despres, Kindleberger and Salant, 1966; see also Gourinchas and Rey, 2005; Hardie and Maxfield, 2016; Hausmann and Sturzenegger, 2005). An internationalised open-market committee would take a call on the key spread of the US economy as a world bank. It is the US' currency, but the Fed is the world's bank, and any such national central bank would need to be governed as such. Empire can be a public good if appropriately configured.

Given that the history of monetary systems is one of crisis-borne evolution, it should come as no surprise that what we see in the wake of the most recent crisis is not the internationalisation of Kindleberger's ex-ante monetary-policy mechanism (this will perhaps come last) but the internationalisation of the ex-post LOLR function through the Fed's dollar swap lines.

The Internationalisation of the Dollar's LOLR Function

In the autumn of 2013, six rich-nation central banks announced that their emergency swap lines created in the wake of the financial crisis would now be converted into 'standing arrangements'—that is, made permanent (Federal Reserve Board, 2013; Mehrling, 2015). Here, we have the first glimpse of Kindleberger's world, the internationalisation of the key LOLR function.

The swap lines are a banking operation. The first leg of the transaction is borrowing one currency against the collateral of another, while the second leg returns the money or collateral and terminates the loan (Stigum and Crescenzi, 2007, pp. 904–906). The difference between the spot and forward rates amounts to an interest rate.

The Fed and the ECB threw together a swap line in the wake of the Credit Crisis to help haemorrhaging European banks who had loaded up on American mortgage assets denominated in dollars (Shin, 2012). When the Eurodollar market froze, European banks could no longer fund their major currency mismatch, having borrowed dollars with euros to buy dollar-denominated mortgage assets. Dollar markets were now closed to them (Baba, McCauley and Ramaswamy, 2009).

Dollars are outside money to European-domiciled banks, so they were indulging in a dangerous game by committing to pay them—a risk that was worth it given the US housing boom. But in the downturn, the ECB would be of no help to them as it cannot create dollars; obviously only the Fed can. The Fed for its part did not want to aggravate the run on the US mortgage market (Dudley, 2012). So the ECB turned to the Fed for a lifeboat operation, and the Fed obliged by reinstituting an old inter-central-bank mechanism. In the process, the ECB was positioned as a domestic franchise of the Fed just as Kindleberger had envisioned: 'In a way,' one European central banker remarked, 'we became the thirteenth Federal Reserve district' (Tooze, 2018).

The extension of this swap facility to other key-currency central banks formalises access to the Fed's backstop for those core economies one level down in the hierarchy. The *private* Eurodollar market, operating offshore in London, the lender of *first* resort for all international commercial transactions, was in effect being backstopped by the Fed (Bernes et al., 2014). Surplus and deficit balance sheets, both public and private, match up their borrowing or lending requirements in these London markets as a matter of course. When they break, international commerce and finance would come to a halt unless they are backstopped. A new layer of multicurrency mutualisation was enabled by the swap lines.

Part of the attraction of the dollar, of course, is that this central-bank backstop remains credible even when massively scaled up. So it proved during the Credit Crisis. The availability of a standing facility for key-currency central banks to borrow dollars in a pinch means that there is now an incipient *mutualisation of core central-bank balance sheets* that can generate fresh dollar reserves and convert them into all key currencies in a crisis as we saw in the Covid-19 crisis. This is the beginning of the internationalisation of the dollar's LOLR function, albeit without the required level of accountability.

The swap line has brought key-currency central banks together on asymmetric terms: these banks have to pay the Fed for the privilege of opening an account there, not vice versa (Federal Reserve Bank of New York, 2020). Yes, American interests were being protected, but the implicit recognition is that the dollar is America's problem precisely because it is everyone else's problem. It is the US' IOU, but it is our money.

Internationalisation involves some loss of American monetary autonomy even if the contracts are asymmetrical. In this sense, the centrality of an offshore dollar market to international trade and finance has drawn American authorities closer towards backstopping balance sheets that are strictly speaking non-American.

In a hybrid credit system formed by interlocking private and public balance sheets, some measure of subsidy for private balance sheets is going to have to be on offer as many would simply not last through a downswing in the business cycle, leading to systemic risk. In a domestic setting, this subsidy takes the form of permitting private balance sheets access to the central bank: average citizens do not bank with the Fed (yet). The exorbitant privilege of a banking licence certainly comes with perks, but, in its ideal type, it also comes with constraints. This public subsidy can hardly be given away free, and ideally some measure of public control is the price the insurer extracts from the insuree (Minsky, 1992).

A more publicly minded Fed would not be happy letting European banks fund in dollars to take risks to the US markets in the first place, exposing themselves to currency mismatches which would eventually entail swap lines with the ECB. It would put pressure on the ECB to reign in its banks. Likewise, it would put pressure on the BoE to reign in the degree of leverage permitted in the London-based Eurodollar market which the Fed also backstopped. The absence of a more publicly minded Fed is a contingent political fact.

This crisis-fuelled internationalisation of the dollar has two elements: the fact of the swap-line bailout and the terms of the bailout. Bailouts are a technical requirement of inherently unstable, complex systems operating on the horizon of an uncertain future (Minsky, 1992), but their terms are negotiated and of course deeply political. The political balance within the hegemon and between the hegemon and the world can be such that its disciplinary power is used in the global public interest.

China as a Global Finance Company

China is missing from this multilateral swap arrangement, although it has *bilateral* swap arrangements with five major central banks save the Fed. The Fed also has a repo facility for holders of US treasuries, an implicit nod to China. So China has plugged into the core system, albeit at one notch down on the hierarchy (Bernes et al., 2014).

Like many financially developing nations, China has one big non-profit balance sheet (the central bank) to manage daily global liquidity as opposed to the rich-nation model of having a larger number of smaller profit-driven balance sheets managing flows in currency markets (this has to do with market failure in global currency markets driven by the 'original sin'). The rich-nation private model defaults back to the central bank in times of trouble in any case, leaving the public balance sheet to mop up the mess. It is not at all clear therefore that the apparently canonical 'deep and liquid' financial markets are a source of power *independent* of the big ballast of the central bank's balance sheet.

China certainly has the scale elements in place to build a currency superstructure that can provide world money. Yet China appears to be exploring a path that is less the US model of a global bank than the old merchant-turned-financier model of recycling liquid outside money surpluses. China is a moneylender, not a bank. At present, it is looking to develop international capital markets, not domestic money markets.

The banking model does not apply to the Chinese economy: it has neither a trade deficit nor a well-developed financial system with its own set of hegemonic elites. Rather, China's well-known problems are those of plenty: how to recycle trade surpluses while keeping the growth party going in order to maintain the social peace (Helleiner and Kirshner, 2014).

Its first solution was to invest in US treasuries, the by-product of a weak currency regime, a strategy that ended up over-feeding the American consumer China depended on to feed its export engine. When crisis eventually happened, China had to look for another strategy to sustainably recycle its export earnings.

The internationalisation of the renminbi (RMB) is one move: the more people hold the RMB, the more RMB-denominated assets Chinese exporters and monetary authorities can invest in, thereby exiting the deadly embrace of the dollar at the margin; this *is* the banking strategy, namely turning its own liabilities into money.

But in the meantime, there is also a real investment strategy to recycle surpluses more durably in non-currency or debt forms. This goes under the various banners of the Asian Infrastructure Investment Bank, the New Development Bank, and the One Belt One Road plan. Rather than turning surpluses into RMB-denominated financial assets, this strategy seeks to convert earned inflows into illiquid, long-term infrastructure assets across the developing world, a classic spatio-temporal fix (Harvey, 2006).

China's trade surpluses give it the ability to be a global finance company rather than a global bank, recycling earned money on the money-lender model rather than borrowing and issuing its own near-money liabilities. Finance company liabilities do not function as money; they do not operate a fractional reserve and do not create checking account liabilities for their loan customers. They lend out surpluses dollar for dollar. Many large non-financial corporations have spawned non-banking finance companies as a means of more effectively managing their cash. Finance companies are moneylenders and investors, not banks.

The US was able to become a global bank because its liabilities were accepted as world money before its 'banking' operations took hold in the mid-1960s. This possibility became a necessity when it went from a trade surplus to a deficit. The US had the exorbitant privilege of running a trade deficit without being called to book by its global creditors.

But US history is not China's fate as some scholars have suggested. A trade deficit, for instance, is not at all a *necessary* outcome of providing the global reserve, although it does permit one. Germain and Schwartz (2014) claim that '[t]he international currency emitter's cannot validate its long-term external assets unless that country runs trade deficits, allowing the periphery to service its long-term external debts to the emitting country' (p. 1100). Yet this is based on an overgeneralisation of the Anglo-American experience (see also Germain and Schwartz, 2015).

In general, as Claudio Borio reminds us,

> current account patterns are *largely silent* about the role a country plays in international borrowing, lending and financial intermediation ... current account positions are not informative of the direction of financing: *investment could be fully financed from advanced economies even if these are in deficit.* One needs to look at the details of bilateral *gross* financing flows. (Borio, 2016, pp. 2–4, emphasis added)

The idea that there is some necessary link between trade deficits and financial flows, Borio notes, rests on the merest confusion between *savings*, which drive the current account, and *financing*, which is determined by a portfolio decision of market actors. China *chooses* to be a global finance company. The US economy was a global banker in Kindleberger's sense in periods when it had both trade surpluses and deficits. The point is to focus on the pattern of gross financial flows about which the current account itself tells us little.

The finance company model could be the Chinese path while its liabilities still do not function as world money. It is a model in which growth is shared not by granting peripheral exporters access to the hegemon's home market, whereby the hegemonic nation's industry takes a hit and therefore has to have a political settlement capable of absorbing these costs (the American path). It might in fact be one in which growth is more evenly shared through some version of 'South–South' cooperation, without idealising what that means.

The fact that the private Eurodollar market in London now sits at the centre of the system gives rise to a whiggishness about how the international system might develop (Bernes et al., 2014). Yet as historians know, this market was a deeply contingent development backstopped by central banks to the point where subsidies amounted to an industrial policy for the financial sector. Given that the rising hegemon of China has nothing resembling the political settlement between the City and the Bank, it would be surprising if the system evolves along similar lines. China has a distinct legitimate political settlement which will construct a credit superstructure that achieves scale in an entirely distinct way.

There are limitations in viewing China through the Anglo-American lens. Just as the American experience was something more than a rerun of the British experience, so too will China innovate around the particular conjuncture in which it finds itself at both domestic and international levels.

The broader point is that a credit system is deeply institutionally indeterminant. As long as the basics of scale, political contracting and hierarchy are in place, many different institutional possibilities can be imagined.

Conclusion: Nice Leviathans

Reformist ideas for the global reserve system require a theoretical framing if they are to be adequately assessed. We have suggested one such framing here, outlining the centrality of scale and robust contracting as the key elements that generate credit power for institutions. In ideal type, the state has the unique ability to forge robust contracts at scale, a political ability that gives it unmatched structural power.

Needless to say, actually existing states are not equal. States are themselves expressions of political settlements, mainly domestic but also international, and the shape of these political settlements determines the degree to which any given instantiation of state power fills out this ideal-type potential.

If we line up economic entities in the world today purely by economic scale, many non-state actors feature above states: Berkshire Hathaway is bigger than India in revenue terms, for instance (Babic, Fichtner and Heemskerk, 2017). Bundles of economic contracts can outstrip political contracts in terms of size and creditworthiness.

But if states get their politics right and hold together a political contract that engenders a large, thriving economy, then they can scale up to much greater size and robustness than non-economic entities. The largest corporation by revenues, Walmart, number ten in terms of revenue, is about one-sixth the size of the US at number one and less than half the size of the United Kingdom at number six.

The world's monetary system is a complex, hierarchical geography of public and private balance sheets with some states currently on top. State actors have long known about the power of public credit, and some have learned how to wield it. Other state elites try to innovate their own credit structures in a game of emulative competition. But we should be cautious in extrapolating too much from the Anglo-American experience: emulation always happens with a good deal of innovation. Yet the robustness of political contracting means non-state actors cannot compete with a well-established leviathan.

The privilege of leviathans is substantial but ultimately limited: they can bend the survival constraint, not break it. Even leviathans can sink. Liberal internationalist technocrats seek non-state solutions to the absence of an outside world money. But the logic of the system means that this path is closed. Kindleberger's path is open if we can find a democratic, global political settlement.

10 | PROOF OF INSTITUTIONS
Cryptocurrencies as Digital Fiat Money

Can we design money without hierarchy, instability and state power? Tech utopians have tried with Bitcoin. Their failure arguably proves that these are indeed fundamental elements of money. Hierarchy emerges willy-nilly in Bitcoin and other cryptocurrencies: 'central planner' software architects write the code; 'mining' is monopolised; exchanges issue crypto-backed IOUs like banks. Bitcoin could function as a token 'outside money' in principle, but its rigidity would be over-disciplining, emulating the anti-democratic gold standard. Bitcoiners' hostility towards credit is understandable given the political capture of credit systems, but it perhaps ought to be directed at this capture rather than the institution itself. Their techno-libertarianism misses the upside of the political nature of credit money, which allows citizens to relax their collective survival constraint.

Credit is a fundamental part of human sociality because economic life is a going concern, pointing relentlessly to the future. Money as credit is one method by which collectives, political and economic, undertake future-oriented action. Money as a digital fiat token cannot perform this coordinating task in principle, no matter how well engineered, because of its finitude, inflexibility and centrality, especially under conditions of capitalism plus democracy. If flexibility were engineered in, then cryptocurrencies would simply have recreated credit money in a new avatar.

Cryptocurrencies cannot function as money because they have as their target a limited notion of money and a thin idea of the work of social institutions. Designers of cryptocurrencies seek to replace human institutions with ingenious cryptographic functions. In identifying the enemy as *fiat* money, cryptocurrencies are simply solving the wrong problem. Yet in their failure, they prove the robustness of creditary institutions.

Despite their operational failure, cryptocurrencies succeed in highlighting the fact that money is always *designed* in accordance with some underlying politics.

They thereby implicitly point to the possibility of more democratically designed money systems.

Monetary systems are inherently hierarchical and therefore highly susceptible to political capture. The solution to capture is institutional *balance* and accountability precisely because alternatives founded on decentralisation are not robust as the failure of cryptos as money illustrates. Indeed, such a decentralisation might be pernicious in its political and economic outcomes.

The technical fact of hierarchy in money condemns the polity to subjecting hierarchy to democratic discipline. There is no pathway that precludes hierarchy: accountable or unaccountable hierarchies are our only options (see Chapter 12).

This is proved by the ongoing failure, over a decade in, of cryptographically decentralised money. Cryptocurrencies are the best attempt yet to decentralise and disintermediate money; yet centralised structures, including forms of credit, keep emerging in their ecology willy-nilly. Because they misrecognise money, the designers of cryptocurrencies fail to account for the foundational fact of credit and its native hierarchy.

Their failure is deeply instructive. While there is a homology between algorithms and institutions, both being rules of the game, social institutions do something that algorithms cannot in principle: they express and contain human conflict in an ongoing fashion. The assault of the cyborgs has left social institutions standing precisely for this reason. Such a view implicitly sees the law as a mere instruction set ready to be rendered in computer code. 'Code is law' is their mantra, but law is not code—it is an organic human institution. The law expresses and encodes different forms of collective action, economic and political. These come to be institutionalised and then turn their social power back on society to reshape it. But this does not mean that the state is something apart from society.

Credit money as a sociopolitical institution turns the social product of a political collective into a financial asset of disproportionate strength and versatility. It does this through a series of political and economic mediations from the taxpayer all the way to the deposit account. At each level, social conflict is expressed and contested through the price and contracting terms of credit. Competing plans are adjudicated in a credit market overseen by hierarchically arranged market makers topped by the central bank, the state's bank. National monetary spaces can be carved out as dry docks for particular political projects. Money as an institutionalised social relation is valuable because it is deeply embedded in real economies producing material value.

Human institutions have a high-dimension capacity to express human conflict. Algorithms can help articulate those projects, but their ontology is too thin, their abstraction too inadequate, to operate at the bandwidth of social institutions like the law, states and banks. Further, lacking a contractual element of any kind, cryptocurrency algorithms are not anchored to value. The contractual element of money gives it both stable value (fiscally anchored at the system's apex) and flexibility (enabled by credit creation or destruction at the capillaries), a combination no cryptocurrency can match in principle. Stable coins backed by national monies are currency derivatives pure and simple—not alternative currencies and definitely not decentralised in any way.

This is not to say that modern credit money works perfectly or democratically— quite the contrary. It is that social institutions are ontologically distinct from algorithms even though the two are similar in ways that make social institutions subject to collective design efforts. The failure of cryptos as money therefore calls our attention to not only the robustness of social institutions but their very designability. With the possibility of design comes the hope of democracy.

In order to get the design right, we must understand the materials at hand. The most exciting thing about cryptocurrency experiments is that they bring computer scientists and engineers to the study of the economy, diluting the economists' pernicious monopoly. The pragmatism of the engineer is, as with that of the banker shared by the Banking School, a salutary corrective to the otherworldliness of the brahmin economist who rarely gets their hands dirty with real economies. As they crash into the credit system, computer science people will hopefully learn about the robustness of social institutions just as much as social scientists will learn about the redesignability and modularity of the institutions.

We will use a political theory of money to argue that Bitcoin and cryptocurrencies will simply not work as money. We also argue that there is an implicit neoliberal ethics at work in the design of Bitcoin, something that could have deleterious effects if generalised. We list several reasons why Bitcoin or cryptos will not work as money in principle.

Cryptocurrencies cannot, by design, provide liquidity to a complex economy. Bitcoins represent a move to constrain the endogenous creation of credit in an economy by centrally and permanently fixing the money stock, a goal shared by monetarists and a money interest seeking to limit the ability of the state to create credit; the hash functions at their core are insufficiently abstract to function as money; despite being designed to be completely decentralised, hierarchy continues to emerge in Bitcoin's operations through mining, system design, code governance and exchanges; despite this emergence of institutions, they are the wrong ones for performing the functions of money; monopoly emerges in mining because the method for deciding how to update the distributed ledger privileges scarce resources. And, finally, cryptocurrencies rely only on charismatic coder-prophets and loosely bound social groupings, or more recently private firms like Facebook—all of which are insufficient in either scale or robustness.

We have been following Philip Mirowski and Dieter Plehwe in defining neoliberalism as an effort to centrally plan, design and construct markets of all kinds where design elements are meant to bring about the particular normative goals of the designers (Mirowski and Plehwe, 2015). Whether intentionally or not, a neoliberal ethic permeates the design structure of Bitcoin. This is largely because the technical price of decentralisation is the ubiquity of a flattened logic of the transaction. This is not the transaction of Commons (1931) which encodes rights to goods and services but the denatured transaction of the fairground or of video game money.

The 'coin' itself is a compendium of the entire series of past transactions undertaken with that coin. In order to achieve decentralisation, all nodes in the network must have a copy of all transactions ever undertaken by all coins forever— an anonymous panopticity that hampers transaction speed. Nodes in the network are paid to be honest, the very pith of neoliberal ethics. In its design, Bitcoin is meant to align individual incentives and social incentives without a central planner allocating positions but very much with a central architect setting the rules of play. Operating on an implicit Smithian ethics, social virtue is meant to emerge from individual vice, but only through clever mechanism design that ensures discipline through collective, perpetual-though-anonymous surveillance. Fair competition is positioned as a social contract.

This lurking neoliberalism is dangerous because it portends an overly disciplined form of money. The fixity desired by cryptos can only come at the cost of autochthonous credit and therefore economic growth. Ironically, it is precisely its fixity that makes its price so volatile as it is unable to respond at the capillary level to economic needs. With contemporary capitalism already biased to inequality, especially in its present avatar, the prospect of further credit discipline is bleak. The political complaint with the capture of the credit system is on the mark, but credit can be used for democracy. Since only credit money can be both stable and flexible, we are condemned to make it democratic.

We should note at the outset that we limit ourselves here to crypto*currencies* and Bitcoin in particular rather than the entire universe of so-called decentralised *finance*. While much of the same critique would apply, this fast-evolving domain is beyond the scope of this study.

What Is a Cryptocurrency?

The study of cryptography is as replete with references to 'the adversary' as neoclassical economics is with references to 'the planner'. The cryptographic structure therefore becomes a reaction formation to the potential moves of the imagined attacker. And the enemy is 'fiat money', so Bitcoin and other cryptocurrencies are designed as better *tokens* rather than credit instruments. Cryptocurrencies are digital tokens that contain an archive of their previous transactions. They are video-game token money with algorithmically contrived scarcity value.

Cryptocurrencies emerged out of the cypherpunk movement, a libertarian or anarchist social formation that seeks to replace social institutions—institutions that the movement finds corrupt and captured being based on frail human trust rather than solid mathematics (Vigna and Casey, 2016)—with cryptography. As such, cypherpunks are cyborgs, looking to take the error-prone human out of the command loop and replace them with a more trusty, because less human, algorithmic machine (Mirowski, 2002). The humans have messed up money. Because fiat money can be created, well, 'by fiat', it is far too susceptible to capture by special interests. 'Famously, in the very first block ever mined in Bitcoin, the coinbase parameter referenced a story in the *Times of London* newspaper involving the Chancellor bailing out banks. This has been interpreted as political commentary on the motivation for starting Bitcoin' (Narayanan et al., 2016, p. 89).

As such, cryptocurrencies are part of a more general efflorescence in alternative ideas about money that emerged in the wake of the 2008 financial crisis: gold-backed currency, narrow banking, 100 per cent money, sovereign money, local area monies, IMF's SDRs, and so on (Weber, 2018). When a social institution is subjected to huge amounts of stress, breaks down and is then patched up to perform unusually, people will start to rethink and seek to reform these institutions. The impetus for social theory has always been social life itself: we only figure out the plumbing when it breaks. Crises switch social matters from ready-to-hand daily operation to present-at-hand analysis.

Cryptocurrencies are not just digital tokens; they are simultaneously a method for moving these tokens around and contain an accounting of all previous transactions in the life of the coin within the coin itself. The coin in Bitcoin *is* the chain of transactions accounted for in a distributed ledger called a blockchain. As we will argue subsequently, the level of detailing and lack of abstraction that this design entails renders cryptos far too granular for capitalism. It turns abstract money into a kind of ticket-cum-ticker tape, potentially proliferating specific-purpose 'monies' to an incoherent extent: there are already about 10,000 cryptocurrencies at this speculative moment, but Bitcoin remains the most iconic.

Bitcoin as Money

My knowledge about the inner workings of Bitcoin and associated cryptocurrencies is based on a reading of the tremendously clear textbook authored by computer scientists and engineers entitled *Bitcoin and Cryptocurrency Technologies* (Narayanan et al., 2016). Since cryptocurrencies are the application of the science and engineering of cryptography to the operations of money, they are based on some cryptographic primitives that we need to briefly outline in order to assess them.

Hash Functions and Limited Abstraction

The first cryptographic primitive is a hash function. This is a compression function, a mathematical function that allows larger pieces of data to be both compressed and uniquely digested or summarised in a smaller string of data. The important properties of hash functions for the operation of cryptocurrencies are collision resistance, hiding and puzzle-friendliness.

The properties of hiding (the inability to go backwards from the hash function to the summarised data) and puzzle-friendliness (see the following discussion) are critical for the notion of 'work' in Bitcoin. Being collision resistant means that the likelihood of two hash numbers being the same is vanishingly small. This is a 'probabilistic guarantee', but as with many things in monetary life, very low probabilities function as certainties. This feature apparently makes them extremely useful in creating all manner of data structures in computer science, earning them the sobriquet of 'the Swiss Army knife of cryptography' (ibid., p. 31).

Hash functions are abstractions from the underlying substrate (the individual transaction), but abstractions with a very high degree of information embedded in them. This makes them much more particular, more granular, than the analogue abstractions used in money to date.

The conceit of cryptocurrencies is that cryptographic properties of hash functions (and digital signatures examined later) are the functional equivalent of the physical properties of precious metals in bearing the functions of money. The signatures that Bitcoins bear are less akin to those on a cheque (or other IOU-like instruments) and more like a stamp at the mint: this is the explicit analogy made by its designers. Minting rights are then decentralised by the protocol.

The work of abstraction in capitalist money means that 'money has no smell': any given unit of metallic money does not bear any marks of the labour processes it has passed through, nor the set of transactions through which it has passed in order to reach a particular conjuncture. This high degree of abstraction has a vital role in capitalism as it facilitates the separability between the sphere of production and the sphere of circulation. Abstraction in capitalist money allows radically distinct branches of the division of labour to communicate with each other and be commensurable through the operations of value. It allows capitalism to operate at a planetary scale.

Note that this is true whether or not we buy Marx's account of *labour power*, namely value. Whatever we take to be the source and font of value, the value-expressing unit (money) has to operate at a particularly high degree of abstraction from the underlying value-producing process in order for commensuration to be possible at scale.

This degree of abstraction is what makes modern cash untraceable, anonymous and quick to use. With credit cards, bank cheques, and so on, the process is certainly less abstract and more traceable, but commensuration happens within a hierarchical set of institutions that work to generate the effect of tracelessness or outsideness for the end user, all wrapped in the fetish of fiat as outlined earlier. Of course, the centralisation and hierarchy are an anathema to cypherpunks.

Hash functions have to abjure this level of abstraction precisely because they are a critical part of data structures that form a tamper-proof, append-only distributed ledger that is the blockchain. This is a ledger to track every expenditure of every token, albeit anonymously (although not quite), precisely to engineer a system that requires no central authority. Anonymous panopticity is the price of decentralisation.

With cryptocurrencies, the monetary 'instrument' is also the transactional archive. This archive, the blockchain, is a list constructed so that one can tell if any of the items on it have been changed merely by looking at the topmost entry. This is possible because the list is linked, with each item 'pointing' to the previous one. When these 'pointers' are hashed, they function as summaries of the previous listed item. If the previous item is itself a block of data with its own internal structure (called a Merkle tree), then large amounts of data can be concatenated, summarised and made tamper-proof by arranging them in a blockchain. We could therefore tell if the contents of any previous block in the chain had been tampered with merely by checking the 256-bit hash in the hash pointers in the current block.

The very structure of the blockchain *limits* the degree of abstraction in cryptos, bizarre as that may sound for such complex data structures. Anonymity is actually pseudonymity since public keys can be mapped and be made to reveal the transactor's identity. And panopticity, the fact that the instrument carries around the entire history of transactions, means that 'clearing' each transaction entails a time-consuming, cumbersome process of verification. The archival weight borne by each Bitcoin, by construction, severely hampers its functioning as money. Cryptocurrencies are 'smelly' (traceable) on purpose, but that makes them too slow, not abstract enough to act as money.

There have been two recent responses to this issue, speeding up transaction times by making the blocks larger and insisting that Bitcoin is not really good for payments but is still a good store of value. The first, Bitcoin Cash, wants to retain the idea of Bitcoin as money and implicitly realises that this entails scale: larger blocks require more computing power and therefore more hierarchy since small computers cannot compete. The second response implicitly gives up on the idea that Bitcoin is 'money' at all and makes it a financial instrument. Tellingly, the two responses are backed by warring communities that are poorly mutualised together so that cults of personality preside (Jeffries, 2018). Indeed, Bitcoin Cash itself split later on the issue of programmability.

Digital Signatures

The other cryptographic primitive critical to Bitcoin is digital signatures. Like regular signatures, digital signatures can be both uniquely signed and verified publically. This is done by generating two keys, one secret and one public, and the sender then signing a message with their secret key while sharing the public key with the recipient. The recipient has to run a verification process to match the two, and only then will the message be decrypted.

A critical innovation in Bitcoin is that public keys act as identities in the Bitcoin network. They enable identity management in a completely decentralised way: one does not need any kind of central administrator who controls and verifies account information. There are no accounts in Bitcoin, merely strings of verified transactions between public-keys-as-nodes in a network.

Digital signatures are at the core of cryptocurrencies since they validate the messages that function as transactions. Signatures help define what a 'coin' is in Bitcoin. A coin is merely a digital statement saying 'create coin', which is then signed and hashed. A coin is a digital string that is cryptographically signed, including hash pointers to previous verified transactions all the way back to the coin's minting.

Anonymous Panopticity

The a priori desire for decentralisation set designers several problems. The first is who gets to issue the token money, solved by distributing this right across the network according to a 'work' rule. But given that the currency is merely a data entry, a digital token, how can we ensure that the same token is not 'spent' or pointed to more than once?

The way around this is to literally *broadcast* each transaction to the entire network—that such and such public key intends to spend this particular coin with this particular serial number—and check this desired expenditure against the archive of transactions that every node possesses. Satoshi Nakamoto, the pseudonymous designer of Bitcoin, analogises this to a stock market ticker tape where traders can see all the transactions without knowing the identity of the transactors. 'The only way to confirm the absence of a transaction is to be aware of all transactions' (Nakamoto, 2008, p. 2). The difference with Bitcoin of course is the linking of transactions to public keys or identities.

We are calling this combination of (near-)anonymity of actors and full visibility of all transactions in a completely decentralised structure 'anonymous panopticity'. Thanks to the properties of hash functions and digital signatures, users in this network can verify transactions without actually knowing the content of either the transaction itself or the persons transacting. No one knows anyone, but everyone can see all transactions.

This panopticity solves the double-spending problem seen as 'the main design challenge' for cryptocurrencies. The blockchain keeps a record of all transactions that ever occurred forever and does so in a secure, tamper-proof fashion, all but eliminating double-spending.

This solution is rather brutal. It means that anonymity in Bitcoin is an all-or-nothing affair: if someone manages to join the dots and link together transaction behaviour of a particular (set of) public key(s), or if someone comes up with an algorithm that publishes the real-world transaction information of such public keys, then a public key's entire transaction history would be exposed.

But cryptocurrencies must take this risk because there is no *decentralised* way of safeguarding against a double-spending attack other than by having a distributed ledger that covers the universe of transactions from the 'genesis block' down to the present. Anonymous panopticity is the price of decentralisation—a heavy price in terms of transaction speeds and therefore 'moneyness' itself.

Bitcoin's Slow Social Contract

Who has the right to update the ledger? How can a decentralised, distributed ledger be managed? Can this be done in real, transactional time?

The key problem here is *agreement*, an eminently political problem given a computer science gloss. How can anonymous nodes in a peer-to-peer network, some of which might be individually or collectively hostile, all come to some agreement as to the global state of a ledger that no one entity controls?

Here again we have a wonderful cybernetic slide that equates between a deep political problem and a problem in network engineering. The problem of forging an 'agreement' between distributed nodes in a potentially hostile environment is framed as a problem of data management in a database distributed over several thousand servers, a 'distributed system'. A database manager has to ensure all servers 'agree' (in the sense of being on the same page rather than forge a contract) on the overall state of the system so that end users are all looking at the same front end.

This agreement between a number of servers is called a 'distributed consensus': 'Distributed consensus has various applications, and it has been studied for decades in computer science. The traditional motivating application is reliability in distributed systems' (Narayanan et al., 2016, p. 52).

In the world of cryptocurrencies, this means that nodes in a peer-to-peer network have to agree on the state of the ledger so that the network arrives at a consensus on which public keys own which Bitcoins and which transactions are valid and not double-spends. The very notion of ownership itself is deeply 'social' and subject to a distributed consensus.

Recall that there are no 'accounts' in Bitcoin. The coin *itself* is defined as a series of signed transactions: 'We define an electronic coin *as a chain of digital signatures*' (Nakamoto, 2008, p. 2, emphasis added). Owning coins means a public key has valid transaction rights over identifiable coins, rights that are agreed upon by nodes because they are present (at a certain depth) in the long-term, consensus ledger. The archive of transactions is the property register. It is transactions all the way down.

At any given point in time, nodes will have a list of transactions on which there is a consensus (and are therefore included on the blockchain) and those that are outstanding and not yet included, payments proposed by various nodes but not yet cleared. A peer-to-peer network is not perfect: not all nodes are connected to each other to exactly the same extent. The network is unevenly dense. So different nodes might have a slightly different picture of the network depending on where they are located and hear about different sets of transactions.

How then can such a network arrive at consensus in this context? The designer's solution, as we have seen, is to periodically *broadcast* unverified transactions to the entire network and then execute a consensus protocol between the nodes to decide which transactions of those nominated make it onto the ledger. Some valid transactions might not make it in time for the current block of transactions, but they will make it into the next time slice if they are valid. Blocks in Bitcoin are updated every ten minutes.

The mathematics of networks has arrived at certain properties for peer-to-peer networks that lack a notion of global time and the possibilities of arriving at a distributed consensus between its nodes. Apparently, this 'pessimistic' literature concludes that with such networks, very few algorithms can be used for the consensus protocol, thanks to several impossibility results (Narayanan et al., 2016, p. 54).

Yet Bitcoin is not merely a peer-to-peer network: it is attempting to be a currency. It turns out that the particular properties of such networks in the context of cryptocurrencies can indeed solve the problem of a distributed consensus: 'Ironically, with the current state of research, consensus in Bitcoin works better in practice than in theory' (ibid., p. 55). Bitcoin appears to have solved the problem of consensus for a subset of peer-to-peer networks that run as currencies.

The solution to the distributed consensus problem revolves around a blending of normative political theory and network design. Nakamoto's (2008) assertion is that '[t]he system is secure as long as *honest nodes collectively control* more CPU [central processing unit] power than any cooperating group of attacker nodes'.

How is honesty determined? It is done by having other nodes ratify the block in which a node's proposed transaction is included. Ratification takes the implicit form of building on top of an existing block in the chain: if nodes refuse to build on a particular block and continue from the previous block, that is a signal that the block is suspected to contain fake transactions, double-spends. Building on the latest block means appending a group of transactions onto the last verified block. Conversely, if nodes do build on a particular proposed block of transactions, they are implicitly confirming that the constituent transactions are valid.

But which nodes get to add a block of transactions to the blockchain? The rules of Bitcoin stipulate that only those nodes which can show some 'proof of work'—that is, only those nodes which can prove that they have solved a particular cryptographic search problem (a guessing game to finding a needle in a cryptographic haystack again using hash functions)—have the ability to propose blocks on the blockchain. If a node has spent real computational resources (done 'work') and successfully solved the search puzzle outlined in the Bitcoin code, it gets to propose the new block and harvest a 'block reward' of new coins. These new coins only have value if this proposed block is built on by others—that is, if they think it contains no double-spends.

Proof-of-work was seen to be a solution to the political problem of representation and decision-making in anonymous, peer-to-peer networks:

> The proof-of-work also solves *the problem of determining representation in majority decision making*. If the majority were based on one-IP-address-one-vote, it could be subverted by anyone able to allocate many IPs. Proof-of-work is essentially *one-CPU-one-vote*. The majority decision is represented by the longest chain, which has the *greatest proof-of-work effort invested in it*. If a majority of CPU power is controlled by honest nodes, the honest chain will grow the fastest and outpace any competing chains. (Ibid., p. 3, emphasis added)

Proof-of-work is meant to select nodes on the basis of the distribution of CPU power. The assumption, remarkably naive in retrospect, is that CPU power is a non-monopolisable resource. 'One CPU, one vote' is cyborg democracy. Mining by solving hash puzzles solves the distributed consensus problem in this peer-to-peer network.

This imaginary of 'one CPU, one vote' has all the trappings of a Smithian universe populated by a large number of small operators, each with individual propensities that coalesce into a socially good equilibrium. Just as monopolists were an anathema to Adam Smith, a special class of nodes, miners, would presumably be an anathema to Nakamoto and the cypherpunk ethos. There is no distinction between types of nodes in the original vision: all nodes compete to solve hash puzzles. The only salient distinction is between honest and dishonest nodes. A different class of miner nodes is not part of this classless vision. Yet class has indeed emerged from economies of scale.

The whole weight of the security of the blockchain and the possibility of a coherent consensus comes down to the assumption that the majority (51 per cent) of nodes are honest. There is no explicit social contract or surveillance mechanism to ensure such honesty—these would be far too centralised. So the solution, pure neoliberalism, is *to pay nodes to be honest*. If a node's proposed block gets accepted by other nodes, it can harvest a 'block reward' of newly minted coins (currently 25 Bitcoins). This is how new coins get created. This block reward halves every 210,000 blocks, so there will only ever be a finite stock of Bitcoins minted (21 million as the rules now stand). Once all the coins are mined, transaction fees will replace block rewards as the main incentive to propose additions to the blockchain.

Undertaking honest computational work gets you a block reward. This is Bitcoin's solution to the problem of the distributed consensus, allowing it to pay its way out of the impossibility results in the literature.

Nodes do not have permanent or real identities, so the normal, real-world pattern of crime and punishment will not work as a surveillance mechanism. We therefore move from a crime-or-punishment paradigm that generates mechanical solidarity to a payments-or-incentive paradigm that appeals to greed and self-interest. We cannot punish double-spenders (public keys are not real identities), so we can only incentivise nodes to act honestly. In this anonymous, decentralised world, incentives replace punishment, leading to a much *weaker* form of mutualisation than either economic or political forms. But paying for honesty is common sense under neoliberal ethics.

Bitcoin's incentive mechanism sets up a constant competition between nodes to solve puzzles in order to successfully propose new blocks and harvest the block reward. But this simultaneously incentivises honest behaviour as a node cannot collect its block reward unless other nodes accept its proposed block by building on it with their own proposed blocks. And on the assumption that the majority of the nodes are honest, nodes will only accept the block if all transactions in that block are valid. Nodes will build on the longest valid chain. The risk of behaving otherwise is wasting real resources, namely CPU runtime.

If a malicious actor wanted to change the blockchain, they would have had to amass enough CPU power or 'hash power' to solve a large number of hash puzzles, propose new blocks, have these blocks verified by other nodes that they control and thereby build another branch of the blockchain that surpasses the existing one to become the longest valid chain on which other nodes would now build as the representative of collective consensus. In short, they would have to spend an inordinate amount of real resources to build their own branch of the chain and overtake the existing branch, something considered infeasible.

Even such a '51 per cent attacker' ought to find it more profitable to play by the rules, asserts Nakamoto in a game-theoretic fashion, because it would simply be cheaper to mint more coins by controlling all that hash power than subverting the ledger in the aforementioned manner.

Again, consonant with its implicit Smithian ethics, social virtue emerges from individual vice: each node is looking out for its own self-interest but is incentivised to act in a manner that other nodes will consider honest. Moral order emerges not from some centralised or divine moral injunction but from an interaction between individual propensities and rule structures. The impartial spectator is also the market competitor who regulates a moral order that is made synonymous with market order.

The tightly structured, video-game nature of the world of cryptocurrencies entails that designers inhabit a game-theoretic framework in order to bring about stable social states. Game theory becomes applied ethics. Game theory and video games share a common parentage in Cold War simulations, so it should be of little surprise that the video-game sociology of the cryptocurrency world should slide seamlessly into game-theoretic formulations (Mirowski, 2002).

Of course, such formulations fail. The costs of computing the proof-of-work can be prohibitive. They now far exceed the capacities of garden-variety CPUs and are the preserve of specialised mining rigs equipped with industrial-scale application-specific integrated circuits (ASICs). Unlike the microprocessors found in computers and cell phones, these ASICs are purpose-built for one specific function (in this case, solving hash puzzles) rather than for general computing and are orders of magnitude more costly to design and construct than our plebeian graphics processing units (GPUs) and CPUs.

As the difficulty of solving the hash puzzles increases (as per the protocol), more and more computing power needs to be thrown at these problems, placing the ideal of 'one CPU, one vote' well out of sync with any substantial notion of decentralisation. Perhaps only states themselves have the scale and ability to substantiate the upfront losses entailed in ASIC development (which involves long lead times and can be rendered worthless as the hash puzzles get more complex) and electricity usage. Ironically, the economics of Bitcoin mining might bring the (rogue) state back in.

In this sense, cryptocurrencies are digital *fiat* currencies: they are digital tokens where the 'fiat' right to create tokens has been distributed according to some rule defining a process of 'work'. This 'work' might appear to give Bitcoin the feel of 'real' commodity money. But it ends up acting like shareholder democracy: those with the most resources have the most votes. Thus, cryptographic 'work' is merely meant to create an aesthetic of the commodity ('coin'), not the value substrate of a real commodity. 'Work' is just a means to distribute the rights to update the ledger and incentivise honest behaviour. A video-game logic of earning points by undertaking some difficult task breaks the fourth wall. In fact, 'work' qua time and energy is not designed as a real anchor at all: it is just an extremely clever but very slow method to solve the political problem of consensus over the state of the distributed ledger.

Conclusion: Law Is Not Code

There are at least two more ways in which hierarchy makes a comeback in cryptocurrencies. Liquidity is of course a critical issue by construction since only a finite amount of coins is ever mined, and credit has always been the answer to liquidity shortages. Credit structures stretch liquidity by promising to pay the underlying scarce unit; they have routinely grown up as a means to economise specie.

In the crypto world, this has taken the form of exchanges complete with regular accounts, which, as with bank accounts, are nothing more than promises to pay some outside asset, in this case Bitcoin. As with other spontaneously emerging economic structures like shadow banks, these are jerry-built and subject to fraud and collapse as with the infamous FTX but going back to the Mt. Gox episode of 2014, among others. 'Stablecoins' are also a method to achieve stability while using blockchain technologies, but they are still token-based and proscribe leverage—that is, the creation and destruction of means of payment according to the demands of commerce. They are also just like dressed-up money market mutual funds, unregulated narrow banks based on cryptocurrencies.

The point is not simply that regulation is required. It is that to operate as money, an instrument needs to be liquid, ebbing and flowing with the pulse of economic life. If a currency's original state does not permit such liquidity, economic actors will very quickly busy themselves in inventing credit structures atop any such outside asset. Credit and its hierarchy are autochthonous, completely native to economic life to the point where even the outermost monies are now a form of credit. Bitcoin exchanges wonderfully prove the nativity of credit because they confound the most ingenious attempt yet to design our way out of credit.

The other source of hierarchy is the very coding of these cryptocurrencies. Bitcoin has a foundation that manages the code, and the mystique of the coder prophet is well established. Facebook, perhaps predictably, took this to the next level by inventing a 'stablecoin' that is highly managed and backed by real-money market makers. Recognising 'trade-off between decentralisation and performance', its Libra currency distributed updating rights oligopolistically to a closed group of 'validators'. Facebook's Libra, renamed 'Diem' before it was eventually wound down, brought hierarchy back full circle, turning the cryptographic token into a bank-like promissory note by dressing up its IOUs as cryptographic tokens.

All new cryptocurrencies face what computer scientists, straining their idiom to accommodate social phenomena, call 'the bootstrapping problem': how do new currencies get off the ground? Because 51 per cent of nodes need to be honest for Bitcoin to be stable, there is a trade-off between its rate of growth and its robustness. If it grows too fast, it might be subverted by dishonest nodes; but if it grows too slowly, it is useless as a currency.

What our computer scientists miss is that the state is the solution to the bootstrapping problem in currencies. The state's liabilities get to social scale immediately because the state is *sociality itself in politico-institutional form*. The cryptocurrency movement only further proves this point. We outlined two forms of sociality earlier, economic and political, each generating a credit money with particular properties. But cryptocurrencies are weakly socialised and barely mutualised at all. This leads to various issues of which 'bootstrapping' is one.

Thus, there is more than complexity at stake in the difference between code and law, between institutions and cryptocurrencies. Institutions are not merely social software, although they are that. Because they contain society-wide conflict, state institutions can scale more robustly than other species of institution. These also anchor money in real economies, something that mere tokens cannot do in principle. These conflict-containing and value-anchoring properties set money institutions, human institutions, apart from algorithmic pretenders. The failure of cryptocurrencies as money proves the former's robustness.

At bottom, the designers of cryptocurrencies, being cyborgs, equivocate between code and law, between instruction set and contract. This equivocation is suggestive up to a point but not beyond. It is ultimately false, reduced in the cyborg imagination in the same way that 'information', 'language' and 'intelligence' are reduced. In effecting this cybernetic slide, designers of cryptocurrencies miss what is fundamental about institutions—not their complexity or verbosity but their ability to express and indeed contain human conflict and anchor material value; with credit money, this is done abstractly yet flexibly and stably.

Designing human institutions is simultaneously a political and technical exercise. Modern money works ultimately because its institutions watch over the social peace, albeit a capitalist one. As creatures of a disturbance of that peace, cryptocurrencies mark an insurgency that could result in a more brutal peace. But their failure might also fire our imaginations to think of money and markets beyond capitalism.

11 | EUROPE AND DEMOCRATIC FUNDING

Robust mutualisation at scale drives hierarchy in money; political mutualisation is more robust than economic; capitalism plus democracy requires a hybrid of both to operate.

The national state just happens to be the most robust mode of political mutualisation at present; others could emerge. The EU can be read as an experiment in a different type of political mutualisation outside the standard, federated state. Its crisis response arguably tells us something about the dimensions of all functional political mutualisations as regards money.

Responding to the credit crisis, the EU muddled through to innovate non-market, institutional sources of state finance that de-marketised government debt, limited the ability of credit markets to be sovereign counterparties and preserved state space to stabilised economies. These were secured by a de facto European fiscal compact at least at the margin. Some kind of fiscal compact and a substantial *de-marketisation of sovereign debt* appear to constitute institutional minima for effective robust political mutualisation, whatever institutional form they take.

Finance is constructed by law, but what, if any, are the logical bounds of the constructive power of law as regards finance? If political mutualisation is critical to functional money, what dimensions must this mutualisation have? Earlier we concluded that the mutualisation of economic contract is weaker than that of a political contract; while the former can expand to greater scale in good times, it dissolves in stressed states of the world (Pistor, 2013). Hence, states which mutualise citizen balance sheets over the largest economies have the best money. Mutualisation at scale therefore represents the logical limit of the plasticity of law in money.

The EU is an interesting intermediate case between pure economic and pure political mutualisation—a case of complex and uneven political mutualisation

Parts of this chapter were originally published as the article 'Europe and the Logic of Hierarchy' in the *Journal of Comparative Economics* 41, no. 2: 436–446 © Association for Comparative Economic Studies 2013. All rights reserved. Reproduced with the permission of the copyright holders and the publisher, Elsevier, Amsterdam.

under conditions of its particular political settlement between national sovereigns. Intermediate cases often tell us a lot about pure ideal types. The EU's failure of crisis management was in large part a result of the infirmities introduced into its monetary institutions by its fragile political settlement. As with our other cases, the EU's failures in crisis management are instructive as they show the link between the nature of the mutualisation of a community and the money it issues. It is not just that the EU is weakly politically mutualised; the institutional details of its mutualisation, themselves the outcome of multiple political equilibria, feed into the behaviour of the EU's credit system and define the limits of technocratic and democratic management.

Acting outside the nation-state frame that Europe itself did so much to standardise historically, the EU is an ongoing experiment in non-national political mutualisation rather than a half-baked national state. If anything, the euro's success as a working global currency shows that what is at stake in money is not the *form* of national sovereignty per se but the substance of robust political mutualisation at scale as the base for economic mutualisation. The EU's complex mutualisation might lead to undemocratic and messy crisis management, and it may indeed represent the mutualisation of Europe's elites more than its people, but it remains a form of political mutualisation that has generated a working, world-scale currency whose binding grows tighter with each crisis.

By definition, the market pool is made up of individual entities linked together by counterparty relations formed between and across levels of the hierarchy. While we might conceive of a banking system as a mutualised bloc—'a single big bank'—for the purposes of abstraction, it actually matters that this pool can and will disarticulate under conditions of stress (Mehrling, 2011). Shared culture can make the pool function like a herd and generate self-fulfilling prophecies that are both stabilising and destabilising, but these bonds are definitionally weaker than the bonds of criminal law and are therefore not the functional equivalent in a crisis.

Put differently, private mutualisation and coordination that are impervious to crisis-born disarticulation can only exist at a scale that is too small to mitigate the crisis itself: this is the lesson that led to the belated founding of the Fed. But to say this is merely to repeat the very raison d'etre of the state going back to Hobbes: the state exists precisely because complex social systems require the credible and highly coordinated deployment of certain functions that are creatures of scale. This only happens when coordination is solid enough that ties of mutualisation do not dissolve under cyclical pressure.

That national sovereignty has proved to be a winning response to this problem thus far is no reason to assume that other forms of binding political mutualisation at scale might not be invented, but clearly we are not there yet. We might view the European experiment in this light rather than shoehorning it into the federated-nation-state narrative. Europe appears to be asking the question: what do non-national forms of political mutualisation at scale look like? It has acquired political mutualisation and scale, but it clearly needs to work on its coordination. Its lack of crisis coordination comes down to the criss-crossing elite or popular demands on the EU which are constitutive of its complex political mutualisation.

The Price of Space

Following Weber, space is definitional of state power, something that 'globalisation' appeared to have undermined. Weber of course defines the state as a legitimate monopoly of violence *within* a given territory. But national structures are themselves of differing scales and qualities of mutualisation, differences that determine where national balance sheets sit in the international hierarchy of money.

If the interest rate is the price of time, money today in terms of money tomorrow, then the exchange rate might be seen as the price of space. Exchange rates commensurate the liabilities of states that reference different national economic catchment areas. And the national space that the global FX market is built on is the US: the price of the dollar is the price of world money (see Chapter 9).

The argument from scale and coordination allows us to see why. The two single largest economic entities in the world are the US economy and the EU economy, representing a quarter of global GDP each. Yet these entities are not equal in terms of their status as world money. The dollar is backed by a single coordinated sovereign whose reserve asset is the US economy. The EU, by contrast, has no singular mechanism to bind the currency to its economy. The complex quality of its mutualisation is a key reason why the euro is not on par with the dollar.

Yet the fact that a non-national state even invites comparison with a bona fide national state ought to tell us something about the role of robust mutualisation at scale in money. In that sense, the global central-bank swap lines are the closest analogy to the euro in terms of being a non-national state yet political form of mutualisation of balance sheets to produce a world-scale backstop for world money.

Europe's historical task, it appears, is to prove that the national state is *not* the only possible institutional expression of the logic of hierarchy. The euro crisis stress tested this notion and exposed many cracks. In every case, further mutualisation at scale between national states was the solution. Some members of the EU continue to resist full and permanent fiscal mutualisation, but it may be that partial, episodic fiscal mutualism will institutionally express the logic of hierarchy in a non-national state way, especially if capital flows can be controlled.

We first outline the fissures in the EU's credit system and link them to Europe's particular political settlement. We will then show how the European response embodied a form of mutualisation at scale that expressed and contested its political settlement.

Funding the Gap

The collapse of the European credit system in 2007–2008 rendered it incapable of playing a critical, binding role. This was to *fund the gap* between the 'coordinated market economies' of the north and the 'mixed market economies' of the south, to use Peter Hall's terms for these national economic models (Hall, 2014). In the vocabulary of the 'varieties of capitalism' literature, a critical 'institutional complementarity' developed between the European banking system and the very project of monetary union. The only way to run a monetary union between divergent national economic models—where one model consistently generated balance of payment surpluses and the other deficits—was for some institution to function as a liquidity transformer from surplus nations to deficit ones while ensuring that the gap did not get too big. Europe was thrown into crisis when this complementary funding machine broke.

Initially, European banks themselves played this role. The continent's credit system mobilised global and northern European savings to invest in the debt of southern European governments, converging European sovereign bond spreads. Yet its banks were also heavily invested in the American mortgage market (Tooze, 2018). When the blowback from the US financial crisis hit the system, the liquidity-transforming process jammed and crisis resulted. A bypass was eventually found at one level higher in the credit system, namely the ECB and the new, hastily built European Financial Stability Facility (EFSF) and its successor agency, the European Stability Mechanism (ESM). To fund the gap, the EU had to invent new institutions of substantial scale and significant mutualisation to staunch the bleeding.

Yet, given the fractured European political settlement, its credit mutualisation, whether through banks or the EFSF, was tenuous and was seen as such by financial markets. For the markets, robust mutualisation at scale means a full fiscal compact on the model of the national state. This is less for neoliberal reasons than for Hobbesian or informational ones: moments of deep uncertainty can only be met by some overwhelming source of certainty. A full fiscal compact is of course ruled out politically in the EU. Yet a resolution to the crisis only needed a form of mutualisation that durably funds the gap. A full fiscal compact is the blank cheque that the markets need in the face of uncertainty, but it might well be overkill in terms of actual funding needs. The demand for a full fiscal compact therefore can be attenuated by limiting the voice of the markets—that is, capital controls, something ruled out by the EU's neoliberal common sense.

The ideology of the Economic and Monetary Union's (EMU) progenitors told them that economic unification would mean that national economic models would converge even in the medium term. The key variable here is time: convergence in terms of economic models is clearly utopian in the medium term, but convergence in terms of performance rather than underlying institutions is conceivable in the long term. But this needs more than a liquidity-transforming function; it needs development banking and disciplined industrial policy. Yet this institutional complementarity between the banking system and monetary union was not explicitly designed in, and EU elites do not view the function of the European banking system in these terms.

Hall shows us that the EU's divergent models actually led to divergence, not convergence. The north saw innovative export-led growth through wage coordination, vocational training and neutral macroeconomic policies. In the south, demand-led growth was the net result of only episodic 'social pacts' between capital and labour, leading to lower levels of skill development being institutionalised and consequently competition based on low-cost labour rather than innovation. Expansionary fiscal policy and periodic balance-of-payments crisis necessitating currency devaluation was the southern pattern.

The fixed exchange rate regime of the euro therefore placed the north at a significant advantage vis-à-vis the south in terms of productivity growth. Contrary to expectations of convergence, reduced borrowing rates for southern governments after the EMU entry led to an implicit cross-subsidisation of their debt costs. The EMU gave southern nations little incentive to alter their growth models by softening their budget constraints even while a critical dimension of flexibility, a national exchange rate, was no longer available. The resulting southern inflation damaged the low-cost growth model, further damaging competitiveness. Large fiscal and current account deficits in the south resulted in a structural gap that needed funding.

How then was it possible for the European project to proceed this far without a systemic crisis?

Mind the Gap

The answer is the European credit system. The asymmetries between the north and the south were sustainable up to a point but not beyond. The solution to the crisis in the near term therefore was to get back to a world where these asymmetries were sustainable, the gap fundable, while at the same time signalling a long-term plan for investing in convergence. If the credit system kept debt flowing into the south, Europe could paper over the asymmetries almost indefinitely so long as two conditions were met. First, some degree of structural reform or industrial policy proceeded in the south so that the gap remained within funding range. Hall notes that this was in fact occurring, but it is a long-term process. Second, the European banks had to avoid over-leveraging themselves so that they could continue to roll over funding to the south. This meant banking supervision and regulation at the European level. The European political settlement meant that EU designers had Europeanised money but not banking.

Given the short-term rigidities in economic structures, the European financial crisis was a liquidity problem, not a solvency problem. These asymmetries are not set in stone: the south is not insolvent but in the midst of a transformation. But it takes time to change, and with all production processes the south needs liquidity during that time. That is all a credit system can do: buy you time.

What European banks were invested in, apart from the US mortgage market, *was* southern Europe. The European banking system was implicitly providing the long-term funding for southern structural transformation by funding southern debt at near-northern prices. This was the carrot, perhaps too much of one as transformation did not occur at a sufficient pace when funding was cheap and plentiful. There was, however, very little stick until the crisis when there was too much of one. The market-based credit system lurched from one extreme to the other yet all the while performing a key institutional role within the European matrix.

What was needed, again, was long-term institutional financing through a development bank that would both provide stability through consistent liquidity and extract discipline on the south to make sure convergence was on track. Neoliberal nostrums ruled such a solution out at the time, but it is never too late.

When the US mortgage market blew up, Europe's banks were heavily exposed: they owned 20 per cent of non-conforming mortgage-backed securities while sponsoring a whopping two-thirds of the asset-backed commercial paper (Tooze, 2018). This was the impetus for the significant swap lines between the Fed and the ECB: European banks had to fund dollar-denominated mortgage assets, but their liabilities were in euros. The ECB cannot create dollars, of course, and privately mutualised money markets had frozen, so some institution had to take on the currency mismatch lest Europe's banks melt away. The currency swaps, another form of improvised mutualisation of apex central-bank balance sheets, was the emergency institution that stepped into the void.

Similarly, once the European banking system was overleveraged, some other local institution has had to perform the role of funding the gap between the north and the south. Belatedly, and only once much pain had been exerted on the south (thereby increasing the gap), the ECB came in with its own version of quantitative easing, augmented by the so-called TARGET2 imbalances, payment system credits or debits between national central banks reflecting trade and/or capital flows (Cecchetti, McCauley and McGuire, 2012).

Yet this was a temporary fix. European banks had to be repaired so that they could return to their role of funding the gap, but now oriented by a south-focused industrial policy so that credit is provided with specific incentives and controls to induce structural change. This meant a bank bailout of significant magnitude. This in turn meant that northern states have to find the fiscal space so that no bank is 'too big to bail' (Blyth, 2013).

This meant getting the politics right in the north. There is a constituency in the north, including elements of German labour, that sees merit in a long-term investment in the south as a market for northern industrial goods (Streeck, 2014). This investment is not for its own sake, of course, but a means to hold the EU together. Workers in the north seem to realise that the EU keeps northern currencies lower than they would be otherwise, thereby subsidising their export-led growth model. This constituency could find an ally with a reform constituency in the south. Their combined strength might break insider control in the south and set structural change on a long-term course. Having been cleaned up, the banks could then return to their job of funding the gap, now fortified by an intra-European rather than domestic political coalition.

Reaching for Democratic Funding

The European crisis called the very legitimacy of the European project into question, bringing to the fore a concern that afflicts many parts of the world—namely the financial foundations of modern states. The lopsided nature of the European project served to highlight the undemocratic side of how we finance the state. It also foreshadows a potential solution to the problem of making our present form of mutualisation at scale more democratic.

While scorn is routinely reserved for the unelected Eurocrats who seek to squash national sovereignty in southern Europe, very little seems to be said about the legitimacy of unelected markets dictating terms to sovereign states. Morality, it seems, is on the side of the creditor: sovereigns, like ordinary folk, ought to pay their debts.

But political communities have a responsibility to maintain their own autonomy to the extent they can, even those that have entered into an 'ever closer' union with other nations. When governments fund themselves in ways that put their autonomy at risk, they are abrogating their democratic duty. This is the double-edged nature of all credit: democracy can be aided by the flexibility and liquidity of putting government debt to market, but beyond a point medicine becomes poison.

So how can democratic states take advantage of the bond markets without being consumed by them?

The answer from creditor morality is simple: do not borrow beyond your means. And there is some truth in this homily. The problem of course is that the very extent of one's means is subject to the judgement of the selfsame creditor. To a large degree, solvency is in the eye of the creditor.

For any economic unit, the pattern of cash inflows rarely maps perfectly onto the pattern of cash outflows, demanding an economy-wide liquidity matchmaker. 'Banking' is the socialisation of this liquidity-matching function. If the matching stops, a borrowing unit's cash commitments could swamp its cash inflows: the unit is insolvent. If your creditors stop rolling over your debt, the music stops very quickly indeed. If the unit is perceived to be insolvent, its access to life-giving liquidity is cut off and the suspicion of insolvency becomes self-fulfilling.

Prudence dictates that any political or economic unit steer clear of such peril. Yet when faced with myriad constraints, units will load up on credit if that dimension is eased. The market price of the unit's debt is meant to be an indicator of proximity to peril. Yet as we have seen, this indicator is notoriously fickle: one day the unit is extremely creditworthy; the next day it is bust.

This was the case with southern Europe: faced with a particular national economic model that generated pressures for expansive fiscal policy, the political settlement in these locales pushed the national economies to the limit even as their budget constraints were softened by soft-headed markets after the EMU entry. It could only have ended badly; yet short-term political incentives and long-term structural constraints combined to drive the south down this route.

Now, especially if the economic unit is a democratic state, it has a duty to avoid such peril. This means that it has a duty to avoid fickle funding. And this in turn means avoiding the bond market beyond the point of democratic prudence. In the wake of the crisis, this is exactly what Europe groped towards. Ironically, it was precisely because Europe lacked a common fiscal authority that it sought a novel solution to the problem of political mutualisation at scale.

Leviathan Interrupted

Most see Europe as an unfinished federal project and thereby weak. From this point of view, the solution to the crisis is the completion of that project through full fiscal union. This of course would imply that every European state would undertake to be jointly and severally liable for the debts of others via the intermediation of a common fiscal authority, the dreaded 'transfer union'.

Yet we need not let money markets set the agenda by limiting our imaginations to institutional forms that gives them succour in a crisis. There is nothing natural about the requirement to stem market uncertainty being met by a full fiscal compact. Controlling markets ex ante is a perfectly workable solution, but keeping capital controls off the table artificially naturalises the appeal for a full fiscal compact.

What if Europe is something new in the world, a totally novel experiment rather than a slow-motion replay of American history? The people of Europe do not want to be part of a federal state, rendering the nation-state analogy nugatory. Our imaginations are constrained by this nation-state frame. This frame blinds us to the key function driving money, namely robust mutualisation at scale. We fetishise form at the risk of ignoring function. As a result, we might end up ignoring workable resolutions to crises.

The impossibility of federated nationhood is what ultimately ties the hands of the ECB as an effective LOLR; the institution's strong anti-inflationary stance is merely the icing on the cake. A prudent LOLR mitigates the fickle nature of market funding by stabilising the credit system as a whole, for a punitive price, when the market's mood inevitably turns. The LOLR function only works if the lender has credibility. A central bank has credibility, in turn, not merely because of its ideology but because of the material fact of scale: it is backed by a balance sheet bigger than any private balance sheet, namely the fisc. The ECB's ideology enabled it to fake credibility in the *absence* of a European fisc as long as the system remained untested. In the absence of a common fisc, its hawkish stance stood exposed, serving only to extend the south's pain. In other words, its credibility came at the cost of democracy and thereby the very legitimacy of the EU.

If the ECB had acted as an adequate LOLR at the beginning of this crisis, it would have implicitly called into being the absent European fiscal authority. Germany in particular would have been doing the underwriting. And this could not happen because the European people do not want to be the United States of Europe: the Bundestag is merely the outward institutional expression of this more general resistance because as the largest economic catchment area, Germany's balance sheet is the first in line for backstopping.

In any event, the ECB is constrained by inadequate mutualisation. If the ECB *had* acted as an LOLR in this crisis without at least implicitly calling into being a common fiscal leviathan—that is, without getting a blank cheque from its constituent sovereigns, and Germany in particular—the ECB *itself* would have taken the place of the impaired sovereigns as the target for the market's wrath. Again, capital controls, had they existed, would have allowed for more options. But neoliberal ethics mean that even hedge funds can limit redemptions but national states cannot.

A LOLR *without* some fiscal backing is simply not credible; the markets would have gnawed away at the euro until it perished or until the implicit backing was made explicit. The assets that the ECB purchased might have lost value and damaged the ECB's own balance sheet; the euro itself would have started to melt away.

In the event, Germany did its best to make explicit that no fiscal leviathan would be erected, so the southern economies had to be force-shrunk down to a size at which the ECB's eventual response without fiscal backing could appear credible. While this obeys the logic of scale, it does so at a huge cost to people in the south and therefore at the cost of increasing the gap between the north and the south that some institution will have to play going forward.

The ECB has an implicit political community undergirding its action, the shadow 'nation' of Europe. This community is implied by the structure of the European monetary system, an implication that has a quantitative expression in the price of a constituent nation's debt. Analogously, the implicit backing of Fannie Mae and Freddie Mac by the US treasury had a dampening effect on the price of their debt. And as with the pressure to explicitly nationalise Fannie and Freddie during the crisis, the markets pushed the ECB or the EU to its limit to test whether this *implicit* backing by the *shadow* polity could be made explicit. Whence the narrative for fiscal union: it is the path of least resistance for the market to get the scale or certainty it wants.

The backing could be, and finally was, rendered explicit in the case of the US because the polity behind the Fed was explicitly and effectively mutualised and could operate in a highly coordinated fashion. This is why the EU crisis expresses itself as a crisis over the kind of mutualisation that the EU will have and on what terms it will have it when the usual nation-state shaped solutions are not available to it.

This is where the EFSF comes in. One can see how this institution might be the kernel of a common fiscal authority, at least in its borrowing power if not its taxation power. And that is what the fight was about at its inception. The Germans wanted to keep it small and limited so as not to prefigure a common fiscal mechanism, but then it became too small to be credible as an LOLR. The markets were too roiled in any case to accept the debt it attempted to sell. Its funds were eventually beefed up even as the ECB belatedly came to the party.

The structure of the EFSF made it a kind of collateralised debt obligation: it pooled together the creditworthiness of sovereigns through proportionate contributions and issued highly rated bonds, the proceeds of which were used to buy encumbered sovereign debt. In the immediate wake of the crisis, a quarter of all Greek debt was owned by the EFSF, with the 'official sector' of the IMF, the ECB, national central banks and the Bank of Greece holding 70 per cent (Serdarevic, 2012).

Conceivably, sovereign wealth funds and other 'international public investors' could be induced to come in as the patient, long-term institutional capital—in other words, not the fickle market money. Since these investors have deep pockets and long-term horizons (some of them are sovereigns themselves after all), they are not subject to the same incentives as market players who tend to be highly leveraged and work on very narrow margins. Having drastically underpriced sovereign risk before the crisis, they then drastically overpriced it as yesterday's promise of growth turned into today's demand for austerity. Long-term investors look at long-term value rather than short-term prices. These investors would typically hold the bonds to maturity and can ride out short-term fluctuations because of their deep pockets. Soon after the crisis they were getting a deal.

The absence of a common fiscal authority in Europe has led to a credibility crisis at its heart. Given their constraints, the Europeans were finding that the other route to stability is in effect to *de-marketise* some portion of their sovereign debt and place it with long-term, buy-and-hold institutions like the EFSF fabricated to replace the unregulated and short-termist credit system. Operating within the contours of their complex political settlement, Europeans sought fiscal space by de-marketising their debt to buy fiscal space rather than giving into the market's demand for full fiscal union which was anyway off the table.

A new institutional balance sheet was being geared to be the functional equivalent of the debt markets in terms of offering greater crisis-proof fiscal space. It might not replace the entire private credit system, but it can ease the terms on which the sovereign borrowing operates by being the bond buyer of last resort. Along with a revamped banking system, this might lead to more stable and thus more democratic funding.

That is but a necessary step, far from sufficient. Once the European credit system is rebuilt, southern states will need *industrial policy* to make that bet pay off this time. All credit does is buy you time. Capital controls buy further time.

The analogy with bank funding is clear: the pre-crisis problem was that banks were sourced funds in highly liquid markets at ever-shorter maturities and in ever-greater proportions. European banks compounded the folly by adding a currency mismatch to that of time and liquidity. This made them highly vulnerable to runs, whence the subprime crisis. One proposed solution was mandatory funding durations imposed by the regulators (enshrined in Basel III): long-term assets ought to be funded by long-term liabilities to the extent possible, the so-called 'net stable funding ratio'.

The state is a long-term asset—the people's long-term asset. It needs a funding structure adequate to its long-term democratic duties. In effect, this means finding a form of mutualisation at scale that maintains autonomy and sovereignty even though the catchment area is broader than the national economy. The EFSF was still a form of crisis-born, temporary mutualisation. Its *permanent* successor, the ESM, is a creature of a brand-new treaty, again a non-nation-state form of political mutualisation.

Common-Pool Discipline

There is another important bank analogy that helps to reframe the question around austerity and highlight the new path that Europe might be charting. The 'fiscal compact' extracts fiscal commitments from states that bind tighter than the pre-existing treaty; with the ESM now in place, the moral hazard of an ESM bailout is deemed to be minimised.

This mimics the compact between banks and sovereigns in domestic settings: local banks are backstopped by the central bank through emergency liquidity insurance. All insurers have the right to regulate their insurees' behaviour, so central banks regulate banks for the privilege of liquidity insurance.

In the post-war period, the politics behind this was simple: unfettered private banking led to war-generating crises that states ended up paying for ex post, so banks had to be tied up in regulations to the point of de facto nationalisation. Unstitching this compact characterised the politics of the neoliberal period that followed. This in turn led to the undemocratic 'too big to fail', which preserved insurance but without accountability.

Through this insurance mechanism, private bank liabilities are in effect written against the sovereign balance sheet, the politically mutualised common pool. The logic of regulating constituent entities that have the privilege of issuing a liability on the common pool is the logic of the fiscal compact.

Yet the politics of its application is reversed. Whereas the post-war application of this logic saw states regulate constituent banks in the name of democracy, undemocratic Europe seeks to regulate constituent sovereigns in the interest of the north. As an ideal type, this disciplinary compact works because of a public–private partnership between states and banks, albeit one with good terms for banks. Disciplining banks is legitimised in the name of democracy and executed by a balance sheet bigger than the constituent banks.

At one level up, the partnership between constituent states and the EU is missing both the ideological prop of legitimacy and the institutional mechanism of the big fiscal stick. The locus of democratic politics remains the national state. Set on current institutional rails, democracy means 'less Europe'. Yet by tying themselves to the euro, sovereigns have locked themselves into the logic of credit that demands that the common pool regulate its constituent elements. And European banks are also part of this common pool as we have seen earlier. The irony is that where common-pool discipline qua bank regulation failed, leading to our present crisis, common-pool discipline qua national fiscal austerity has only strengthened. This of course is because of the lopsided relationship between the money interest and the public interest.

Fair mutualisation means common-pool discipline on *both* bank and national dimensions. Constituent units issuing a common liability do indeed have to be disciplined for the sake of the common pool, but this must apply to both nations and banks. When these units are sovereign democratic states, they must also find the means to fund themselves in a manner that does not overdo austerity in the name of stability. While the need for discipline does indeed arise from the lack of discipline either by the markets or by the terms of Maastricht, to see the solution merely in terms of discipline of nation-state elements is inadequate.

The divided nature of the European economy has precluded the embedding of necessary common-pool discipline in a narrative of give and take. This narrative has to change before things can move forward. The south has to be allowed to invest and grow its way out of its mess—and do so through a model that suits each national community. Convergence of performance should not be mistaken for convergence of institutions. There are many paths to growth. It will take disciplined investment to find those paths.

Conclusion: The Impossible Arbitrage of Space

What we might consider is that Europe's ex-post crisis response might be a way of insulating democratic states from the fickle markets ex ante.

We know that how we fund our governments matters for their legitimacy, but our democratic common sense ties only taxation to representation. Yet the structure of state borrowing is equally critical. Grasping for institutional solutions, Europe's experiment turned to a patient structure of funding, albeit only at the margin. There might be a lesson in there for all democratic nations: fund long term through institutions rather than markets.

Given where in the world most savings are located, democratic national funding might entail more globalisation, not less. Or, rather, it would entail a different version of globalisation than the current one that renders market-based pooling between national states merely in terms of austerity and discipline, creating a terrible choice between austerity and democracy. Thinking about democratic funding means denying the necessity of this choice.

The centrality of core national economic space provides us with another route to the answer to one of the more vexing empirical questions in international finance: why does the arbitrage condition of uncovered interest parity fail? Why does the forward rate not adjust to equal the expected future spot rate and thus eliminate an arbitrage opportunity? The answer is liquidity risk, and this depends on access to an LOLR in the currency in which the bank or dealer has incurred a liability (Mehrling and Neilson, 2014). Because such access is different over time and space, liquidity risk persists, and the arbitrage condition fails.

Unified economic space naturally eliminates this liquidity risk by eliminating exchange rates themselves; this is the European route. Thus, at the limit, realising the utopia of no arbitrage can only be achieved by an equally utopian world state. Note that this is the spatial equivalent to the idealised provision of totally free liquidity by a central bank domestically with the aim of eliminating risk in the pricing of time (Mehrling, 2011). Both are dangerous utopias as the Credit Crisis and the European crisis show, respectively. If liquidity is not a free good, the diversity of economic space cannot be wished away. This is the deep lesson of the 'varieties of capitalism' literature.

The next best thing in terms of this spatial idealisation would be to seamlessly backstop all key currencies by mutualising central-bank liabilities at the apex of the system. Such episodic mutualisation is of course the function of central-bank swap lines. The regulatory equivalent would be coordination of banking policy across nations for that set of interlocking activities. This is what the Europeans are trying with their banking union.

At the global level, this would be the mother of all coordination games. In the wake of the failure of this idealisation, the state continues to function as the backstop for credit systems precisely because it expresses the maximum scale at which robust coordination is possible.

Thus, hierarchy of scale and coordination explains risk premia in the FX markets. Only a few states have effectively integrated themselves with economic spaces at the scale required to have their liabilities function as world money. Other economic state spaces remain relatively demutualised and relatively uncoordinated and therefore have their liabilities tradable only at premia that violate uncovered interest parity. In other words, 'parity' implies the impossible elimination of difference in economic space.

Elasticity and discipline can still be exerted from the apex of this jerry-built international system for a price. Central banks, individually or collectively, might not have a choice as to whether they support liquidity in the forward markets or not. But they do have a choice as to the terms of refinance and the conditions under which market-making more generally operates. That is where all the political action is. And this is the arena within which the elasticity of law can be exercised to serve either the public interest or the money interest.

Financial systems are always hierarchical, a brute technical fact that can lead to adverse normative consequences. The normative task is to mitigate this hierarchy with structures of accountability.

Democratisation is therefore not synonymous with a flat institutional world. Accountability per se is not unthinkable in hierarchical systems; the fact of hierarchy just makes democracy even tougher. Given its logical necessity, there is a grave danger in thinking without hierarchy. Hierarchy defines the logical terrain within which we must engineer a democratic outcome. Learning from Europe means thinking through hierarchy to enable that outcome. The European experience shows that non-nation-state political mutualisation can operate at scale. But that entails at least two further institutional moves: to demarketise government debt structures and to undertake industrial policy to compensate for differences in the productivity of political–economic space. Capital controls might also be considered. Such are the tasks for those who want to make the EU an accountable, democratic hierarchy.

12 | DEMOCRATIC SOVEREIGNTY MAKES MONEY

Democratic sovereignty embeds national money securely in a national economy over a long time horizon. Yet, ironically, it also severely limits the tools of monetary management. Democracy's post-war rise destroyed the central bank's ability to *sharply* raise interest rates to stem a credit bubble as this would crash the economy (Polanyi, 2001 [1944]; Eichengreen, 1998). Without this commitment to crash the economy, global money markets became so destabilising that they had to be contained; post-war controls on global capital flows were the flipside of democracy (Ruggie, 1982).

The deregulation of the neoliberal era signalled a reversal, but democracy endured albeit weakened. 'Privatised Keynesianism' and a welfarist 'politics of the governed' in the Global North and the Global South, respectively, were required to keep a tentative social peace (Chatterjee, 2004; Crouch, 2011). Democracy still limited price-based control, but now deregulation dismantled non-price control, resulting in a substantial amplification of the inherent instability of credit. Money's inherent hierarchy was weaponised and therefore delegitimated. Instability and inequality eventually shattered the neoliberal peace, giving rise to our populist present.

Democracy therefore gives money durable scale while simultaneously limiting the set of feasible institutional arrangements. We conclude by suggesting that a democratic response to both the impairment and delegitimation of monetary governance would be to nationalise banking behind capital controls while, following Keynes, globalising 'ideas, knowledge, science, hospitality, travel'. Democracy means nationalising banks and controlling capital flows. It does *not* mean narrow, exclusionary nationalism.

Collectives standing behind their money have a political choice: how do we configure a system that is inherently hybrid, hierarchical and unstable? What are our goals for this system? Do we want to maximise growth for the time being at the cost of inequality? How much instability do we tolerate in the service of this growth? How much pollution and intergenerational inequality are we willing to endure?

None of these are mechanically available, of course, but we can set the system in a direction with appropriate margins of safety. If these sound like questions for 'fiscal policy', it is because we are used to inhabiting a dichotomy set up by a political move to depoliticise 'monetary policy' as *solely* a technical exercise rather than an expression of politics through the design of monetary technicalities. Money is just government debt that does not mature and pays no interest. Just like government debt, it is a bet on a collective's future.

Legitimacy is definitional of the state; it is also foundational to the acceptance of the state's money. If modern legitimacy is based on democratic sovereignty, then modern money is intimately tied to democratic sovereignty. In a literal sense, democratic sovereignty makes money.

Institutions like the state are composed of what Roberto Unger calls frozen politics: where the fight stops, the institutional line is temporarily drawn until the fighting starts up again. The nature of the political settlement determines the shape of the governing institutions, including monetary control mechanisms.

If money is currently grounded in a democratic settlement, how is this democratic settlement expressed in the configuration of money? What are the tensions between democracy and money, and how might we confront them? This chapter outlines tensions between democracy and the inherent monetary features of hierarchy, entropy and technocracy.

The first tension is how democracy deals with two technical elements of credit money systems: hierarchy and entropy. Hierarchy can lead to capture, while entropy necessitates bailouts. It is hard but not impossible for democracies to pair hierarchies with accountability. Perhaps even harder for democracy is to deal with credit system entropy by means of a well-configured bailout. The particular political settlement in the North Atlantic headquarters of global capitalism does not help.

In trying to reconcile hierarchical money and democracy, we have to come to terms with how central banking is a form of central planning. Neoliberals achieved this, arguably, by reconciling themselves to a form of central planning. A key predicate here is understanding how markets themselves are social institutions subject to design and construction.

Following Commons, Polanyi and especially Mirowski, we see the market mechanism as highly engineered and thus capable of being configured for democracy. There is no such thing as a generic market except at a very high and therefore unhelpful level of abstraction. There are only *particular* markets with *particular* microstructures and *particular* dynamics.

What separates the classical liberal creed from today's neoliberals of course is that the latter are market planners: they self-consciously design and construct markets to perform certain functions and then naturalise these designs in the name of efficiency as understood by mainstream economics. What is less well appreciated is that when paired with money markets that are inherently hierarchical, the endeavour to plan markets becomes a form of *central* planning.

Neoliberals therefore had to find ideological space for this form of monetary planning. They did so in at least two ways: by endorsing modern portfolio theory as a form of privatised scientific planning that would be enabled by tying up the central banker qua central planner in algorithmic decision rules. That was in theory; in practice, robot central banking was always for down-hierarchy units. For the hegemon, neoliberals developed a cult of the Schmittian decisionist in the form of the oracular, 'maestro' central banker.

A second major way in which the tension between the money interest and the public interest is expressed, parallel to the tension between expansion and control, is that between technocracy and democracy.

Money is hard. Controlling it is harder: as Keynes famously noted, we have 'blundered in the control of a delicate machine, the working of which we do not understand'. Only public-minded technocrats can effectively control money in the public interest. What we have presented earlier is in the end of one long argument for bank nationalisation, given that banks write liabilities on the public exchequer. Technocrats can make honest mistakes and need to be insulated from the public's wrath in order to learn from these mistakes. But good-faith autonomy can become bad-faith capture very quickly—hence the present popular scorn for experts.

A democracy needs to strike a balance between autonomy and accountability in central-bank planning. This might mean that we accept the technocratic verdict of periodic bailouts and austerity to reset the system, but only if the burden is equitably shared. Bailouts and austerity then become bureaucratic housekeeping exercises rather than slow-motion civil wars.

Bailouts and other lifeboat operations are standard in the history of money and banking, and indeed justifiable on the technical grounds that many complex systems develop entropy and chaos over time and require a periodic reset (Minsky, 1992). With social institutions, technical choices are also political choices generating winners and losers. Yet the requirement of a reset is a technical feature of the credit system as a complex system and is therefore impossible to design away.

The technical features of a complex system like money therefore set the limit of what a political imaginary can accomplish. We can design more or less fragile systems, more or less democratic systems, but we cannot design away entropy itself. We are condemned to account for it technically and politically. We now have to do so in a world that is deeply interconnected economically but necessarily partitioned into units of variously mutualised political communities.

The rest of the chapter is organised as follows. The first section briefly sets out our admittedly thin use of the term 'democracy'. The second section looks at how such a democracy hampers price-based control. The third section outlines how capitalism and democracy both demand flexibility and stability from money. Given the limitations of price-based control under conditions of democracy, the burden of control actually falls on non-price forms of control: regulation or outright nationalisation. The final section therefore concludes by making the case for global capital controls and bank nationalisation.

Democratic Sovereignty in Most of the World

Democratic sovereignty, like all sovereignty, is a modus vivendi. Political bargains result in a particular constellation of institutions. Unger (2007, p. 49) argues for the political ontology of all social institutions: 'the whole order of society and culture represents a frozen politics—the containment and interruption of fighting'. Democracy is the current name we give to how we resolve the conflicts that are constitutive of society.

Without making a transcendental or teleological argument, we can identify a general pattern of 'frozen politics' that, beginning in the early modern period in Europe and by way of decolonisation, became a global social fact. This is democratic or popular sovereignty, when rule is authorised and legitimated by the ruled.

As the EU illustrates, the nation-state form ought not to be the limit of our imagination of how popular sovereignty can be expressed concretely. Political theorist Karuna Mantena reminds us that the nation state did not in fact exhaust the anti-colonial imagination; many state forms, including dominions, were deemed to be consistent with popular sovereignty (Mantena, 2016). Yet since the post-war period, the space of imagining state formations has been demarcated by popular sovereignty residing in a nation state.

This is not to confuse democratic sovereignty with *procedural* democracy. As Partha Chatterjee has pointed out, even putatively non-democratic regimes are now constrained to invoke the people:

> There is no question that the legitimacy of the modern state is now clearly
> and firmly grounded in a concept of popular sovereignty.... Even the most
> undemocratic of modern regimes must claim its legitimacy not from divine
> right or dynastic succession or the right of conquest but from the will of the
> people, however expressed. (Chatterjee, 2004, p. 27)

While common sense points to the *process* by which governance is anchored with the
people, it is worth reiterating that there are versions of popular sovereignty that look
to the *outcomes* of governance rather than the procedures. The legitimacy of relatively
authoritarian states in East Asia in the twentieth century, for instance, rested less on
formal representation than a sense of public duty to achieve a revolutionary outcome,
namely economic development. These regimes had what Chalmers Johnson called
'revolutionary legitimacy', a legitimacy of 'outputs' rather than mere representational
'input' (Johnson, 1999, p. 53). These remain forms of democratic sovereignty.

This firm establishment of sovereignty as democratic alters our understanding of
the ontology of money. When we see democratic sovereignty from the point of view
of Unger's radicalised pragmatism as a particular configuration of politics, we undo
the Chartalist hypostatisation of the state. By rethinking sovereignty as democratic
sovereignty, we move from a state theory of money to a political theory of money.

A sovereign, as Richard Tuck (2016, p. 121) observes, is construed as being
perpetual in nature. When this sovereign is a *demos* bound together in a legitimate
political settlement, this infinite future horizon is not only embedded in real relations
of production but also made available for the operations of credit and banking.

This is why the state has the best money on regular commercial calculation. It is not
only the largest *economic* entity but the only *perpetual* one. Unlike a normal bank, the
democratic sovereign state mutualises not through commercial contract but through
the political contract of democratic sovereignty. Contractual robustness, a perpetual
temporal horizon and national scale combine to generate a unit with borrowing
capacity like no other, a democratic leviathan.

It turns out that money is a deep feature of popular sovereignty. Democratic
sovereignty makes money, and money enables the *demos* to potentially achieve feats
of collective action when it borrows from its own future.

Democracy Hampers Technocracy

By controlling an economy's endogenous capacity to generate the medium of its own
expansion, the central bank modulates the servo-mechanical coherence of money

with value, by influencing the robustness of the constituent economic units. It can effect this control with the grain of the credit system—that is, 'on banking principles'. Exercising this infrastructural power, the state's bank can learn to control the amplitude of economic cycles, themselves the product of interacting uncertainties.

Set in the money markets, interest rates are the most important prices in an economy, helping determine how much businesses invest and how much households spend, save and borrow. They set the temperature in the hothouse that is a modern economy. And the hand on the gauge is that of the central bank. By controlling the price in this one essential market, it controls the prices in all markets. This is sophisticated economic control, neither untrammelled nor despotic. It is economic action at a distance mediated by banks and markets. Raise the interest rate, and the cost of bank borrowing increases, delimiting the degree to which banks can expand their balance sheets. Raise the short-term interest rate, and the rates at different maturities move in sync as arbitrageurs transmit the elevated price to all fixed-income instruments. Hierarchy means 'planning' can occur through actions in one upstream market.

The endogenous tendency to overextend credit in a system of private banks led to multiple credit booms and busts, more than populist democracy could stand. The balance between the public and money interests in rich nations played out as the burden of bank creditworthiness being split, shifting in the last instance to the nation state. If a bank failed, its shareholders might suffer, but depositors were to be protected by state-backed deposit insurance. The welfarist idiom of protection was applied to banking, an implicit recognition that the money function was a public utility. The pastoral care of money became an aspect of the state's broader pastoral functions. Insuring depositors in private banks against the loss of their money is tantamount to de facto nationalisation of a systemically critical portion of the liabilities side of the banking system even in public–private hybrid systems.

Banks became a kind of retail outlet for the function, contributing their own credit in large measure, by which they continued to profit, but restricted in their field of operation for the sake of the public money function. Indeed, price-based control only operates in tandem with other regulatory forms such as restrictions on entry (licensing), capital adequacy, liquidity ratios, and so on. Given that marginal sources of liquidity can be international, capital controls themselves are part of the overall 'regulatory' framework within which other forms of control operate.

The rationale for regulation comes ultimately from deposit and liquidity insurance rather than 'market failure': an insurer has the right to demand prudent behaviour from the insuree. Moral hazard abounds: banks can take on more risk knowing that the state has covered their depositors. Extreme moral hazard requires highly detailed regulations—indeed so detailed that the case for keeping banking in the private sector disappears altogether. Full nationalisation would of course entail a different set of control issues.

Unlike regular business, banks cannot be allowed to fail since their deep interconnections with each other mean that the failure of one potentially could lead to cascading failures. Banks could be allowed to fail, and cascading failures could occur if the polity were willing and able to tolerate the whipsawing business cycles that would ensue. A democratic polity cannot withstand such volatility. Therefore, regular capitalist market discipline for banks fails thanks to democracy, leaving our control mechanisms to carry the disciplinary load.

But democracy further hampers one of these methods of control—interest rates. As we saw in Chapter 8, a proliferation of alternative sources of domestic and international funding makes it hard for the central bank to take the proverbial punch bowl away from the party. We saw that the Fed had such difficulty in disciplining system liquidity, especially given the offshore Eurodollar market, that it gave up altogether on countercyclical policy and moved to cleaning up the mess after the party.

Such leniency was not totally politically inspired. Even public-minded central-bank planners are constrained by democratic populism. This is because any small rise in rates might not *by itself* be enough to stem a rising credit tide; any large rise in interest rates, on the contrary, would crash the economy itself.

Money market veteran Al Wojnilower noted:

> [O]nce expansionary forces have taken hold, the Federal Reserve can contain them only by remaining 'tight' beyond the time that will subsequently be recorded as the cyclical peak. *There is no kill except overkill.* (Wojnilower, 1980, p. 291, n. 7, emphasis added)

Of course, in a populist democracy overkill is out of the question. As we saw earlier, if democracy limits the central bank's arsenal to only *gradual* countercyclical rate hikes, market operators observing this know that they can leverage up to the point where their margin over the borrowing rate remains positive.

Ironically, raising rates gradually in a world of populist democracy and cheap and available liquidity actually amplifies the cycle. Only the threat of a sudden hike, a threat to crash the economy, would curtail this procyclical behaviour, but sudden hikes are ruled out by democracy lest democracy itself is damaged. Popular sovereignty has hampered price-based monetary control.

We should therefore be sceptical about what the blunt tool of short-term interest rate control can achieve in terms of countercyclical purchase in the absence of other forms of control. Direct controls, modulating or even blocking off access to local and global liquidity, have to play an outsized role in a democracy, especially one which is less financially developed but even otherwise.

The Medium Is the Measure

The complex of capitalism plus democracy defined roughly the last century since the collapse of what Polanyi called nineteenth-century civilisation. If money is a form of institutionalised social power, the architectonics of society at any given historical conjuncture will govern its form and function. The functional horizon of modern money is by no means universal or trans-historical. Harking back to ancient Sumeria to search for the roots of modern money might not be a sound method.

Even neoliberals have to contend with democracy. Welfare has been atrophied from a universalist to a particularistic right in this era of neoliberal governmentality, but it still exists. Citizens are reduced to biopolitical entities that have to be 'cared' for, whether by means of privatised Keynesianism, universal basic incomes or the panoply of targeted poverty maintenance schemes in the Global South of which microfinance and conditional cash transfers are emblematic.

Complete theories of capitalism and democracy are of course beyond the scope of this work. But any reading of the history of capitalism shows that access to liquid 'cash' (defined historically) drives capitalist growth over the long term. The arc that begins with the invention of commercial credit to ration scarce specie in the early modern period stretches all the way to East Asian development banking in the twentieth century. Where robust credit institutions of whatever configuration fail to develop, robust capitalism remains elusive. Again, this is an irreducibly political story: Does the set of people who know how to run credit acquire political power? Do statist technocrats learn how to harness the Promethean power of credit?

Capitalism and democracy set the broad functional requirements for modern money. An over-rigid monetary system leaves too little space for capitalist investment validation even while limiting the fiscal room for manoeuvre required of the modern welfarist state. Yet a credit system that is too flexible will embed excessive risk across the system that will eventually lead to a crash, taking many private and public balance sheets down with it. Our dominant social formation demands both stability and flexibility. Achieving both simultaneously and at scale is the trick.

Money must of course be stable in order for it to work as a means of payment. This can be achieved by rigidly defining the monetary instrument in terms of some finite quantity of items that never changes or only does so in incremental and predictable ways. This is the monetarist dream, now replicated in computer code with cryptocurrency efforts.

But this ancient desire for stable and exogenous money mistakes the medium for the measure. In our monetary economies, the medium *is* the measure. While most measures of physical phenomena are also abstractions (you cannot touch 'weight' or 'height'), they are not the very medium of the measured object's existence. Yet without money, there is literally no economy. The economist's fiction of barter is just that—a complete fiction. A *monetary* economy has a different ontology, one that endogenously generates the medium of its operations even if the corresponding measure must be made to appear exogenous and thing-like in order to function. The state itself is endogenous to society.

As such, if we limit the *medium* in the service of the stability of the *measure*, we limit the very expandability of economic life. This corseting is perfectly possible as a technical matter and has occurred under all kinds of historical formations. But such austere rigidity cannot withstand the conjoined demands of capital and democracy *unless these two dynamics are themselves suppressed in politically durable ways.*

Permanently petrifying money will either lead to the stultification of capital or the limiting of the fisc in undemocratic ways, or some combination of the two. The period of the classical gold standard in the late nineteenth century, as we have seen, saw a global credit system disciplined by gold. But this was only sustainable because the *absence* of democracy in both the Global North and the Global South ensured the credibility of the gold peg. The global rise of democracy was the death knell for gold; this is Polanyi's central lesson. In other words, a relatively inelastic and stable system could only be sustained under undemocratic conditions.

Once democracy placed its demands on money, either democracy would have to be suppressed or money would have to be set on some other basis that combined stability with much greater elasticity. Through disaster, there emerged a monetary system based on national economies rather than the 'barbarous relic' (Keynes' term for gold), a system with substantially more degrees of freedom. That capital was relatively suppressed in this period meant that this monetary freedom could be put in the service of democracy.

But economic growth is itself a *political* requirement emerging from capitalism subject to democracy. Our impending planetary doom has still not shaken the deep naturalisation of the political requirement for economic growth. Universal welfare could have been achieved long ago through an equitable redistribution of our highly advanced means of production, but that of course runs against capitalist dogma. 'Growth' is a modus vivendi between the demands of capital and democracy, enabling capital to legitimise itself by (falsely) promising a better life to people *without* having to redistribute. But consistent capitalist growth is simply unattainable if we choke off the very medium of economic life. This bill is now coming due as consistent growth chokes off planetary life itself.

The dynamic needs of commerce are impossible to plan centrally, yet ironically this is precisely what fixing the stock of money for all time amounts to. Credit systems are both hierarchical and hybrids between economic and political mutualisation, creating space for both centralised direction and freedom at the capillary levels within a space outlined by central regulations. Credit, as a promise to pay money, represents an inherent flexibility in social relationships that can only be engineered away entirely with extreme government coercion that would cross the bounds of legitimacy.

People always find means to ration scarce 'money' by creating their own credit promises to pay whatever is running as 'money'. This is as true for Bitcoin exchanges (is your trading account really a Bitcoin or just a promise to pay one?) as it was for gold and central-bank money. Even during India's demonetisation episode, people created informal, interpersonal credit spontaneously: 'pay me later'. The point is to curate this credit growth; killing it off is impossible. Because credit systems are always hierarchical, credit can always be centrally managed. Such management will always be subject to political priors set by global or local equilibria between capital and democracy.

The alternative to flexibility is for credit flow to dry to a trickle. If this is the political path of least resistance, such a state still has to ensure legitimacy by managing money in some other way, often by some combination of internal and especially external patronage, which makes it a dependent backwater in terms of both capital and democracy. Elites in the Global South have long been happy to sacrifice national self-sufficiency and the development of robust capitalism in the service of their own reproduction, but even they have to maintain local legitimacy in an era of democracy.

An epoch ended with the post-war growth cycle of the Global North petered out, and the developmental dreams of the Global South lay largely in tatters. The stage was set for a rebound of global capital which duly suppressed democracy in the Global North. In the Global South, where democracy had configured itself more explicitly along the lines of patronage, whether electorally mediated or otherwise, oligarchy also bloomed.

But things have not quite reverted back to the nineteenth century so that democracy continues to place its demands on money even if this demand is filtered through our neoliberal common sense and biopolitical governance. Capital's response was marketised welfare by means of subsidised credit in the Global North; sustained capital flows to the Global South paid for by selling off more and more national equity; massified Chinese labour; and, more recently, the ability to pay for things by submitting ourselves to perpetual surveillance. The commoditisation of experience through perpetual electronic surveillance can retail itself as democratic because it makes things free at the point of use, a perversion of the welfarist principle.

Democratic fiscality creates a nationwide asset base which can be leveraged much further than any narrow commodity, even after the tax secession of the oligarchs. The modern credit system combines degrees of expandability that remain stable because national money has a national economic base. Commerce may elude crude, quantitative central planning, but credit is always offered on terms set by the most creditworthy operators; domestically this remains the state and its central bank. These lords of finance will often get it wrong, but the institutional opportunity for control is native to the hierarchical logic of money.

This is not to say that some private forms of bank money can be of such a scale that they swamp other forms of state-backed banking. The dollar-based shadow banking system is orders of magnitude larger than India's publicly owned banking system, for instance. But the private, international dollar is a promise to pay the public, national dollar. The fidelity of the *global* private dollar system, in the last instance, rests on the backstop done by a *national* public bank, the Fed. When the cycle turns, this private credit system retreats to the largest pool of liquidity that retains robustness even in highly stressed states of the world when mere economic contracting evaporates. There is of course nothing inevitable about this dynamic: it is a political outcome that sees the money interest expand to the point of incoherence only to have the public provide anchorage at the point of inevitable collapse.

Hierarchical credit systems offer several opportunities for control, but each of such instances is an opportunity for the dual politics of capital and democracy to play a hand so that the outcome is highly contingent. When well managed, a monetary system based on national economies combines systemic stability at the core ('money') while permitting flexibility at the margins ('credit'), but the system can be geared between discipline and elasticity in a number of ways. Capital and democracy both demand stability and flexibility, and the question becomes 'discipline or elasticity for whom?'

Monetary systems that are solely private or based on finite (digital) items fall outside this functional space because their institutions simply lack the bandwidth to fully express the demands of capital and democracy.

Needless to say, not all citizens and residents contribute equally to production, and most do not enjoy the full fruit of their labours. This is another manifestation of the ever-present contradiction between capitalism and democracy: national money is given secure value by democratic legitimacy, but capitalism distributes money in a manner that tears at the very legitimacy of the system.

As long as we use credit money to coordinate a social division of labour through markets, we are going to have to manage the basic technical fact of hierarchy in monetary systems. How democracies manage this technical fact is a matter of politics.

Democracy in the World

Under free movement of capital and a currency pegged to gold (or, equivalently, a credible inflation target in place), countries are constrained to move their domestic interest rates to maintain the peg or target; this is the famous 'trilemma' in open economies. If money flows out of the country, the peg or target will be threatened as the exchange rate falls, and interest rates will have to be increased. This in turn imparts discipline on the credit system, constraining government borrowing and seizing up the economy.

In short, free movement of capital and rigid policy rules for the currency set the economy for potential austerity at the mercy of global money markets that have an unelected seat at the fiscal table. Such discipline will clash with a democracy sooner or later unless democracy itself is suppressed.

The aforementioned arrangement was the default setting under the gold standard, the high-water mark of global imperialism. As we saw, the system was highly managed, far from self-equilibrating. Democracy has to be absent for the discipline of gold, the discipline of pegs or targets or policy rules to function. Well-meaning neoliberal technocrats arguing for policy rules like inflation targeting in the context of open capital accounts are in fact arguing for a diminishment of monetary sovereignty and risking the suppression of democracy. This of course chimes with the conservative impulse that the *demos* do not really know what is in their own best interest.

This world of gold collapsed with the rise of democracy: speculation turned from a stabiliser to a disruptor as markets realised that central banks could no longer induce draconian discipline with impunity. Only post-war capital controls kept democracy and capital from colliding, enabling the fisc to expand domestically without capital flight to world outside money. Capital had to be disciplined so that democracy could have elasticity.

When capital was released from its democratic shackles, it was the gold standard redux, but this time with democracy very much a feature. Now capital and democracy were face to face without the intermediation of capital controls and repressed finance. Incomes stagnated in most nations while inequalities exploded, and a planet wrapped in global supply chains boiled over: such are the fruits of the neoliberal's dominance over democracy.

But the death of gold was also a triumph for democracy itself in that it enshrined a national credit note at the centre of capitalism. Far from being 'the immediate social incarnation of human labour in the abstract' as per Marx, modern world money is irreducibly a *national* money, the political logic of the nation stamping itself on the abstraction of money. This potential can be captured, but the alternatives, whether from the IMF or the cypherpunks, are worse. The Bitcoin dystopia of permanently fixed money threatens to take us back to the depredations of gold.

The current world order might have elevated one national money above others, but this is reflective of a deeply unstable global division of labour—unstable socially, politically and ecologically. The division of labour is itself a hierarchy, ramifying far and wide but with a dense, highly interconnected core. This shows up in an economic geography which corresponds to certain political communities of nation states. Capital necessarily pushes at the boundaries of these communities, but it is also critically enabled by them. This gives nation states substantial leverage over capital that is often left unused.

Our present global division of labour results in a pattern that might be termed 'imperial', used here as a shorthand for an interdependent arrangement that exhibits systemic inequalities and asymmetries with clear core or periphery functions and locations. It is fragile because the natural infirmities of this unequal economic arrangement are not held in place by an explicit political arrangement. Colonialism was of course one such arrangement, which resolved the tensions of the system in a radically unequal manner.

The present system is the result of the interaction of independent polities networked together in an unstable fashion. Domestic rebalancing, political and economic, and international coordination adequate to this networking are therefore the need of the hour. National macroeconomic lopsidedness is the outcome of a series of domestic political struggles that have resulted in a narrow concentration of political power. This in turn has led to a lack of effective political checks and balances and therefore a pattern of institutional abuse that itself has led to unsustainable risk or return trade-offs at both the national and international levels.

In the north, the result of this political struggle has led to a runaway financial sector, the star of the tertiary economy, while the south is witnessing the blossoming of authoritarian capitalisms that maximally expose their economies to government failure and thereby risk overheating their industrial engines.

Further, excessive financial risk-taking in the north has been fuelled by export-derived surpluses from the south, a dynamic that leads to a win–win situation for a period (and for some) but whose incoordination exaggerates its networked unidirectionality so that no one element in the dynamic can apply the brakes before the excessive risks embedded in the system send it spinning out of control.

Having to import a significant and increasing percentage of its secondary and primary products, the north is an economy flying on a one-sector engine. The continued competitiveness of Japanese and German manufacturing is both limited to the high-tech sector and is the result of concerted governmental effort to swim against the tide of tertiary dominance; these efforts are in turn propped up by the balance of their respective political economies.

The analogous, but inverted, situation in the south is India, a developing nation whose domestic political class balance has led to an over-investment in tertiary education and resulted in a massive pool of low-cost, high-skilled workers capable of sustaining service-based exports, atypical of a developing nation. On either side of the north–south divide, Europe and India represent somewhat more balanced mixtures of macroeconomic activity that correct for the extremes at either end of the spectrum: America and China.

Globalisation qua connecting everything to everything else turns out to be a spectacularly bad idea. Administrative closure of these hubs by means of capital controls would enable a better macroeconomic balance between all sectors of the economy and therefore be in favour of local economies, democratic communities and a cooler planet. The neoliberal creed of hyperconnectivity is merely a shill for capital. One of the Covid-19 pandemic's grim lessons, seemingly common sense, is that a system without firewalls is highly fragile; local failures can go systemic very quickly. Credit systems have capital buffers and LOLR functions for precisely this reason. Compartmentalisation is often sound design and need not be read as parochialism.

There is nothing essential about the local being parochial or provincial or indeed proto-fascist. Following Rabindranath Tagore, we can be both local and cosmopolitan at the same time. Civic nationalisms, uniting people on the basis of a shared vision of the future rather than an invented past, can be a progressive alternative to ethnic nationalisms. We can arrange our monies to serve that end.

National money systems work for capitalism plus democracy, as we have seen, because they are hybrids between economic and political mutualisation no matter their *formal* ownership structures. Only such hybrids can combine the properties of stability and flexibility. This suits the demands of our governing social formation, but given the unevenly dense nature of any complex social division of labour, any post-capitalist economy would arguably require some combination of stability and flexibility that only social relations, promises, can provide.

In any event, the history of credit culminating in the most recent crisis proves that the hybridity between *privatised* banking and *nationalised* money generates contradictions that are very hard to manage. Democracy itself hampers price-based controls to the point where heavy regulations asymptotically approaching nationalisation are required at a minimum. Money markets are inherently hierarchical and always centrally planned by nature. The most upstream price of money is already an administered price rather than a market price. Market discipline fails with banks that are so definitionally tightly networked that they simply cannot survive without each other and the central bank. Banks are always networked, so they are always too networked to fail. Private banks always receive public liquidity insurance, often drastically underpriced.

Public–private hybrid systems are simply engines for moral hazard. It becomes increasingly difficult to argue for banking to remain in private hands at all. Nationalised banking will of course have its own set of issues, and combinations of political and economic mutualisation will anyway have to be imagined locally.

A key resource in this reimagination, we hope, is the lesson that money is a deep feature of popular sovereignty. Political collectives ought to be able to design money with a view to their collective norms. Such collectives need not be narrowly national in an exclusionary way, of course. We must be careful not to let arguments for functional capital firewalls and nationalised banking slide into narrow narratives of national pride.

If we cannot leave economic nationalism to the doctrinaire, we cannot leave globalisation to the globalists. Perhaps we can do no better than Keynes' argument from national self-sufficiency: 'Ideas, knowledge, science, hospitality, travel—these are the things which should of their nature be international. But let goods be homespun whenever it is reasonably and conveniently possible, and, above all, let finance be primarily national' (Keynes, 1933).

One lesson of the political theory of money might be that the nation state, recently neoliberalised and darkened by creeping fascism, must once again become the route to democracy by means of a civic rather than ethnic nationalism. After all, only political bonds at scale can make money and democracy pull in the same direction.

Bibliography

Acemoglu, D., S. Johnson and J. Robinson (2005). 'The Rise of Europe: Atlantic Trade, Institutional Change, and Economic Growth'. *American Economic Review* 95(3): 546–579.

Aglietta, M. (2018). *Money: 5,000 Years of Debt and Power*. London: Verso.

Arnon, A. (2011). *Monetary Theory and Policy from Hume and Smith to Wicksell: Money, Credit, and the Economy*. Cambridge, UK: Cambridge University Press.

Baba, N., R. N. McCauley and S. Ramaswamy (2009). 'US Dollar Money Market Funds and Non-US Banks'. *BIS Quarterly Review* (March): 65–81.

Babic, M., J. Fichtner and E. M. Heemskerk (2017). 'States versus Corporations: Rethinking the Power of Business in International Politics'. *International Spectator* 52(4): 20–43.

Bagehot, W. (1920 [1873]). *Lombard Street: A Description of the Money Market*. London: John Murray.

Balganesh, S. (2016). 'The Constitutionalization of Indian Private Law'. In *The Oxford Handbook of the Indian Constitution*, edited by S. Choudhry, M. Khosla and P. B. Mehta, pp. 680–696. New Delhi: Oxford University Press.

Bech, M. L., A. Martin and J. McAndrews (2012). 'Settlement Liquidity and Monetary Policy Implementation: Lessons from the Financial Crisis'. *Economic Policy Review* 18(1): 1–26.

Bell, S. (2001). 'The Role of the State and the Hierarchy of Money'. *Cambridge Journal of Economics* 25(2): 149–163.

Berger, A. N., A. K. Kashyap, J. M. Scalise, M. Gertler and B. M. Friedman (1995). 'The Transformation of the US Banking Industry: What a Long, Strange Trip It's Been'. *Brookings Papers on Economic Activity* 2: 55–218.

Bernanke, B. (2005). 'The Global Saving Glut and the US Current Account Deficit'. Speech 77, Board of Governors of the Federal Reserve System, Washington, DC.

Bernes, T. A., P. Jenkins, P. Mehrling and D. H. Neilson (2014). *China's Engagements with an Evolving International Monetary System: A Payments Perspective.* Waterloo and New York: Centre for International Governance Innovation (CIGI) and Institute for New Economic Thinking. https://www.cigionline.org/sites/default/files/china_engagement_cigi-inet_special_report_web_0.pdf. Accessed on 22 February 2023.

Blyth, M. (2013). 'The Austerity Delusion: Why a Bad Idea Won Over the West'. *Foreign Affairs:* 92(3): 41–56.

Borio, C. (2016). 'On the Centrality of the Current Account in International Economics'. *Journal of International Money and Finance* 68: 266–274.

——— (2019). 'On Money, Debt, Trust and Central Banking', BIS Working Paper No. 763, Bank for International Settlements, Basel, 11 January.

Borio, C., and P. Disyatat (2011). 'Global Imbalances and the Financial Crisis: Link or No Link?'. BIS Working Paper No. 346, Bank for International Settlements, Basel, 8 June.

Borio, C. E., and P. Van den Bergh (1993). 'The Nature and Management of Payment System Risks: An International Perspective'. BIS Economic Papers No. 36, Bank for International Settlements, Basel.

Bolton, P. (2016). 'Presidential Address: Debt and Money: Financial Constraints and Sovereign Finance'. *Journal of Finance* 71(4): 1483–1510.

Braudel, F. (1992). *Civilization and Capitalism, 15th–18th Century,* vol. 3: *The Perspective of the World.* Berkeley: University of California Press.

Brewer, J. (1989). *The Sinews of Power: War, Money and the English State 1688–1783.* Cambridge, MA: Harvard University Press.

Brunnermeier, M., and I. Schnabel (2016). 'Bubbles and Central Banks: Historical Perspectives'. In *Central Banks at a Crossroads: What Can We Learn from History?,* edited by M. D. Bordo, Ø. Eitrheim, M. Flandreau and J. F. Qvigstad, pp. 493–562. Cambridge, UK: Cambridge University Press.

Burger, A. E. (1969). 'A Historical Analysis of the Credit Crunch of 1966'. *Federal Reserve Bank of St. Louis Review* (September 1969).

Carruthers, B. G., and A. L. Stinchcombe (1999). 'The Social Structure of Liquidity: Flexibility, Markets, and States'. *Theory and Society* 28(3): 353–382.

Chatterjee, P. (2004). *The Politics of the Governed: Reflections on Popular Politics in Most of the World.* New York: Columbia University Press.

Cecchetti, S. G., R. N. McCauley and P. McGuire (2012). 'Interpreting TARGET2 Balances'. BIS Working Paper No. 393, Bank for International Settlements, Basel, December.

Cohen, B. J. (2006). 'The Macrofoundations of Monetary Power'. In *International Monetary Power*, edited by D. M. Andrews, pp. 31–50. Ithaca, NY: Cornell University Press.

——— (2015). *Currency Power: Understanding Monetary Rivalry*. Princeton, NJ: Princeton University Press.

Copeland, M. A. (1952). *A Study of Moneyflows in the United States*. Cambridge, MA: National Bureau of Economic Research.

Commons, J. R. (1931). 'Institutional Economics'. *American Economic Review* 21(4): 648–657.

Corrales, J. S., P. A. Imam, S. Weber and E. Yehoue (2016). 'Dollarisation in Sub-Saharan Africa'. *Journal of African Economies* 25(1): 28–54.

Crouch, C. (2011). *The Strange Non-Death of Neoliberalism*. Cambridge, UK: Polity Press.

D'Arista, J. W., and T. Schlesinger (1993). 'The Parallel Banking System'. Briefing Paper. Economic Policy Institute, Washington, DC. http://www.epi.org/files/page/-/old/briefingpapers/1993_bp_parallel.pdf. Accessed on 22 February 2023.

Dickson, P. G. M. (1967). *The Financial Revolution in England: A Study in the Development of Public Credit, 1688–1756*. New York: St Martin's Press.

de Cecco, M. (1975). *Money and Empire: The International Gold Standard, 1890–1914*. Lanham, MD: Rowman & Littlefield.

Desan, C. (2014). *Making Money: Coin, Currency, and the Coming of Capitalism*. New York: Oxford University Press.

——— (2019). *The Monetary Structure of Economic Activity*. Harvard Law School mimeo.

Despres, E., C. P. Kindleberger and W. S. Salant (1966). 'The Dollar and World Liquidity: A Minority View'. *The Economist*, 5 February.

Dooley, M., D. F. Landau and P. Garber (2009). 'Bretton Woods II Still Defines the International Monetary System'. *Pacific Economic Review* 14(3): 297–311.

Dowd, K. (2000). *Money and the Market: Essays on Free Banking*. New York: Routledge.

Dudley, W. (2012). 'Letter to the Editor Regarding Central Bank Liquidity Swaps'. 5 January. https://www.newyorkfed.org/markets/statement_0105_2012.html. Accessed on 22 February 2023.

Durkheim, E. (2014 [1893]). *The Division of Labour in Society*. New York: Simon & Schuster.

Drezner, D. W., and K. R. McNamara (2013). 'International Political Economy, Global Financial Orders and the 2008 Financial Crisis'. *Perspectives on Politics* 11(1): 155–166.

Eichengreen, B. (2008). *Globalising Capital: A History of the International Monetary System*. Princeton, NJ: Princeton University Press.

——— (2011). *Exorbitant Privilege: The Rise and Fall of the Dollar and the Future of the International Monetary System*. Oxford: Oxford University Press.

European Commission, (n.d.). The Euro as Legal Tender, available at https://ec.europa.eu/info/business-economy-euro/euro-area/euro/use-euro/euro-legal-tender_en. Accessed on 22 February 2023.

Federal Reserve (2018). 'Statistical Release, Assets and Liabilities of Commercial Banks in the United States'. 7 December 2018. https://www.federalreserve.gov/releases/h8/Current. Accessed on 22 February 2023.

Federal Reserve Board (2013). 'Federal Reserve and Other Central Banks Convert Temporary Bilateral Liquidity Swap Arrangements to Standing Arrangements'. http://www.federalreserve.gov/newsevents/press/monetary/20131031a.htm. Accessed on 22 February 2023.

Federal Reserve Bank of New York (2020). 'Central Bank Swap Arrangements'. https://www.newyorkfed.org/markets/international-market-operations/central-bank-swap-arrangements. Accessed on 22 February 2023.

Frankel, J. A. (1995). 'Still the Lingua Franca: The Exaggerated Death of the Dollar'. *Foreign Affairs* 74(4): 9–16.

——— (2012). 'Internationalisation of the RMB and Historical Precedents'. *Journal of Economic Integration* 27(3): 329–365.

Foucault, M. (2003). *Society Must Be Defended: Lectures at the Collège de France, 1975–1976*. London: Allen Lane.

Garbade, K., F. Keane, L. Logan, A. S. Kirby and J. Wolgemuth (2010). 'The Introduction of the TMPG Fails Charge for US Treasury Securities'. *Economic Policy Review* 16(2).

Germain, R., and H. M. Schwartz (2014). 'The Political Economy of Failure: The Euro as an International Currency'. *Review of International Political Economy* 21(5): 1095–1122.

——— (2015). 'The Political Limits to RMB Internationalisation'. In *Enter the Dragon: China in the International Financial System*, edited by D. Lombardi and H. Wang, pp. 133–158. Montreal: McGill-Queen's University Press.

Goodhart, C. A. E. (1983). *Monetary Theory and Practice: The UK-Experience*. New York: Macmillan Publishers.

——— (1988). *The Evolution of Central Banks.* Cambridge, MA: MIT Press.

——— (1995). *The Central Bank and the Financial System.* London: Palgrave Macmillan.

——— (1998). 'The Two Concepts of Money: Implications for the Analysis of Optimal Currency Areas'. *European Journal of Political Economy* 14(3): 407–432.

——— (2000). 'Can Central Banking Survive the IT Revolution?' *International Finance* 3(2): 189–209.

——— (2002). 'The Endogeneity of Money'. In *Money, Macroeconomics and Keynes: Essays in Honour of Victoria Chick,* edited by P. Kriesler, J. Nevile, P. Arestis, M. Desai and S. Dow, pp. 26–36. London: Routledge.

Goodhart, C. A. E., and E. Meade (2003). 'Central Banks and Supreme Courts'. FMG Special Papers, No. sp153, Financial Markets Group, London School of Economics. http://www.lse.ac.uk/fmg/documents/specialPapers/2003/sp153.pdf. Accessed on 22 February 2023.

Goodhart, C. A. E., and M. Jensen (2015). 'Currency School versus Banking School: An Ongoing Confrontation'. *Economic Thought* 4(2): 20–31.

Gorton, G., and A. Metrick (2012). 'Securitized Banking and the Run on Repo'. *Journal of Financial Economics* 104(3): 425–451.

Gourinchas, P. O., and H. Rey (2005). 'From World Banker to World Venture Capitalist: US External Adjustment and the Exorbitant Privilege'. *G7 Current Account Imbalances: Sustainability and Adjustment,* edited by R. H. Clarida, pp. 11–66. Cambridge, MA: National Bureau of Economic Research.

Gurley, J. G., and E. S. Shaw (1960). *Money in a Theory of Finance.* Washington, DC: Brookings Institution.

Hall, P. A. (2014). 'Varieties of Capitalism and the Euro Crisis'. *West European Politics* 37(6): 1223–1243.

Hancock, D., and W. Passmore (2011). 'Did the Federal Reserve's MBS Purchase Program Lower Mortgage Rates?'. *Journal of Monetary Economics* 58(5): 498–514.

Hardie, I., and S. Maxfield (2016). 'Atlas Constrained: The US External Balance Sheet and International Monetary Power'. *Review of International Political Economy* 23(4): 583–613.

Harvey, D. (2006). *The Limits to Capital.* London: Verso.

Hausmann, R., and F. Sturzenegger (2005). 'US and Global Imbalances: Can Dark Matter Prevent a Big Bang?'. Working Paper No. 124, Centre for International Development, Harvard University, Cambridge, MA, 13 November.

Hawtrey, R. G. (1919). *Currency and Credit*. London: Longman.

——— (1933). *The Art of Central Banking*. London: Longman.

Hayek, F. A. (1976 [1944]). *The Road to Serfdom*. London and New York: Routledge.

——— (1945). 'The Use of Knowledge in Society'. *American Economic Review* 35(4): 519–530.

Helleiner, E. (1996). *States and the Reemergence of Global Finance: From Bretton Woods to the 1990s*. Ithaca, NY: Cornell University Press.

——— (2003). *The Making of National Money: Territorial Currencies in Historical Perspective*, Ithaca, NY: Cornell University Press.

——— (2008). 'Political Determinants of International Currencies: What Future for the US Dollar?' *Review of International Political Economy* 15(3): 354–378.

Helleiner, E., and J. Kirshner (eds.) (2009). *The Future of the Dollar*. Ithaca, NY: Cornell University Press.

——— (eds.) (2014). *The Great Wall of Money: Power and Politics in China's International Monetary Relations*. Ithaca, NY: Cornell University Press.

Hester, D. D. (2008). *The Evolution of Monetary Policy and Banking in the US*. Berlin: Springer.

Hetzel, R. L., and R. Leach (2001a). 'The Treasury-Fed Accord: A New Narrative Account'. *FRB Richmond Economic Quarterly* 87(1): 33–56.

——— (2001b). 'After the Accord: Reminiscences on the Birth of the Modern Fed'. *FRB Richmond Economic Quarterly* 87(1): 57–64.

Hicks, J. R. (1989). *A Market Theory of Money*. Oxford: Oxford University Press.

Hodgson, G. M. (2017). '1688 and All That: Property Rights, the Glorious Revolution and the Rise of British Capitalism'. *Journal of Institutional Economics* 13(1): 79–107.

Hördahl, P., and M. R. King (2008). 'Developments in Repo Markets during the Financial Turmoil'. *BIS Quarterly Review*, 8 December.

Ingham, G. (1984). *Capitalism Divided? The City and Industry in British Social Development*. London: Macmillan Publishers.

——— (2004). *The Nature of Money*. Cambridge, UK: Polity Press.

——— (2013). 'Reflections'. In *Financial Crises and the Nature of Capitalist Money: Mutual Developments from the Work of Geoffrey Ingham*, edited by J. Pixley and G. C. Harcourt, pp. 300–322. Basingstoke, Hampshire: Palgrave Macmillan.

——— (2016). 'The Nature of Money: A Response to Stefano Sgambati'. *European Journal of Sociology* 57(1): 199–206.

———— (2018). 'A Critique of Lawson's Social Positioning and the Nature of Money'. *Cambridge Journal of Economics* 42(3): 837–850.

———— (2020). *Money (What Is Political Economy?)*. Cambridge, UK: Polity Press.

———— (2021). 'In Defence of the Nominalist Ontology of Money'. *Journal of Post Keynesian Economics* 44(3): 492–507.

Jeffries, A. (2018). 'The One True Bitcoin'. *The Verge*, 12 April. https://www.theverge.com/2018/4/12/17229796/bitcoin-cash-conflicttransactions-fight. Accessed on 22 February 2023.

Johnson, C. (1999). 'The Developmental State: Odyssey of a Concept'. In *The Developmental State*, edited by W.-C. Meredith, pp. 32–60. Ithaca, NY: Cornell University Press.

Khan, M. (2017). 'Chinese Foreign Exchange Reserves Swell by $24bn to 2017-high'. *Financial Times*, 7 June. https://www.ft.com/content/1bb073cb-01bb-371f-9c59-91142f38d6d9. Accessed on 22 February 2023.

Keynes, J. M. (1933). 'National Self-Sufficiency'. *Yale Review* 22(4): 755–769.

Kindleberger, C. P. (2000 [1967]). 'The Politics of International Money and World Language'. In *Comparative Political Economy*. Cambridge, MA: MIT Press.

———— (1981). 'Dominance and Leadership in the International Economy'. *International Studies Quarterly* 25(2): 242–254.

———— (1994). 'Foreword'. In *Private Money and Public Currencies: The 16th Century Challenge*, edited by M. T. Boyer-Xambeu, G. Deleplace and L. Gillard. ME Sharpe, pp. ix–xii. Armonk, NY: M. E. Sharpe.

King, M. (1999). 'Challenges for Monetary Policy: New and Old'. *Quarterly Bulletin: Bank of England* 39: 397–415.

Kirshner, J. (2014). 'Same as It Ever Was? Continuity and Change in the International Monetary System'. *Review of International Political Economy* 21(5): 1007–1016.

Knapp, G. F. (1924 [1905]). *The State Theory of Money*. London: Macmillan Publishers.

Konings, M. (2011). *The Development of American Finance*. Cambridge, UK: Cambridge University Press.

Konings, J. P. (2019). 'Starbucks, Monetary Superpower'. 21 August. http://jpkoning.blogspot.com/2019/08/starbucks-monetary-superpower.html. Accessed on 22 February 2023.

Kraemer, K., L. Jakelja, F. Brugger and S. Nessel (2020). 'Money Knowledge or Money Myths? Results of a Population Survey on Money and the Monetary Order'. *European Journal of Sociology* 61(2): 219–267.

Krippner, G. R. (2010). 'The Political Economy of Financial Exuberance'. In *Markets on Trial: The Economic Sociology of the US Financial Crisis: Part B*, edited by M. Lounsbury and P. M. Hirsch, pp. 141–173. Bingley, UK: Emerald Group Publishing Limited.

——— (2011). *Capitalising on Crisis*. Cambridge, MA: Harvard University Press.

Lake, D. (2009). *Hierarchy in International Relations*. Ithaca, NY: Cornell University Press.

Lange, O. (1967). 'The Computer and the Market'. In *Socialism and Economic Growth*, edited by C. Feinstein, pp. 158–161. Cambridge, UK: Cambridge University Press.

Mann, M. (1984). 'The Autonomous Power of the State: Its Origins, Mechanisms and Results'. *European Journal of Sociology* 25(2): 185–213.

Mantena, K. (2016). 'Popular Sovereignty and Anti-Colonialism'. In *Popular Sovereignty in Historical Perspective*, edited by R. Bourke and Q. Skinner, pp. 279–319. Cambridge, UK: Cambridge University Press.

Marx, Karl. (1992 [1867]). *Capital*, vol. 1. London: Penguin Books.

McLeay, M., A. Radia and R. Thomas (2014). 'Money Creation in the Modern Economy'. *Bank of England Quarterly Bulletin* Q1. https://www.bankofengland. co.uk/-/media/boe/files/quarterly-bulletin/2014/money-creation-in-the-modern-economy.pdf. Accessed on 27 December 2022.

McCulley, P. (2007). 'Teton Reflections'. Global Central Bank Focus, PIMCO, August–September. https://www.pimco.com/en-us/insights/economic-and-market-commentary/global-central-bank-focus/teton-reflections. Accessed on 22 February 2023.

Mehrling, P. (1998). *The Money Interest and the Public Interest: American Monetary Thought, 1920–1970*. Cambridge, MA: Harvard University Press.

——— (1999). 'The Vision of Hyman P. Minsky'. *Journal of Economic Behavior* and *Organization* 39(2): 129–158.

——— (2000a). 'The State as a Financial Intermediary'. *Journal of Economic Issues* 34(2): 365–368.

——— (2000b). 'Modern Money: Fiat or Credit?'. *Journal of Post Keynesian Economics* 22(3): 397–406.

——— (2000c). 'Minsky and Modern Finance'. *Journal of Portfolio Management* 26(2): 81–88.

——— (2003). 'Mr Goodhart and the EMU'. In *The State, the Market, and the Euro: Chartalism Versus Metallism in the Theory of Money*, edited by S. A. Bell and E. J. Nell, pp. 26–38. Cheltenham: Edward Elgar Publishing.

———— (2005a). 'Monetary Transmission without Sticky Prices'. Columbia University.

———— (2005b). *Fischer Black and the Revolutionary Idea of Finance*. Hoboken, NJ: John Wiley and Sons.

———— (2006a). 'Mr. Woodford and the Challenge of Finance'. *Journal of the History of Economic Thought* 28(2): 161–170.

———— (2006b). 'The Problem of Time in the DSGE Model and the Post Walrasian Alternative'. *Post Walrasian Macroeconomics: Beyond the Dynamic Stochastic General Equilibrium Model*, edited by D. Colander, pp. 70–79. Cambridge, UK: Cambridge University Press.

———— (2010). 'Monetary Policy Implementation: A Microstructure Approach'. In *David Laidler's Contributions to Economics*, edited by R. Leeson, pp. 212–234. London: Palgrave Macmillan.

———— (2011). *The New Lombard Street: How the Fed became the Dealer of Last Resort*. Princeton, NJ: Princeton University Press.

———— (2012a). 'The Inherent Hierarchy of Money'. In *Social Fairness and Economics: Economic Essays in the Spirit of Duncan Foley*, edited by L. Taylor, A. Rezai and T. R. Michl, pp. 394–404. London and New York: Routledge.

———— (2012b). 'A Money View of Credit and Debt'. INET Working Paper, Institute for New Economic Thinking, New York, 4 November, https://www.cigionline. org/sites/default/files/inet2012mehrling_amoneyviewofcreditanddebt.pdf. Accessed on 22 February 2023.

———— (2012c). 'Three Principles for Market-Based Credit Regulation'. *American Economic Review* 102(3): 107–112.

———— (2013). 'Essential Hybridity: A Money View of FX'. *Journal of Comparative Economics* 41(2): 355–363.

———— (2014). 'Why Central Banking Should Be Re-Imagined, in Re-Thinking the Lender of Last Resort'. BIS Paper No. 79, Bank for International Settlements, Basel.

———— (2015). 'Elasticity and Discipline in the Global Swap Network'. *International Journal of Political Economy* 44(4): 311–324.

———— (2016). 'Beyond Bancor'. *Challenge* 59(1): 22–34.

———— (2017). 'Financialization and Its Discontents'. *Finance and Society* 3(1): 1–10.

Mehrling, P., and D. H. Neilson (2014). 'A New Measure of Liquidity Premium'. In *Banking, Monetary Policy and the Political Economy of Financial Regulation: Essays in the Tradition of Jane D'Arista*, edited by G. A. Epstein, T. Sclesinger and M. Vernengo, pp. 290–318. Cheltenham: Edward Elgar Publishing.

Mehrling, P., Z. Pozsar, J. Sweeney and D. Neilson (2013). 'Bagehot Was a Shadow Banker: Shadow Banking, Central Banking, and the Future of Global Finance'.

Available at SSRN: https://ssrn.com/abstract=2232016. Accessed on 22 February 2023.

Minsky, H. P. (1986). *Stabilizing an Unstable Economy*. New Haven: Yale University Press.

——— (1992). 'The Capitalist Development of the Economy and the Structure of Financial Institutions'. Paper No. 179, Hyman P. Minsky Archive. http://digitalcommons.bard.edu/hm_archive/179. Accessed on 22 February 2023.

Mirowski, P. (1989). *More Heat than Light: Economics as Social Physics, Physics as Nature's Economics*. Cambridge, UK: Cambridge University Press.

——— (1990). 'Learning the Meaning of a Dollar: Conservation Principles and the Social Theory of Value in Economic Theory'. *Social Research* 57(3): 689–717.

——— (1991). 'Postmodernism and the Social Theory of Value'. *Journal of Post Keynesian Economics* 13(4): 565–582.

——— (2002). *Machine Dreams: Economics Becomes a Cyborg Science*. Cambridge, UK: Cambridge University Press.

——— (2011). 'Realism and Neoliberalism: From Reactionary Modernism to Postwar Conservatism'. In *The Invention of International Relations Theory: Realism, the Rockefeller Foundation, and the 1954 Conference on Theory*, edited by N. Guilhot. New York: Columbia University Press.

Mirowski, P., and D. Plehwe (eds.) (2015). *The Road from Mont Pèlerin: The Making of the Neoliberal Thought Collective, with a New Preface*. Cambridge, MA: Harvard University Press.

Nakamoto, S. (2008). 'Bitcoin: A Peer-to-Peer Electronic Cash System'. https://bitcoin.org/bitcoin.pdf. Accessed on 26 December 2022.

Narayanan, A., J. Bonneau, E. Felten, A. Miller and S. Goldfeder (2016). *Bitcoin and Cryptocurrency Technologies: A Comprehensive Introduction*. Princeton, NJ: Princeton University Press.

Nersisyan, Y., and L. R. Wray (2016). 'Modern Money Theory and the Facts of Experience'. *Cambridge Journal of Economics* 40(5): 1297–1316.

North, D. (1989). *Institutions, Institutional Change, and Economic Performance*. Cambridge, UK: Cambridge University Press.

North, D., and B. R. Weingast (1989). 'Constitutions and Commitment: The Evolution of Institutional Governing Public Choice in Seventeenth Century England'. *Journal of Economic History* 49(4): 803–832.

North, D., J. J. Wallis and B. R. Weingast (2009). *Violence and Social Orders: A Conceptual Framework for Interpreting Recorded Human History*. Cambridge, UK: Cambridge University Press.

Ocampo, J. A. (2014). 'The Provision of Global Liquidity: The Global Reserve System'. WIDER Working Paper No. 2014/141, World Institute for Development Economics Research, United Nations University (UNU-WIDER), Helenski.

Organisation for Economic Cooperation and Development (OECD). *Revenue Statistics 2022.* https://www.oecd.org/tax/tax-policy/revenue-statistics-highlights-brochure.pdf. Accessed on 22 February 2023.

Otero-Iglesias, M. (2014). *The Euro, the Dollar and the Global Financial Crisis: Currency Challenges Seen from Emerging Markets.* New York: Routledge.

Panitch, L., and M. Konings (2008). 'Demystifying Imperial Finance'. In *American Empire and the Political Economy of Global Finance,* edited by L. Panitch and M. Konings, pp. 1–15. London: Palgrave Macmillan.

Patton, M. (2016). 'US Role in Global Economy Declines Nearly 50%'. *Forbes,* 29 February. https://www.forbes.com/sites/mikepatton/2016/02/29/u-s-role-in-global-economy-declines-nearly-50/?sh=60bfc06f5e9e. Accessed on 22 February 2023.

Pickering, A. (1995). 'Cyborg History and the World War II Regime'. *Perspectives on Science* 3(1): 1–48.

Piketty, T. (2014). *Capital in the 21st Century.* Cambridge, MA: Harvard University Press.

Pistor, K. (2013). 'A Legal Theory of Finance'. *Journal of Comparative Economics* 41(2): 315–330.

Polanyi, K. (2001 [1944]). *The Great Transformation: The Political and Economic Origins of Our Time.* Boston: Beacon Press.

Pozsar, Z. (2015). 'A Macro View of Shadow Banking: Levered Betas and Wholesale Funding in the Context of Secular Stagnation'. 31 January. https://ssrn.com/abstract=2558945. Accessed on 22 February 2023.

Pozsar, Z., T. Adrian, A. Ashcraft and H. Boesky (2010). 'Shadow Banking'. Federal Reserve Bank of New York Staff Reports, Staff Report No. 458, July. https://www.newyorkfed.org/medialibrary/media/research/staff_reports/sr458.pdf. Accessed on 22 February 2023.

Rodrigues, A. (1993). 'Government Securities Investments of Commercial Banks'. *Quarterly Review of the Federal Reserve Bank of New York* 18 (Summer): 39–39.

Ruggie, J. G. (1982). 'International Regimes, Transactions, and Change: Embedded Liberalism in the Postwar Economic Order'. *International Organization* 36(2): 379–415.

Seabrooke, L. (2006). *The Social Sources of Financial Power: Domestic Legitimacy and International Financial Orders.* Ithaca, NY: Cornell University Press.

Serdarevic, M. (2012). 'So, Who's Going to Sell Their Greek Bonds?' *Financial Times*, 29 November. http://ftalphaville.ft.com/2012/11/29/1287493/sowhos-going-to-sell-theirgreek-bonds/. Accessed on 22 February 2023.

Shin, H. S. (2012). 'Global Banking Glut and Loan Risk Premium'. *IMF Economic Review* 60(2): 155–192.

Sproul, M. (2018). 'The Real Meaning of the Real Bills Doctrine'. MPRA Paper No. 87608, Munich Personal RePEc Archive, University of Southern California, 26 June (revised November 2018).

Stiglitz, J. E., and B. Greenwald (2010). 'Towards a New Global Reserve System'. *Journal of Globalization and Development* 1(2): Article 10.

Stigum, M., and A. Crescenzi (2007). *Stigum's Money Market*. New York: McGraw Hill.

Strange, S. (1996). *The Retreat of the State: The Diffusion of Power in the World Economy*. Cambridge, UK: Cambridge University Press.

Streeck, W. (2014). *Buying Time: The Delayed Crisis of Democratic Capitalism*. New York: Verso Books.

Swoboda, A. K. (1968). 'The Euro-Dollar Market: An Interpretation'. *Essays in International Finance*, no. 64. Princeton, NJ: Princeton University Press.

Tett, G. (2009). *Fool's Gold: How the Bold Dream of a Small Tribe at JP Morgan Was Corrupted by Wall Street Greed and Unleashed a Catastrophe*. New York: Simon & Schuster.

Tilly, C. (1990). *Capital, Coercion, and European States*. Cambridge, MA: Basil Blackwell.

Tooze, A. (2018). *Crashed: How a Decade of Financial Crises Changed the World*. London: Penguin Books.

Triffin, R. (1960). *Gold and the Dollar Crisis*. New Haven, CT: Yale University Press.

Tuck, R. (2016). 'Democratic Sovereignty and Democratic Government'. In *Popular Sovereignty in Historical Perspective*, edited by R. Bourke and Q. Skinner, pp. 115–141. Cambridge, UK: Cambridge University Press.

Tymoigne, E., and L. R. Wray (2013). 'Modern Money Theory 101: A Reply to Critics', Working Paper No. 778, Levy Economics Institute of Bard College, New York. http://www.levyinstitute.org/pubs/wp_778.pdf. Accessed on 22 February 2023.

Unger, R. M. (1987). *False Necessity*. Cambridge, UK: Cambridge University Press.

——— (2007). *The Self-Awakened: Pragmatism Unbound*. Cambridge, MA: Harvard University Press.

Van Horn, R., and P. Mirowski (2009). 'The Rise of the Chicago School of Economics and the Birth of Neoliberalism'. In *The Road from Mont Pelerin: The Making of the*

Neoliberal Thought Collective, edited by P. Mirowski and D. Plehwe, pp. 149–163. Cambridge, MA: Harvard University Press.

Varadarajan, T. (2007). 'Milton Friedman at Rest'. *Wall Street Journal*, 22 January.

Vigna, P., and M. J. Casey (2016). *The Age of Cryptocurrency: How Bitcoin and the Blockchain Are Challenging the Global Economic Order*. New York: Macmillan Publishers.

Weber, M. (1978). *Economy and Society: An Outline of Interpretive Sociology*, vol. 1. Berkeley: University of California Press.

——— (1991 [1919]). 'Politics as a Vocation'. In *From Max Weber: Essays in Sociology*, edited by H. H. Gerth and C. W. Mills, pp. 77–128. New York: Routledge.

——— (2018). *Democratising Money? Debating Legitimacy in Monetary Reform Proposals*. Cambridge, UK: Cambridge University Press.

Wighton, D. (2007). 'Citi Launches $49bn SIV Rescue'. *Financial Times*, 13 December. https://www.ft.com/content/6626b45e-a9dd-11dc-aa8b-0000779fd2ac. Accessed on 22 February 2023.

Wojnilower, A. M. (1980). 'The Central Role of Credit Crunches in Recent Financial History'. *Brookings Papers on Economic Activity* 11(2): 277–340.

Wray, L. R. (ed.) (2004). *Credit and State Theories of Money: The Contributions of A. Mitchell Innes*. Cheltenham: Edward Elgar Publishing.

Xiaochuan, Z. (2009). 'Reform the International Monetary System'. People's Bank of China Speeches, 23 March. http://www.bis.org/review/r090402c.pdf. Accessed on 22 February 2023.

INDEX